SIR EDMUND HEAD

A Scholarly Governor

A century ago, in 1854, Sir Edmund Head became governor general of Canada. His earlier career as Oxford don, chief Poor Law commissioner during the "hungry forties," and lieutenant governor of New Brunswick, had prepared him to succeed Lord Elgin in this senior post in the British colonial service. Combining the outlook and training of a scholar with a long administrative experience in difficult posts, Head had a clear insight into British North American problems, and was able to guide British and Canadian politicians toward their solution in the creation of the new Dominion of Canada. Later, as Governor of the Hudson's Bay Company, he carried negotiations for the transfer of the Company's territories to the verge of conclusion before his sudden death in 1868.

Neglected until recently by Canadian historians, the significance of the work of one of Britain's greatest colonial administrators is only now beginning to be appreciated. Professor Kerr's biography creates a lively and convincing picture of Head and colonial life at a critical period. Based on careful research among the public documents of the period, and making use as well of Head's private letters to close friends in England and North America, it is the first full-scale treatment available of this philosophic and capable governor whose influence on Canadian national development was so important.

DONALD GORDON GRADY KERR has made Sir Edmund Head the subject of his study since he received his B.A. from McGill in 1935. His post-graduate studies took him to Ottawa and London for research, to the Zimmern School of International Studies in Geneva, and to the University of London from which he received his doctorate in 1937, with Sir Edmund Head as the subject of his thesis. Later, with a view to publication of his work, Dr. Kerr received a grant from the Social Science Research Council, and, to complete the research and make publication finally possible, a Nuffield Fellowship. Earlier in his career, he was a high school teacher in Montreal; during the war a Lieutenant-Commander and senior assistant of the Naval Historian. Since 1946 Dr. Kerr has been head of the Department of History at Mount Allison University, Sackville, New Brunswick.

SIR EDMUND HEAD

A Scholarly Governor

By

D. G. G. KERR

with the assistance of
J. A. GIBSON

UNIVERSITY OF TORONTO PRESS
in co-operation with Mount Allison University: 1954

. . . Edmund Head; a man whose endowments and attainments taken together might have achieved a high literary reputation, had he not, almost of necessity, for he was not rich, betaken himself to public employments instead of literary labors. It seems to be often assumed as a matter of course, that the latter labors give birth to more lasting results than the former. All that ought to be assumed is that the laborer will probably be longer known by name, and that the results of his labors will be more distinctly traceable to himself. The good done by Sir Edmund Head in his public employments will bear fruit in successive generations of consequences, long after any portions of it have ceased to be referred to their original. It is personal reputation only which is more lasting in the case of literary achievements.

Some men—a very few—in our time may have rivalled Sir Edmund Head in knowledge of books and some in the knowledge of art; but probably no one was equal to him in knowledge of both together: and when I first knew him there was, along with this, a gayety of heart which, in so laborious a student, made, perhaps, the rarest combination of all. It was subdued afterwards, though not extinguished, by some years of ill-health, through which, with manly energy,

> "he kept
> The citadel unconquered,"

doing the state excellent service. . . .

HENRY TAYLOR, *Autobiography*, I, 257–58

PREFACE

N O representative of the sovereign had a wider or more varied association with British North America than Sir Edmund Walker Head, Lieutenant Governor of New Brunswick, Governor General of Canada, and Governor of the Hudson's Bay Company: none had a higher reputation during his lifetime as a man of learning: yet none of his eminence was so consistently over-looked—or at best, misunderstood—by students of Canadian history until quite recently. Professor Chester Martin and Dr. W. M. Whitelaw did much to draw attention to his importance in the 1920's and 1930's; and the purpose of the present study is to make clear what sort of man Head was and what role he played in the events of his time. It is hoped that one result at least will be a more general appreciation of the fact that Sir Francis Bond Head was not the only Canadian governor of that surname.

Some explanation is necessary at the outset with regard to the nature and extent of the collaboration between Dr. Gibson and myself in the authorship of this book. While postgraduate students at Oxford and London respectively, we found that we had both chosen Head as the subject for our doctoral dissertations. We were too far advanced in our work, and too keenly interested in it, for either of us to consider changing to another topic; but we agreed that he should make his a more completely biographical study, while I should concentrate on Head's public career in British North America. This we did. In 1949, when both of us were ready to turn to Head again after a number of years filled with other duties, we agreed to work together and divide the task more or less along the lines stressed in our theses. Since then, however, Dr. Gibson's time has been encroached upon by new responsibilities, and his contribution has had to be limited to a first draft of chapter I, extensive notes for a large part of chapter XI, and a careful reading of the rest followed by much sound advice. His assistance has, needless to say, been a major factor in preparing this work for publication.

vii

The material available for our investigation was copious. Primarily, it consisted of the official correspondence conducted by Head during the several periods of his career. However, especially with respect to his Canadian administration, it was impossible not to perceive that the despatches exchanged by Head and the colonial secretary were sometimes inclined to be perfunctory. Relations between the Canadian and Imperial governments depended, during this period, to an increasing extent on two other—unofficial or semi-official—channels of communication: first, personal conversations between officials of the Colonial Office and Canadian ministers visiting in London; and secondly, private correspondence between those officials and the Canadian governor general. The latter channel we know from the *Elgin-Grey Papers* was of very great importance during Elgin's administration, and there are many indications that it did not cease to be so when Elgin left the province. We have reason to believe that Head wrote extensively to Labouchere and the Duke of Newcastle and to some at least of the other colonial secretaries of his time, as well as to his friend Herman Merivale, who remained permanent under-secretary through frequent changes of ministry until 1859.

Efforts to trace Labouchere, Newcastle, and Merivale papers all failed, and so far as we know none of importance for our purposes still exist. Members of the Head family were most cooperative, and my thanks are due in particular to Mrs. Yvonne Mahuzies, Sir Edmund's grand-daughter, to Mrs. F. M. Morris-Davis, a descendant of Sir Francis Bond Head, and to Mr. Philip Yorke, a nephew of Lady Head. Unfortunately, however, the principal result in this direction too was negative, as it was discovered that all of Sir Edmund's papers were destroyed some years ago.

The gap thus caused was filled in some measure by the small but important collection of Head Papers in the Public Archives of Canada and by letters from Head to Sir George Cornewall Lewis, which are among the Lewis Papers at Harpton Court, Kington, Herefordshire. I wish to thank Sir Henry Duff Gordon most sincerely for the generosity with which he allowed me to make use of these letters. The greatest amount of material of use was found, of course, in three great repositories: the Public Archives of Canada, the Public Record Office, and the Archives of the Hudson's Bay Company. We wish to acknowledge our great indebtedness to the Canadian Archivist, to the Keeper of the Public Records, and to the Governor and Committee of the Hudson's Bay Company for permitting us to make use of the documents in their custody.

For the financial and other assistance necessary to pursue work of this kind, Dr. Gibson wishes to thank the Rhodes Trust and the Royal Society of Canada Fellowships Board. On my part, I should like to acknowledge my gratitude to my father who made it possible for me to spend two years in London, and to the Canadian Social Science Research Council, Mount Allison University, and the Publications Fund of the University of Toronto Press for generous grants in aid of research and to assist publication.

Finally, the record would be incomplete without grateful mention of the expert and sympathetic editorial assistance given by Miss Francess G. Halpenny of the University of Toronto Press, and the long hours spent by my wife checking the manuscript and then the proof with me.

D. G. G. K.

Sackville, N.B.
March 29, 1954

CONTENTS

I

THE MAKING OF A SCHOLAR AND GOVERNOR, 1805–1847

ONE

Early Years and Poor Law Experience

THE Head family was of ancient Kentish stock. Their name they owed probably to the Cinque Port of Hythe—known in Domesday as "de Hede," and meaning in its Anglo-Saxon form of *hethe*, a haven or port. Family tradition speaks of a certain Haymo de Hethe, Bishop of Rochester in the fourteenth century, builder of the tower of Rochester Cathedral and confessor to the unfortunate Edward II. Because of his loyalty to his king at a time when this was not very generally regarded as a virtue, particularly by Queen Isabella and her sympathizers, Haymo's consecration had had to take place in France. Loyalty and ecclesiastical connection remained two strong characteristics of the family after the Head baronetcy was created in 1676. The first baronet, Sir Richard, who sat three times in parliament representing Rochester, had the unique distinction of presenting Charles II with a silver basin and ewer when he entered Rochester at the time of his restoration in 1660, and of receiving an emerald ring from the fleeing James II to whom he gave shelter during his last days in England in 1688. The second baronet offered his house in Rochester to be used as the bishop's palace; three other baronets were clergymen.

The grandfather and father of Edmund Walker Head typified, each in his own way, the dual family tradition. Sir Edmund, the sixth baronet, like the first, was a business man, a leading citizen of his community, and a devoted servant of the king. Emigrating to Charleston, South Carolina, in the 1760's, he became prosperous, was chosen president of the local Court of Trade and Commerce, and in 1775 was elected a delegate from South Carolina to the Second Continental Congress. A loyalist, he refused to take his seat, and instead suffered the confiscation of his property, was thrown into prison, and in the end barely escaped with his life to England. There, however, he soon re-established himself as a merchant in London. His son and sole heir, John,

born in South Carolina and brought up in London, having
attended Magdalen College, Oxford, and been called to the Bar
by Lincoln's Inn, took holy orders and turned back to the old
family countryside of Kent where in 1801 he purchased Wiarton
Place, near Maidstone, for his bride Jane, only child of a London
merchant, Thomas Walker. Perpetual curate of Egerton, Kent,
and rector of Rayleigh, Essex, the Rev. Sir John Head seems to
have been an unconventional, well-dressed, and jovial cleric,
much respected by all shades of opinion in his parish. He resided
in France for extended periods, certainly from 1817 to 1821 at
Boulogne. A record exists of his presiding over a great dinner
of "plum pudding, roast and boiled beef, and beer" given at Rayleigh for 700 poor people on June 21, 1832, to celebrate the
passing of the Reform Bill. He died in London on January 4,
1838.

Edmund Walker Head was born on March 21, 1805, at Wiarton Place. One of his earliest memories was of a Sunday morning
walk with his father to the church at Hythe. When they arrived,
just after eleven o'clock, they found that the majority of the con-
gregation were still standing outside. *"They were anxiously
listening to the faint reverberation of cannon, which came from
eastward."* It was on that Sunday, June 18, 1815, while the church
clock at Nivelle nearby was striking eleven, that the Battle of
Waterloo began.

In the same year Edmund Head was sent to Winchester, where
he became, through his marked proficiency, a favourite pupil of
the celebrated headmaster, Dr. Gabell. "It is hard," wrote the
latter to Sir John Head in 1822, "to part with so delightful a boy;
but there is virtue in parting with him; pray do not detain him
beyond the proper time."

On June 11, 1823, Head was matriculated as a fellow-com-
moner at Oriel College, Oxford, and the following January he
came into residence. The Oxford of that period was still a quiet
academic community, as yet undisturbed by the new railway
which was shortly to supersede the stately coaches which ran
between the Mitre and Charing Cross. The life of a fellow- or
gentleman-commoner (distinguished by the silk gown he was
entitled to wear) was leisurely as a rule; but it appears that
pecuniary losses in the family convinced Head that he would
have to make his way by his own efforts. Having declined,
apparently on conscientious grounds, to take holy orders, he

applied himself to his studies with assiduity and, as it turned out, with distinction. In 1827 he was placed in the first class in the University examination in *literae humaniores* and he proceeded to the B.A. degree in the same year.[1]

Head spent much of the next two years on the Continent, travelling in Italy, and living for extended periods in Germany, for a while with Charles Babbage, the distinguished mathematician. When Babbage returned to England, Head wrote to him frequently in a neat, clear, vertical hand which contrasts strangely with his writing of later years—become broad, rapid, sometimes very nearly if not completely illegible, the result of the exigencies of official life perhaps, or of the impatience of a quick mind with the slowness of pen and hand. In the spring of 1829 Head went on to Paris where his family were then resident and where at intervals during the next few years he spent some time with them. He was there during the July Revolution of 1830, writing to Babbage after it: "I saw the fun in France—i.e. I was at Versailles during the row but did *not* fight for the mob, as you will readily believe."[2]

Although he had returned to Oxford in the spring of 1830 to take up new duties there, travel on the Continent continued to be a major interest with Head. In 1830 and 1831 he visited many parts of Spain in company with David Roberts, the artist; three of the plates in the latter's volume on Spain were based on Head's sketches. During the summer of 1833 he was again in Spain, this time with Richard Ford, author of the *Handbook of Spain*, who regarded him as "a well-informed, agreeable companion."[3] Part of the summer of 1834 Head spent in Italy, and during 1835, in company with G. C. Lewis, he revisited a number of the cities of Germany.[4] From all of this experience abroad he acquired a

[1] The biographical details are from: *Annual Register*, 1838, pp. 185, 194; 1840, p. 131; 1859, p. 433; *D.N.B.* (1921), IX, 323; *Proceedings of the Royal Society*, XVI (1867–68), lxxi–lxxvi; W. H. Ireland, *History of Kent*, II, 221; Philip Benton, *History of the Rochford Hundred*, p. 757; *Illustrated London News*, 1868, pp. 110, 147, 281; *Notes & Queries*, 4th Series, I, 121. In addition, manuscripts relating to family history were made available through the courtesy of Mrs. Mary Morris-Davis (née Head), Guestling House, Guestling, Sussex.

[2] B.M., Add. MSS. 37184, f. 402, Head to Babbage, n.d. [autumn, 1830]. See also: *ibid.*, f. 199, same to same, January 28, 1829; f. 256, same to same, April, 13, 1829.

[3] R. E. Prothero (ed.), *Letters of Richard Ford*, pp. 128, 139. Some years later, Ford wrote the review of Head's *History of the Spanish and French Schools of Painting* (London, 1848), in the *Quarterly Review*, CLXV (June, 1848), 1–37.

[4] G. F. Lewis (ed.), *Letters of Sir George Cornewall Lewis*, p. 46.

firm foundation for his later writings on the art and literature of
western Europe, and a knowledge of modern languages which
made him one of the most accomplished linguists and philologists
of his generation.

Head's resumption of his life at Oxford had resulted from his
election, on April 16, 1830, into one of three vacant fellowships
at Merton College where, as well as being principal of the post-
masters, he held from time to time between 1830 and 1836 the
additional offices of Greek and grammar lecturer, Knightley's
catechetical lecturer, and librarian, and for shorter intervals was
one of the bursars and auditors of accounts. In 1834 he served as a
University examiner, and in 1835 he was one of the examiners
for the fellowship into which the Hon. James Bruce (later eighth
Earl of Elgin) was elected.[5] When Head succeeded Elgin as
governor general of Canada in December, 1854, the latter
referred to the election nearly twenty years earlier in moving
terms. A letter written to Babbage during Head's first year at
Merton reveals a rather typical, light-hearted, but a little self-
conscious young lecturer: "I am steady, grave & well-behaved—
lecture the young men in Classics & Divinity & *above all set a
good example* as you will readily believe."[6]

Oxford in this period was already astir with the Tractarian
movement, more particularly following Keble's famous sermon on
National Apostasy in 1833. Head was brought into close touch
with persons who were prominent or would later become prominent in the religious and literary life of England, including
Manning and Newman, the brothers Wilberforce, R. H. Froude,
Edward Villiers, and Denison, later Bishop of Salisbury.[7] Head
however in these years had his eyes on Europe and its treasures
of literature and art; he took no deep personal interest in the
religious controversy raging about him. Of all the friendships
that he formed at Oxford, the most lasting and undoubtedly the
closest was with George Cornewall Lewis. Lewis had been
elected into a studentship at Christ Church in 1826. After being
called to the Bar in 1830, he began to practise on the Oxford cir-
cuit where Head saw him frequently during the period of his

[5]Merton College Register, *s.a.* 1830–39.
[6]B.M., Add. MSS. 37184, f. 402, Head to Babbage, n.d. [autumn, 1830].
[7]Merton College Register, *s.a.* 1830–39. Manning, Denison, Villiers, and Elgin
were all fellows of Merton at the same time as Head.

residence at Merton. A mutual friend, many years later after both had died, said of Head and Lewis:

No two men could be more singularly fitted to love and esteem each other and, in a certain sense, to supply each other's deficiencies. Both were strongly addicted to the study of the past; but Lewis more in relation to antiquities and politics, Head especially in the province of history and art. Both were classical scholars of mark—Lewis, no doubt, with far more of industry and research, Head with at least equal elegance. Both were early engaged in the same line of political and social speculations; and in both liberal tendencies were accompanied by the same singular candour and modesty of judgment.[8]

It was while Head was still at Merton that the Warden and Fellows resolved to petition the House of Lords (through the Archbishop of Canterbury, Visitor) against any appointment of commissioners to inquire respecting the statutes and administration of the different colleges and halls at Oxford and Cambridge. When a royal commission with somewhat wider terms of reference was created in 1850 Head was serving as lieutenant governor of New Brunswick. He was sent by the secretary to the commissioners a copy of the paper addressed to all the heads of houses, all professors and public officers of Oxford, and to other eminent persons connected with the University "whose station and experience were thought to merit the public confidence." Having had his attention directed to some sixteen questions, Head sent a lengthy and thoughtful reply, dated at Government House, Fredericton, in May, 1851.[9] Although written nearly fifteen years after he had severed his active connection with Oxford his views were based largely on his experience there and may be conveniently described at this point.

According to his recollection, "the ignorance of many students just admitted from private tutors, was astounding. . . . The University, at least in my time, was deficient in Latin scholarship. . . ." He added that it would supply one great want in English education "if the elements of the Roman law were really taught. Without those elements the public and municipal law of Europe generally is unintelligible. It was also clear that the physical sciences had been "most unjustly depreciated and discouraged at Oxford."

[8]*Proc. Royal Society*, XVI (1867–68), lxxi; *Edinburgh Review*, CXVIII (1863), 136–66.
[9]*Oxford University Commission Report* (1852), Evidence, part V.

Turning to the question of government interference in the internal affairs of Oxford, one of the most controversial features of the inquiry, Head dealt at some length with the distinction that must be made in this regard between public corporations such as the University itself, and private corporations such as the individual colleges. He admitted first, "as every Englishman must do," that there might well be an "abstract" right of parliament to override by its legislation the statutes of both public and private corporations. Drawing an example from the time of his distinguished forbear, he noted: "The noble opposition of Magdalen College to King James II was what it was because it was made against the *unlawful* exercise of the Royal Prerogative, not against the *legal* and constitutional enactments of a Sovereign Legislature of which the Crown is a part."[10]

Whatever its abstract right, however, Head believed that in practice even parliament should take account of the difference in status between the University and the colleges. In the case of the former, it might quite properly intervene from time to time by positive enactments directing the manner in which the privileges, granted in the first place by the Crown and the nation, could best be used for the continuing advantage of the nation at large. In the case of the colleges, however, regulated originally by the terms of private endowments, "the analogy of English law and the sound feeling of the English people" would best be answered by making legislative interference negative—that is, parliament should confine itself merely to authorizing the colleges to abstain from enforcing such of their regulations as no longer accorded with the will of their members. Some authorities might argue that even this much interference with private institutions was unwarranted. Head could not agree: "Is it not almost absurd to attribute to the wishes of a fallible man, living in the thirteenth or fourteenth century, a power of binding in perpetuity a corporate body endowed with an artificial existence by the law alone?" In fact, it seemed to Head that very serious disadvantages indeed might result if there were not in all college charters and statutes an implied condition of obedience to the law of the land as it might be modified with the passage of time and change

[10]*Ibid.*, p. 158. The reference is to the attempt of James II to expel the fellows of Magdalen because of their refusal to accept a Roman Catholic president of his nomination. For the connection of the king and Sir Richard Head, and of Sir John Head with Magdalen College, see above, pp. 3, 4.

of social viewpoints. There was much shrewd common sense in these observations by Head, which went far beyond the questions raised by the commission, and they provide a useful insight into a working theory of public law and legislative interference with private rights which more than once in official dealings he had to carry into practice.

In answer to the commissioners' question on the usefulness of Bodley's Library, Sir Edmund forwarded a copy of a pamphlet (*A Few Words on the Bodleian Library*) which he had published, anonymously, at Oxford in 1833. The text, which examines the statutory provisions governing the conduct of the library, and the then apparent limitations on its usefulness, was reprinted in full in the commission's *Report*. One passage from this interesting pamphlet foreshadows the mind of the colonial governor and servant of the Crown of twenty years later. The following cautionary injunction applied originally to Oxford, but it subsequently took on a wider application when his field of interest expanded:

As to incurring the imputation of a want of sufficient regard for the institutions of this place, I must consider that such an attachment is most truly shown, not by shutting one's eyes to any defects in our system, but by an anxiety that Oxford should lead the way in opening every avenue to knowledge, and hold the high station in the eyes of the country which such a course would ensure. To strain for this object without yielding to any affectation of liberality, or stubbornly adhering to established forms, is our duty and therefore our interest. . . .

On many later occasions his views on important issues of colonial policy were marked by exactly this same moderate and enlightened liberal-conservatism.[11]

The considerations which led Edmund Head to exchange the academic life of Oxford for a civil appointment in 1836 probably were related to pecuniary reverses in his family and to his determination to make his own way, unaided by his father. He had already begun legal studies, entering at Lincoln's Inn on April 29, 1835, though he was never called.[12] On January 18,

[11]In sending three copies of his pamphlet to Charles Babbage, Head wrote: "Will you accept a copy of a sort of libel on the University . . . ? I hope it will produce an attack on the authorities here [Oxford] on the points in question. Such are the parricidal [?] lessons you have taught me." B.M., Add. MSS. 37186, f. 192, Head to Babbage, n.d. [1833].

[12]Lincoln's Inn, Admission Register, *s.a.* 1835, p. 93. Head took his name off the books of the Society on November 2, 1842. According to J. C. Dent, *Canadian*

1836, apparently through the influence of his friend Lewis, whose father was the senior commissioner, Head was appointed an assistant Poor Law commissioner at an annual salary of £700. During the next four years his duties took him into the counties of Hereford and Radnor, and parts of Worcester, Glamorgan, Monmouth, Cardigan, and Carmarthen. It was while living in Herefordshire that he met Anna Maria Yorke, daughter of the Rev. Philip Yorke, prebendary of Ely, and great-granddaughter of the famous first Earl of Hardwicke. They were married at Ross-on-Wye on November 27, 1838. During the winter of 1840 and the early part of 1841 Head served as assistant commissioner for the metropolitan area of London. This brought him into renewed contact with Lewis who had in the meanwhile succeeded his father as one of the chief commissioners. Later in 1841, Head himself was promoted to a chief commissionership on the resignation of J. G. Shaw-Lefevre, and he remained in this post along with Lewis and the third chief commissioner, George Nicholls, until the Poor Law commission came to its unhappy ending in 1847[13]

The New Poor Law of 1834, which it was Head's duty to help administer in these various capacities for over ten years, was an important and revolutionary experiment in re-defining the legal relations between rich and poor, and indeed in regard to the whole field of English local government. It was at the same time a chief centre of violent controversy and agitation in that particularly disturbed period in English domestic history. Being shot at, as Head was on one occasion, was amongst the many hazards of an assistant commissioner's life;[14] and being exposed to a long campaign of vilification in the press and parliament,

Portrait Gallery, IV, 158–59, and H. J. Morgan, *Sketches of Celebrated Canadians*, p. 551, an article which Head published in the *Foreign Quarterly Review*, XXVI (May 1, 1834) on Spanish painters is said to have been the means of determining his vocation in life by attracting the attention of the Marquess of Lansdowne, who in consequence of it advised him to turn his attention to ecclesiastical law. Such advice, from such a quarter, was not to be despised, as it implied a tacit promise of patronage. Head devoted himself industriously to the prescribed course of study and was soon afterwards appointed an assistant Poor Law commissioner. No corroborative evidence has been discovered to prove the truth of this story but it does not seem unreasonable.

[13]Sidney and Beatrice Webb, *English Poor Law History*, part II, *passim*. See also: P.R.O., M.H. 1/7,204; 1/27,181; *Eighth Report of Civil Service Commissioners* (London, 1863), p. v.

[14]S. E. Finer, *Sir Edwin Chadwick*, p. 141.

climaxed by the ordeal of questioning and cross-questioning before a select committee of the House of Commons, was the still harder fate of the commissioners. On the whole Head's contributions in the realm of Poor Law administration do not appear to have been of major significance, and they need not be examined in detail. What is, however, significant in this period of his career is the experience he gained from being plunged into the midst of a raging torrent of controversy and obliged to deal with most complex and delicate administrative and political problems, and with all types of people, frequently in the harsh glare of hostile publicity. These years, anxious and unsatisfactory as they must in many ways have been, were the years during which the scholar became as well the administrator. His character was shaped and his knowledge of men and governments rounded out in such a way as to prepare him for becoming one of the leading colonial governors of his generation.

As an assistant commissioner in the west of England and in Wales, Head's work from 1836 on was largely of a routine nature so far as can be judged from the reports he sent to the chief commissioners at Somerset House:[15] the founding of new "unions," as these larger units of Poor Law administration were called, and the setting up of boards of guardians to govern them; the supervising and counselling of the guardians in such matters as discipline and rating; and, as it chanced, inquiring into the disturbances that coincided with the period of Chartist activities in the late 1830's. These Poor Law reports show, as do also Head's later despatches from Canada, that official correspondence need not be shorn of literary elegance. And, on more than one occasion, they foreshadow too his special and characteristic interest in the long-range, psychological implications of even the most immediate and practical problems. For instance, in a report of May 21, 1837, he describes the current discontent and excitement prevailing in the neighbourhood of Cardigan and draws attention to the woefully inadequate resources there for the maintenance of law and order. He is not content, however, merely to urge the need for "the establishment of some more efficient police than at present existing," and for the adoption of other practical remedies. Looking into the future, he sees that the very organization of such bodies as the boards of guardians would help

[15]P.R.O., H.O. 73, *passim.*

improve the situation. They would give training and experience to the crude Welsh farmers and yoemen, and serve to fit them for public business of every kind.

There is a wider gap between this class and those of the next grade in Wales than in any other part of the United Kingdom. The existence of a notion of anything like public principle is extremely rare among them— the motives of following this or that individual or of supporting this or that friend are the most common sources of action, nor does there appear the same reluctance to avow it as in the more enlightened districts. They have little or no belief in the purity of others' conduct, and the administration of justice is always considered by the lower classes to be determined by favour. . . .

A board of guardians must bring the farmers—previously subject to no public opinion at all—into contact with the magistrates and with persons "certainly better educated and obliged at least to *profess* purer motives." This would be a great point gained in public morality. Head's report concludes:

My belief is that by making the *profession* of better motives necessary, by the operation of a more extended public opinion, we are laying the foundation of a really better mode of action. The first step to be gained is that a man should be ashamed to avow a job though he may yet be well-inclined to effect it, and this step I think the organization of Boards of Guardians has a direct tendency to secure. By slow degrees we may hope that it may elevate a class of men cut off from the action of all opinion but that of their immediate neighbours and equals, to better habits of public business and to such a due and conscientious discharge of the duties of a citizen as it is the object of all liberal institutions to secure.

In this report are phrases strikingly similar to those Head would use in official correspondence from the other side of the Atlantic a number of years later.

A private letter to Lewis of the same year puts many of the same views, with less studied candour but with the same general effect:

George Clive ended a letter to me not long ago with the following benevolent and pious ejaculation, written from the depth of Wales: "that the devil would fly away with this miserable race of Celtic savages is the fervent prayer of yours sincerely, G. C.".—I need not say how heartily I repeat "Amen" to the above petition. . . . The gradual action of Boards of Guardians, railroads, and other opportunities of intercourse, may civilise them in about three centuries.[16]

[16]Lewis, *Letters*, p. 79, Head to Lewis, April 27, 1837.

These observations, public and private, were written in, and prompted by, an age in which the working class as a whole still had no parliamentary franchise, in which newspapers were still almost invariably too expensive for individual reading, in which the railway was only beginning to reduce the hazard of distance, and in an era quite devoid of instruments of mass propaganda such as the radio and the cinema. But they touch upon the essence of democratic government on the British model, which even in 1837 was challenging the boldest spirits of the Canadas; and they embody the idea of civic self-importance which was perhaps the most striking characteristic of Head's thoughts on political affairs and one which was ever present during his later career in British North America.

Head's appointment in 1841 to be one of the three chief Poor Law commissioners was of more than personal importance—it marked a turning point in the long struggle that had gone on within the commission since its formation between the Lewis faction and that of the redoubtable Edwin Chadwick.[17] Chadwick was, and had been from the beginning, not a commissioner but merely the secretary to the commission. However, he was a very special sort of secretary, because he had taken a leading part in drafting the Poor Law itself, he had had every right to expect appointment as one of the original commissioners, and when he finally agreed to accept the more humble office, had been given certain promises which, although vague, made it possible for him to assume an independent and almost dominant role within Somerset House. Moreover, Chadwick was a man of extraordinary vigour and determination, passionately concerned with the Poor Law which he considered to have been his own creation, and impatient to the point of fanaticism with colleagues—and more particularly, with superiors—who were less intense in their enthusiasm or more conscious of the need for compromising with circumstances. The activities of this most intractable secretary, along with the other extreme difficulties of administering the Poor Law in the 1830's, had finally led the elder Lewis to seek the shelter of retirement in 1839. Chadwick had hoped to succeed him, and was bitterly disappointed when the Government appointed instead the son, G. C. Lewis. The latter was a quiet, but very firm and assured young man, and an able administrator who was to go on eventually to high cabinet office. He was aware

[17]Finer, *Chadwick*, pp. 200–7.

of the difficulties of the situation into which he was entering and
was determined from the first to assert his full authority. With
Nicholls living now almost entirely in Ireland in charge of the
Poor Law there, and Shaw-Lefevre inclined to remain in the
background, Somerset House became more than ever divided
between the supporters of the two main protagonists. The resignation of Shaw-Lefevre in 1841 was the occasion for the final test
of their strength.

Once again Chadwick hoped for his own promotion. Other
names however were put forward for what was clearly an
"appointment fraught with difficulties,"[18] and gradually it became
clear that Lewis was exerting his influence in favour of Head.
Shaw-Lefevre, who was also a close friend of Head's, did like-
wise. The home secretary, with whom the appointment rested,
was Lord Normanby. Impressed by Head's Poor Law record,
though not yet personally acquainted with him, Normanby
seems to have been on the point of nominating him for the
vacancy when one of the frequent political crises of the time
brought about a sudden dissolution of parliament. In the election
that followed, Normanby and his Whig colleagues were swept
from office. The new home secretary, Sir James Graham, in spite
of every effort by Chadwick, and in disregard of party considerations, came to the same conclusion as his predecessor that Head's
promotion was the best solution of the difficulty. Its announcement made Lewis's victory complete and broke Chadwick's
power so far as the Poor Law was concerned. Lewis and Head
were unable to remove Chadwick, but by altering office pro-
cedures and by other means they reduced his participation to a
minimum. Along with Graham, with whom they worked very
closely, they were then in a position to assume full control.[19]

The precise extent to which Head helped to shape the policy

[18]*Ibid.*, p. 203, Normanby to Russell, June 28, 1841.
[19]Henry Reeve (ed.), *Greville Memoirs*, Second Part, II, 60:
"*November 30th.*—Graham has made Sir Edmund Head Poor Law Commissioner,
an appointment very creditable to him. . . . The appointment of Head is what
Normanby was urged, but was afraid, to make. He shrank from it, however, from
very poor reasons, not honourable to himself or to others concerned. First of all,
John Russell's trying to thrust Rich upon him, a man not for one moment to be
compared with Head, and then because Chadwick was against him. Accordingly
he left it to the Tories, fully expecting they would appoint Colonel A'Court; but
Graham has thrown over all party considerations, and having, after strict enquiry,
satisfied himself that Head is the ablest and fittest man, he has given him the situation."

of the commission during the next six years is impossible to say. Close personal friends as well as colleagues, Head and Lewis must undoubtedly have made major decisions by a process of discussion and mutual agreement. Both too were active in day-to-day administration—one reads, for example, of Head ordering that the day appointed for the christening of the Prince of Wales "be observed as a holiday by the officers of the Commission";[20] calling on his friend Babbage to "crack your brains on a difficult point of statistics";[21] travelling to Scotland, at the request of the home secretary, to inquire into the amount of distress in the weaving industry at Paisley, where the relief fund had been "grievously mismanaged."[22] Matters of this sort, some trivial, some of national importance, but all of a practical, more or less routine nature, constituted the real work of the commission during these years, and Head had a full share in handling them.

Head lived during these years in London first at 41, Cambridge Terrace, Hyde Park, and from 1843 on at 2, Chester Place, Hyde Park Square. Several chance references indicate that his health was of some concern to himself and his friends during 1842 and 1843.[23] It may be that it was at this time that epilepsy first manifested itself. Whether then or later, Head seems to have suffered from the *petit mal* form of this disease for much of the remainder of his life. It caused him at infrequent intervals to lose consciousness for a few seconds—to break off a conversation, for example, stare fixedly in front of him, and then resume talking as though nothing had happened. There was apparently no physical or mental deterioration as a result. Indeed one close friend writing after Head's death noted particularly that when he had visited Head toward the end of his term in Canada "he was . . . full of physical strength, which he delighted to enjoy in the most vigorous bodily exercises, and he took . . . pleasure in the resources of his marvellous memory, as well as in a sort of general intellectual activity, which he spread over . . . many subjects of elegant culture, as well as of judicial and administrative policy."[24]

[20]P.R.O., M.H. 1/32, 79.
[21]B.M. Add. MSS. 37192, f. 43, Head to Babbage, February 14, 1842.
[22]Lewis, *Letters*, p. 119.
[23]*Ibid.*, Lewis to Grote, March 13, 1842; B.M., Add. MSS. 37192, f. 329, Head to Babbage, June 17, 1843.
[24]G. S. Hillard (ed.), *George Ticknor*, II, 482–83, Ticknor to E. Twistleton, March 22, 1868.

Commenting again on Head's memory, which impressed all who knew him as being most phenomenal, this same friend wrote on another occasion: "I think he can repeat more poetry, Greek, Latin, German, and Spanish, than any person I ever knew."[25] The main effect of the disease seems to have been to make Head increasingly irritable in later life.[26]

Meanwhile, in London, Head was "the mirthful member of a small, and, but for him, somewhat grave circle of friends of which Edward Villiers was the centre."[27] This circle, in addition to Lewis who married Villiers' sister in 1844, probably included Henry Taylor, the poet and Colonial Office official, John Austin, the jurist, and his bluestocking wife, Sarah Taylor, Henry Hart Milman, soon to be Dean of St. Paul's, Edward Twistleton, and perhaps a few others. Babbage as well remained a close friend of Head's, as did Sir Charles Lyell, the geologist. Philology, art, literature, history, and government—a wide variety of cultural and intellectual pursuits, ranging from the most recondite to the greatest topics of the day—these were the compelling interest of the members of this group and bound them together in life-long friendships. Head, himself in the very midst of the difficulties in which the Poor Law Commission was embroiled at the time, translated and edited Part II of Kugler's famous *Handbook of the History of Painting*, the part dealing with the German, Flemish, and Dutch schools. He published this in 1846, and two years later brought out a uniform volume on the Spanish and French schools which he had completely re-written.

By the time this second volume appeared Head's connection with the Poor Law Commission had terminated and he had left London to begin upon a new career in North America. The Poor Law Commission, for all its effective work, had never seemed to have, or to be able to acquire, the character of finality in either its structure or its conduct. Its basic weaknesses have already been outlined above. In view of these, it was almost constantly under attack.[28] The final great storm of public protest was roused

[25]*Ibid.*, p. 424, Ticknor to the Hon. E. Everett, August 22, 1859.

[26]Among other references to this, see E. W. Watkin, *Canada and the United States*, pp. 502–3.

[27]Henry Taylor, *Autobiography*, I, 257–58.

[28]Associations were also formed specifically to organize opposition to the Poor Law Act with a view to obtaining its repeal. Cf. An advertisement of the South Lancashire Anti-Poor Law Association in the *Manchester and Salford Advertiser*, November 11, 1837 (copy in P.R.O., H.O. 73/52).

in 1845 as a result of certain unsavoury incidents brought to light in connection with the affairs of the Andover Union in Berkshire.[29] A parliamentary inquiry into this matter was at first refused by the home secretary, but finally took place when a departmental inquiry proved highly unsatisfactory even to the commissioners themselves. Chadwick's vehement testimony before the House of Commons committee to the effect that the commissioners had countenanced many illegal practices served merely to make doubly sure that the committee's report would be adverse and that a subsequent motion by Disraeli "that the Commissioners have been negligent in their duties" would be passed. A comprehensive revision of the Poor Law administration and some change at least in its personnel was now necessary. As soon as this could be effected, the old commission came to an end on December 17, 1847, and with it the appointments of Head and Lewis, and of Chadwick as well, were terminated. Whatever the public belief, those most closely in touch with the situation were conscious of the fact that the failure of the commission was not in the main the fault of any individuals but was inherent in the system and in the circumstances in which it had had to function. The Government made clear that this was its view of the case when Lewis, winning a seat in parliament, was first appointed to the Board of Control and then within six months or so became under-secretary in the Home Office itself. Chadwick's real worth was recognized by putting him in charge of a royal commission on London sanitation, and this led shortly to his great work on the Board of Health. Head was offered the lieutenant-governorship of New Brunswick.

[29]Maurice Marston, *Sir Edwin Chadwick*, pp. 63–65; Finer, *Chadwick*, pp. 257–88.

II

NEW BRUNSWICK, 1848–1854

TWO

The Beginnings of Responsible Government

WHEN Sir Edmund Head arrived at Fredericton and took the oath of office as lieutenant governor of New Brunswick on April 11, 1848, he was entering in his early forties upon a new career in a very different environment from that to which he had been accustomed. The question arises: to what extent was this mere acquiescence in the only course that seemed open to him, to what extent was he following his own personal bent? The answer is more complex than is apparent at first glance. Following the decisions of the spring of 1847 which meant that their connection with the Poor Law administration would shortly be terminated, Head and Lewis had waited with natural anxiety to learn what attitude the Government might take to their further employment. Accordingly, in August, when Lewis won his by-election and received the offer of a junior post in the Government from Russell, he notified Head of this immediately: " . . . I lose no time in communicating it to you, as showing what his intentions are to the commissioners. It seems to me that the great difficulty in your case is to find an office that will suit you."[1] When not long afterwards Head was tendered the New Brunswick appointment, it might seem that he had little alternative but to accept.

This was no doubt true, by and large, but it is a fact nevertheless that Head had much earlier given serious consideration to a career in the colonial service. There may even be some foundation for the delightful rumour that Lord Glenelg had intended to appoint Edmund Walker Head rather than Francis Bond Head as lieutenant governor of Upper Canada in 1835 but confused the two names as many others have done since. Francis Hincks in his *Reminiscences* states that J. A. Roebuck and "another Imperial statesman" both assured him definitely that this was

---

[1]Lewis, *Letters*, p. 157, Lewis to Head, August 16, 1847.

the case.[2] Careful study of the circumstances and of the back-grounds of the two men makes the story seem almost incredible—almost as incredible indeed as Bond Head's own account of how he was awakened in the middle of the night by a courier from the Colonial Office and read by candlelight with growing con-sternation that he was to proceed at once to London and thence to Upper Canada as its new lieutenant governor![3]

Whatever the truth of this strange affair may be, Edmund Head did decide at just about that time not to take a colonial appointment, but to join the Poor Law administration instead. Lewis who had done all in his power to persuade him to remain in England assured him that his choice was wise. "The more I see of colonial life," he wrote from Malta, where he was serving on a special commission of inquiry in 1836 and 1837, "the more I am satisfied that you did rightly in preferring your present employment, with all its drawbacks, to the colonial service. The scum of England is poured into the colonies. . . . I confess it seems to me that no man who is not in debt, or has not a large family, is justified in going out to a colony."[4]

By 1847, however, the situation was somewhat different. Head's experience in the Poor Law Commission had hardly been such as to predispose him in favour of similar employment at home. Moreover, the reputation of the colonial service stood much higher than it had ten years before, particularly because of Lord Grey's success in raising the standard of appointments. Even Lewis was inclined to think the New Brunswick opportunity a good one, although sorry for personal reasons to see Head leave England. "I cannot tell you how glad I was to receive the account of Lord Grey's offer . . . ," he wrote to Head. "I collect that you have made inquiries which satisfy you as to the eligibility of the appointment. I know very little about the place; I fear it is ter-ribly cold, but I suppose pine-wood is cheap, and stoves are

[2]Francis Hincks, *Reminiscences*, pp. 14–15.

[3]F. B. Head, *A Narrative*, pp. 23–25. The blood relationship of Edmund and Francis Head was very remote, going back to a common ancestor in the seven-teenth century. The arms of the two branches of the family were different, though the motto, "Study Quiet," was the same. There is no evidence of any association between the two men before their common experience of appointments in Canada, although they may probably have met. Their descendants in the twentieth century maintain a family contact with one another. For a full discussion of Glenelg's alleged confusion see James A. Gibson's "The 'Persistent Fallacy' of the Gover-nors Head," *Canadian Historical Review*, XIX (September, 1938), 295.

[4]Lewis, *Letters*, p. 90, Lewis to Head, October 3, 1837.

capacious. It is odd it should be in North America. You must take some lessons about *hoisting the British colours*, &c."[5] To their mutual friend George Grote, the historian, Lewis added, "It is complete banishment into the backwoods, but the climate is better than Canada; and, after all that has passed, Head accepted it without hesitation. The employment is honourable and sufficiently lucrative. For my part, I regret very much that he could not be appointed to some office in this country."[6]

The New Brunswick in which Head was to live for the next six years was almost as much a "backwoods" colony as Lewis believed it to be. Its population of some 200,000 lived for the most part along the Bay of Fundy and the North Shore and in some narrow lines of settlement that penetrated up river valleys into the interior. As a result, the colony was virtually an aggregation of individual communities which were almost isolated from one another by great areas of forests and hills. Apart from Fredericton, the capital, situated some eighty miles up the St. John River, the major centres were all seaports. Saint John was the largest of these and the provincial metropolis. Lumbering, shipbuilding, fishing, and agriculture were necessarily the main occupations of the people, and since only the oldest families had arrived more than one or two generations before, provincial society was still generally crude and without much order or stability.

Lack of unity was the source of a number of the colony's most serious problems. In so far as this was due to geography, it could gradually be overcome by building roads, bridges, and later railways. That accounts for what at first seems a disproportionate amount of the New Brunswick government's attention being devoted always to such matters. There were, however, other barriers as well which divided New Brunswick and accentuated the very dangerous tendency for local and group interests to take precedence over the welfare of the colony as a whole. Race, religion, and manner of settlement were all factors in preventing the province's comparatively small number of inhabitants from forming a cohesive and self-conscious political unit.

Differences of racial or national origin were probably the least important in the 1840's. The Indians were a small helpless remnant, while the French, though more numerous and by no

[5]*Ibid.*, p. 157, Lewis to Head, September 28, 1847.
[6]*Ibid.*, p. 162, Lewis to Grote, November 5, 1847.

means decadent, dwelt along the north-eastern shore and were almost entirely cut off from the rest of the province. Their quiet industrious mode of life was typical of French *habitants* whether in Canada or in Acadia. They engaged in farming and fishing on a small scale and were moderately prosperous. For more than twenty years after the foundation of the province, however, they had been disqualified by their Roman Catholic religion from exercising the franchise, and for another twenty years they were unable to accept any government office. They had become accustomed therefore to take no part in the affairs of the colony, but to live their own lives in their own communities, guided by their own priests. Their geographic isolation had preserved these habits, and even when they were given full political rights, their influence remained as late as Head's time almost negligible.

Religious discrimination which took the form of giving special advantages to the Church of England was a more significant source of political division. There was no established church in New Brunswick, but the government-supported King's College and many of the schools were virtually Anglican, and so were almost all government officials prior to 1848. It was not until that year that L. A. Wilmot became the first Nonconformist to hold the office of attorney general, and in 1851 he set a similar precedent for the Bench when he accepted a judgeship.

Religious differences were accentuated in some degree by the manner in which the province had been settled. The first English-speaking settlers had begun to arrive in New Brunswick by 1758, on the eve of the conquest of Canada, and for some twenty-five years they had infiltrated slowly, most coming from the New England colonies to the south. By the outbreak of the American Revolution, there were a number of small communities in existence along the Bay of Fundy, and up the St. John River. With the exception of a Yorkshire settlement on the Chignecto Isthmus, all were essentially replicas of their parent communities in Massachusetts or Connecticut. They were organized into townships; their inhabitants were hardy, independent, God-fearing Calvinists; and their principal occupations, apart from trade, were shipbuilding, agriculture, and fishing. On the arrival of the Loyalists in 1783, these "Old Inhabitants" became at once a minority and—what is sometimes overlooked—they tended to become aggressive and self-conscious in a way peculiar to minorities. They did not lose their identity in the new wave of immigrants; but, particularly in Saint John, where priority helped to compensate for lack of numbers, they continued to have a characteristic influence. The Saint John merchants, like their cousins in Boston, held to a hard-headed, close-fisted philosophy in which there was little room for a sentiment such as that of loyalty to the Empire. During the Revolution, the sympathies of most had been on the republican side; and it is significant that in 1849, when Imperial free trade seemed to threaten their lumbering and shipping interests, they did not hesitate to raise from the midst of the "Loyalist" province the cry of "annexation."

The Loyalists were different in a number of respects. As early as 1776, when Boston was evacuated, refugees had begun to arrive in the northern colonies. Few went to the backwoods of New Brunswick, however, until May, 1783, when the first great body landed at Saint John. This group were rapidly followed by others, bringing the total to almost 14,000 by the end of the year. They did not come in the main from New England, but from New York where they had embarked, or from still farther south. They were, of course, intensely patriotic. Many were soldiers who had fought with the British armies. Whole regiments were disbanded and given lands up the St. John along the old post trail to Canada. Some were professional men, others shop-keepers or farmers. The majority were destitute and unaccustomed to the hardships of pioneer life which they now had to face. They were obliged therefore to spend their whole energy in winning a livelihood. Their interests became centred in their own particular localities, and their sole requirement of the colonial government was that it undertake to build the roads and bridges which they so urgently needed. A smaller but very important group of Loyalists were concerned with the government in a more immediate way. Mainly Anglican, they had been lawyers and office-holders in the old colonies and now they congregated in Saint John and Fredericton, becoming the first official class of the newly constituted province.

The Loyalists had been followed into the province by another tide of immigration which had begun to flow after the Napoleonic wars. The wars themselves had stimulated the economic development of the province, and made possible the absorption in the post-war years of quite large numbers of those trying to escape from the depression and unemployment that beset Britain after peace was made. Once started, the movement from the British

Isles had continued at a varying rate for the next thirty years. It had culminated with the great Irish influx of 1847. The immigrants of these years were of all types, but they had one thing in common—all were newcomers as compared with the Loyalists and the "Old Inhabitants." They found these earlier arrivals firmly ensconced in the political and economic leadership of the colony, and their struggle for equality constituted an important element in the division of opinion that occurred in New Brunswick on the subject of Responsible Government.

Head had an opportunity to learn something of the background of New Brunswick affairs before his departure from England. At the Colonial Office in the first weeks of 1848, he studied the despatches of Sir William Colebrooke, whom he was to succeed, and had long conversations with various officials, especially with his friend Herman Merivale, the permanent under-secretary. The most important thing he found out was that the change of governors was to be made the occasion for introducing what had come to be known in North America as Responsible Government: a system of ministerial responsibility to the legislature which was as close an approximation as was possible in a colony to the British system of cabinet or parliamentary government. This would require the reconstruction of the New Brunswick executive council along more popular lines and certain other innovations not to be hastily undertaken by a new governor. It was decided therefore, with Head's concurrence, that he should postpone his arrival in the province until the legislature had been prorogued in the early spring. Then he would have time to study the situation, make personal contacts with the leading men of the colony, and proceed with whatever changes seemed necessary in an atmosphere free from the tension of legislative debate.[7]

In March, 1848, Sir Edmund Head sailed from Liverpool on board the S.S. *Caledonia* to take up his first colonial appointment. He was accompanied by Lady Head, their two small children, his private secretary Richard Pennefather, and several servants. Landing in Halifax, they spent a week as guests of Sir John Harvey, the lieutenant governor of Nova Scotia, awaiting word that the New Brunswick session had ended, and then went on through Windsor and across the Bay of Fundy to Saint John. It was from the deck of the steamer *Saxe Gotha*, as she entered

[7]P.R.O., C.O. 188/104, Colebrooke to Grey, February 8, 1848, minutes.

Saint John harbour very early on the morning of April 7, 1848, that Head caught his first glimpse of the province he was to govern for the next six years.

A description of Head that appeared in the Halifax *Sun* at this time, and was copied in several of the New Brunswick papers in anticipation of his arrival, is one of the few portraying in some detail his personal appearance, and it reveals a shrewd insight into his character:

His Excellency is of slender make—5 feet 9 or 10 inches in height, and apparently on the sunny side of 50. He has a slight stoop—as though he had laboured long and studiously at the desk. His complexion is fair—his eyes light blue, full and large—his hair is sandy, and scant. His address is easy and familiar—but the close observer could not fail to trace in the lines about his mouth indications of decision and firmness.[8]

At Saint John, the formalities attendant upon vice-regal life began somewhat earlier in the day than would now be probable:

His Excellency Sir Edmund Head accompanied by Lady Head and family, and his Private Secretary, Mr. Pennefather, arrived here yesterday morning at 5 o'clock, in the steamer Saxe Gotha. . . . Lady Head and family came on shore soon after the Steamer's arrival, and shortly after seven o'clock His Excellency landed and proceeded in Sir W. Colebrooke's carriage to the Saint John Hotel, where he was received by a Guard of Honour of the 33rd Regiment . . . the Band playing the National Anthem. The Citizens who had assembled also welcomed His Excellency with three hearty cheers.

Sir William Colebrooke's farewell Levee took place at 2 o'clock, today, at the Court House, when the gentlemen who attended had an opportunity also of paying their respects to Sir Edmund Head.[9]

Similar ceremonies followed at Fredericton after the trip by boat up the St. John River, the beauty of which the Heads thus enjoyed for the first time. They culminated on April 11, when Head went in state to the Council Chamber in the Legislative Building and presented his commission of government, took the usual oaths of office, and received the usual loyal addresses of welcome.[10]

The problem that faced Head, of introducing Responsible Government in New Brunswick, was rather different from that of

[8]Halifax *Sun*, March 29, 1848.

[9]*Ibid.*, April 17, 1848.

[10]P.A.C., N.B. Executive Council Minutes, April 11, 1848; Fredericton *Reporter*, April 14, 1848. Head's commission was dated at Windsor, October 20, 1847.

Elgin in Canada or of Harvey in Nova Scotia. Public opinion was
still much more thoroughly confused on the subject in New
Brunswick than in the neighbouring provinces where years of
debate led by some exceedingly able individuals had gradually
clarified certain basic principles. In New Brunswick, just a few
years before, at the time of a general election, candidates had
been unashamed in professing their ignorance. One had summed
up Responsible Government simply as "Responsible Nonsense."
Another, clearly putting no stock in theory, asked, "Who has
seen it? Or felt it? Nobody! It is not in existence. . . . There is
no way to render our Legislators responsible, but by turning out
the extravagant and putting in the frugal." A justly modest individual explained that: "Very few people understood what Responsible Government meant; he hardly understood it himself.
It was, in his opinion, just introducing another branch in our
Government."[11] Making due allowance for the exaggerations of
campaign oratory and the wider spread of knowledge by 1848,
there can be no doubt, as soon became evident to Head himself,
that the latter's main duty was not merely to give formal acceptance to the principle of Responsible Government but to explain
it and to work out its full implications in what was still a
politically immature community.

In the meantime, Head had to direct his immediate attention
to two distinct, but interlocking, tasks. One was to lay the
foundations for Responsible Government by inaugurating what
had come to be known in the colony as the "departmental"
system—the system by which the heads of major government
departments would be brought into the executive council and
hold office thenceforth along with its other members on a political
tenure. The second was to decide on actual appointments to such
a council.

The way had been prepared for changing to the departmental
system by two important statements of Colonial Office policy
issued in 1839 and 1847. In the first, Lord John Russell had been
concerned to end the custom that had arisen of regarding heads
of departments, like judges, as virtually holding office for life.
This had made them almost independent of any control by either
governor or legislature, and Russell ordered that all major
administrative appointments should from then on be considered,
in practice as well as in form, as being held "during pleasure."

[11]These quotations are from election speeches of 1842 quoted in G. E. Fenety,
Political Notes, I, 36–37.

Existing occupants of paid positions were to be recognized as having a life interest that they could be asked to abandon only in return for equitable compensation; but members of the council, who as such were unpaid, and all new departmental heads, would become removable at the discretion of the governor.[12] Russell's intention had been merely to bring all members of the colonial administration under the effective control of the governor. He had no wish to make them responsible to the assembly as well. In fact he had believed at that time that the introduction of Responsible Government "might be dangerous or even dishonourable."[13]

By 1847, however, Russell and his Government had come to a different conclusion. This was announced by the new colonial secretary, Lord Grey, in the well-known despatch to Harvey in which he pointed to the British system of cabinet government as "worthy of imitation in the British American colonies," and ordered the appointment to the executive council in future of "those only of the public servants who are to be regarded as removable on losing the confidence of the Assembly."[14] The joint effect of these two statements of 1839 and 1847 was to make the introduction of the "departmental" system possible—the first by giving the governor discretionary powers regarding appointments and dismissals, the second by instructing him to use these powers to ensure the responsibility of the executive to the legislature. In theory at least, difficulty might still be encountered only if it were desired to make political an office held by an individual appointed before 1839, and then all that would be needed would be to grant him an adequate retiring allowance.

Examining the application of these rulings to New Brunswick in 1848, Head concluded that for the present the most necessary offices to bring into the council were those of the attorney general, solicitor general, provincial secretary, and surveyor general.[15] The appropriateness of this so far as the two law offices are con-

---

[12]W. P. M. Kennedy, *Documents of the Canadian Constitution*, pp. 423–24, Russell to Poulett Thomson, October 16, 1839. For discussion of the implications of this famous despatch see *Cambridge Historical Journal*, II (1926–28), 248–51.

[13]Kennedy, *Documents*, pp. 421–23, Russell to Poulett Thomson, October 14, 1839.

[14]*Ibid.*, pp. 496–500, Grey to Harvey, March 31, 1847.

[15]P.R.O., C.O. 188/105, Head to Grey, confidential, May 20, 1848. Except where specifically noted the account of Head's reconstruction of his government is taken from this despatch, on which Grey minuted, when it was received at the Colonial Office: ". . . a remarkably clear & able despatch & Sir E. Head's views are highly judicious."

cerned need not be argued. The provincial secretary in New Brunswick was responsible for the financial and much of the general internal policy of the government, and the surveyor general occupied a key position because of the importance of the sale of crown lands and of timber-cutting rights in the provincial economy. An executive council which did not include these four officials would be greatly handicapped.

A fortunate series of circumstances enabled Head to place all but the surveyor-generalship on a political tenure at once without doing anyone an injustice. The office of attorney general was already vacant, its occupant having died in February. The solicitor general, W. B. Kinnear, held office under the terms of Russell's despatch of 1839 and could therefore be dismissed if necessary. He was, however, a member of the legislative council and was a competent man of moderate opinions who might well form part of the new ministry. Since no one had actually been dismissed on political grounds even after 1839, and since personal rights were still respected more highly than political theories in many quarters in New Brunswick, Head determined to keep Kinnear in office if at all possible and to resist attempts to oust him by those with no better motive than a desire to take his place.

The case of the provincial secretary's office was somewhat different. This was the most important office of all, in many ways, and it was essential that its holder be a member of the assembly as well as of the executive council. In explaining this to Grey, Head added emphatically:

The former condition is the more essential, because the financial affairs of this province are not by any means in a clear position and will within a short time form the subject of further discussion in the Assembly. There exists no financial Secretary or other public officer conversant with the details of the government who can explain or support a measure in that body. . . . It is especially necessary for the Government to have a person in the position of Provincial Secretary, who could support and enforce the measures of the Government in the Assembly, and who therefore must be thoroughly acquainted with the views on which those measures are founded. It will be essential, moreover, that the other members of the council should cordially co-operate with the Secretary for the time being.[16]

The incumbent, J. S. Saunders, could fulfil none of these conditions, but he had been appointed after 1839. Head was pre-

[16]P.R.O., C.O. 188/105, Head to Grey, April 22, 1848.

pared in this case to go to the length of asking for his resignation when Saunders, foreseeing what might happen, applied for another lesser office. "I esteem myself very fortunate," Head wrote to the colonial secretary, "in being able in this instance to propose an arrangement which will substantially satisfy Mr. Saunders, and will yet allow of a Government being formed upon the principles recognized by your Lordship and approved by the Assembly."

The one problem for which there was no immediate solution was that regarding Thomas Baillie, the surveyor general. Appointed prior to 1839 Baillie's grasp on office could be broken only by death or by the willingness of the assembly to grant him an adequate retiring allowance. His conduct of his office, his disproportionately large salary guaranteed by the civil list, and the possibility of bringing about his resignation had been subjects of political controversy in the province for years, and no conclusion was yet in sight. For the time being, Head's only course was to retire the surveyor general from the executive council and advise him to take no further part in politics.

When it became clear that at any rate three heads of departments could be brought into the council on a political tenure, Head turned early in May to the consideration of actual appointments. It is here in particular that the difference between his problem and that of Elgin or Harvey is revealed. There was no party leader in New Brunswick whom Head could call on to form a government. Indeed the fundamental fact of the colony's political life was the absence of organized parties. As late as the previous spring of 1847, in the course of a debate in the assembly, Charles Fisher, who in 1855 after Head's departure would himself form the first party government in the province's history, was reported as saying:

". . . He would regret to see the day when the organization of violent antagonistic political parties would be found necessary in this Province—but that there were two separate and distinct parties springing up around them, was beyond dispute. It had been said by hon. gentlemen of the Government, that no such thing as party existed in this Province. It was true they were not like Nova Scotia—torn to the very centre—family divided against family, and brother against brother, by political party. But he would now warn his hon. friends of the Government to beware lest they stumbled upon the same block the Government had there. He did not wish in a small Province like this, to see Party Government; it was no doubt best where there was plenty of material—but in this small Colony, with not over

200,000 inhabitants, there was little talent enough for one good Government."[17]

As these words of Fisher's indicate, all that there was of political party in New Brunswick—and all that he and most others hoped there would ever have to be—was a certain vague distinction that was springing up between reformers, who had advocated Responsible Government, and conservatives, who had opposed it; but the majority did not belong fully in either category, and there were almost as many shades of opinion on this and other matters as there were men in political life. It might be hardly just to say that a man's politics depended on whether he was in or out of office. Generally speaking, however, the small lawyer-merchant class, mainly Anglican and of Loyalist extraction, which dominated the executive and judicial branches of the government, could not but fear a change that threatened their vested interests. In a colony where professional opportunities were limited, the financial security and social prestige that went with official position had always appeared particularly attractive. Family-compact government had developed, to a greater extent possibly even than in Canada. The Odells, for instance, father and son, had held the major office of provincial secretary, one after the other, for a total of sixty years; and a grandson had been deputy provincial secretary for a time before becoming, successively, registrar and clerk of the executive council, judge of the court of common pleas, member of the legislative and executive councils, and finally postmaster general. Other old families, such as the Peterses, the Blisses, the Streets, the Chipmans, and the Botsfords, always had representatives in the offices of the government and on the Bench. Chief Justice Chipman, to take only one more example, was said to have no less than eight nephews (most of them Botsfords), two cousins, and a brother-in-law holding amongst themselves at least seventeen offices, ranging from advocate general and executive councillor to surrogate of Restigouche County.[18] It was the effect of Responsible Government on their personal and family interests rather than any consideration of principle or party that was almost bound to seem of primary importance to many of the members of this class, and to their would-be successors as well.

[17]Fenety, *Political Notes*, I, 236–37.
[18]P.R.O., C.O. 221/8, Halifax *Sun*, December 19, 1849.

In such circumstances, Head's task of trying to form an avowedly responsible ministry during his first weeks in New Brunswick was a most delicate one. He could not turn to a Baldwin or to a La Fontaine or to a Joseph Howe, and let him choose his own party government. The corresponding individuals in New Brunswick were outstanding as a result of their personal qualifications only, and although they might be known for their opinions on certain questions including Responsible Government, none had a significant following in the legislature. Instead, therefore, it was necessary for Head himself to bring together a number of them into an executive council which could then function collectively as a responsible ministry. The very fact of the predominance of personality over party which placed this burden on his shoulders, made it much weightier, and more dangerous. Even the most scrupulous regard for every individual interest and claim would hardly enable him to escape the charge of favouritism; and regardless of its membership, a ministry formed in this way would inevitably appear, at least, to be the nucleus of a governor's party. Instead of being aloof from party struggles, Head would tend to become the centre around which they developed—an unenviable position for a governor under Responsible Government. Head does not seem to have been fully aware of this danger in 1848, but later when it became more evident, he accepted it as a necessary part of the transition to complete parliamentary government.

Head's procedure in choosing the individuals to constitute his first responsible ministry reflects his characteristic attitude of moderate liberalism—the attitude of a scholar who is at the same time a practical administrator, sympathetic with reform but suspicious of revolution, and inclined rather to build on foundations already laid than to break new ground. He began first by examining the old ministry in the light of the new requirement that it have the confidence of the assembly and with a view to finding what changes if any were needed. There were, in fact, only four of the old nine-member council to be considered. Two had died, two had had to retire because they held non-political offices and so were ineligible for seats in a responsible ministry, and the fifth had decided to withdraw from politics for private reasons. After careful study, Head asked all of those remaining to stay on in the government. Indeed the presence of two of them, R. L. Hazen and E. B. Chandler, seemed essential. Hazen,

although he held no departmental office, had been the real
leader of the government in the assembly for some time, and
Chandler had served in the same capacity in the legislative
council. They were moderately conservative and in Head's
opinion were "the most able and the most influential" of the old
ministry.

In finding colleagues to work with them Head had to choose
between looking to the left or to the right. It is an interesting
commentary on the weakness of the reform movement in New
Brunswick that such a choice could exist at the time of the
formation of the first Responsible Government, but in fact the
advice of Colebrooke just before his departure had been in favour
of the second alternative. He had recommended the promotion
of Kinnear to the office of attorney general and the appointment
as solicitor general of J. A. Street whose views were more conservative than liberal. A government centring around these men
would have leaned distinctly toward the right. Head would
eventually turn to Street in the crisis of 1851, but in 1848 he
believed rightly that a conservative government would not have
the confidence of the assembly in which the tide seemed to be
turning slowly in the direction of reform. He decided instead,
therefore, to invite Lemuel A. Wilmot, New Brunswick's leading
reformer, to the council table, along with Charles Fisher, his
chief lieutenant. In this he had the support of Hazen and
Chandler who agreed that since Responsible Government was
being introduced the backing of its most active advocates would
be necessary for a strong ministry.

Head's formation of this moderate coalition of Wilmot reformers and conservatives of the Hazen-Chandler type has frequently been compared unfavourably with Elgin's clear-cut
support of a one-party government, and in fact it has been generally stated that it was not until Head's departure that New
Brunswick was able to *win* real Responsible Government under
a reform ministry led by Charles Fisher. This criticism, made
originally by contemporaries with a political axe to grind, and
repeated by later writers, accustomed to think in terms of party,
contains some truth but is misleading. A coalition government
chosen by the governor was clearly unsatisfactory, but it seemed
natural, and indeed the sole arrangement then possible, in New
Brunswick. It was in conformity with New Brunswick's tra-
ditional aversion to party conflict and it was the only type of

government that could obtain majority support in the assembly. Wilmot, and Charles Fisher himself, had no hesitation whatsoever in 1848 in joining it, and Fisher's comments in the debate of the year before show that it accorded exactly with his belief at that time in the virtues of non-party government. That it coincided as well with Head's philosophy of political moderation was incidental.

The decision made as to the general nature of the new government, all that remained was some last-minute bargaining for the three departmental positions which carried with them salaries and administrative authority. Wilmot held out for the office of attorney general. This senior law office was most attractive to a lawyer not only in itself but because its holder was usually considered to be next in line for the chief-justiceship, a position of very high honour and emolument and having the security of tenure that would now disappear from political office. Pertinent in this regard was the fact that Chief Justice Chipman was aged and infirm. On the basis of personal standing in the legal profession, Kinnear, Chandler, and Hazen all had a better right to the appointment, but Wilmot's claims on political grounds were unanswerable. "He looks upon himself," Head commented, "as a perservering & consistent advocate of those principles of responsible govt. which have been recognized by Her Majesty's Govt at Home, and he expects to reap the benefit of that consistency. It is impossible to deny that there is much justice in this view, & I feel that the position thus taken by him has a real foundation in the influence which he has exercised, and is likely to exercise, in the House of Assembly." After failing to tempt Wilmot with the provincial-secretaryship, therefore, Head had to agree that political considerations being paramount, Wilmot should become attorney general.

Kinnear was content under the circumstances to be allowed to keep his position as solicitor general and Hazen had reached the stage of wishing to take a less active part in public affairs. The real problem that arose out of Wilmot's appointment was how to safeguard the interests of Chandler whose ability and influence made him almost as important to the government in the legislative council as Wilmot would be in the assembly. Chandler had been willing to give up his claim to the attorney-generalship if he were made solicitor general instead and strong pressure was brought to bear on Head in favour of this solution.

Head, however, was loath to countenance what would be considered, in a province not yet accustomed to political tenure, an injustice to Kinnear, and instead it was finally agreed that Chandler should remain in the government without portfolio, but should receive written assurance from both Wilmot and Fisher that they would recognize the superiority of his claim to the first vacancy that might occur on the Bench.[19] Since Chandler's ambitions at that time were directed towards becoming a judge, this was a satisfactory compromise all around.

The third office, that of provincial secretary, went to John R. Partelow, a member of the assembly who had been mayor of Saint John. Partelow was known for his great administrative and financial skill, and his powers of political management would make him a great asset to the government in the assembly. With one seat on the council left to be filled after the new ministry met, Head was able to report to the colonial secretary on May 20 that the first "responsible" government in New Brunswick had been formed.[20]

In the month or so that followed before he left Fredericton to begin a systematic tour of the province, Head worked hard to familiarize himself with all details of provincial affairs. Despatches to the colonial secretary and to Elgin and the other governors, drafted in most cases in his own handwriting, and dealing with a great variety of subjects, bear witness to his activity—as does the item in the Fredericton *Reporter* of June 23 recording that he helped conduct, during an eight-hour period, the terminal examinations of the collegiate school. The administrative experience he had gained with the Poor Law Commission, however, stood him in good stead, and before long, as he noted a year later in a letter to Lewis, he had "comparatively very little" to do:

My predecessor used to be incessantly writing & either he or his private secretary transacted a good deal of Provincial business in this house. This I have altered & adopted the more constitutional course of sending all the

[19]J. W. Lawrence, *The Judges of New Brunswick*, p. 444. The letters from Wilmot and Fisher, dated May 16, 1848, are quoted here.

[20]Its members were: L. A. Wilmot, attorney general; W. B. Kinnear, solicitor general; John R. Partelow, provincial secretary; E. B. Chandler; Charles Fisher; R. L. Hazen; G. S. Hill; Alex Rankin. Early in 1849, the remaining seat was filled by the appointment of Daniel Hanington.

ordinary provincial business through the Provincial Secretary's office. The consequence is that I very soon discharged a clerk who was kept here & paid from the Governor's contingencies & now neither I nor my Secretary are the least overworked. A good deal has been done too by refusing to listen to the complaints which are properly a subject for the civil law of the country. At first people were perpetually coming to get redress in little disputes about the boundary of a grant of land & such like things; but by steadily declining to act as a court of Equity when I had no authority I have got rid of most of these cases. I began for the first two or three times that the Executive Council met by going through each matter with them singly in detail, until I understood the nature of the business & thus had a check on them. Now they meet first in committee & then recommend what they think fit at their meeting here. This is the proper course with 're-sponsible government'. A governor's power is mainly that *nothing can be done without him.* He has only to doubt & hesitate & require further demon-stration. His power of positive action *independently* must be small but so much the better for his tranquillity of mind. Personal influence with the members of the Council will do much too.[21]

On June 24, Head began the first of a series of trips which were to take him to all parts of the province before winter, and which drew from newspaper editors favourable comparisons with his more "sedentary" predecessors.[22] Accompanied by Lieutenant Colonel Hayne, his aide-de-camp, and by Penne-father, he undertook on this occasion "a regular bush excursion," going north from Fredericton into the heart of the province to visit settlements at Stanley and Boiestown. Camping out four nights in the woods, tramping through miles of bush, and paddling by canoe across lakes and along streams, he arrived back in Fredericton at the end of a week with an enthusiasm that he never lost for the scenic beauty of the province. The Frederic-ton *Reporter* noted that he had shown himself an expert disciple of Izaak Walton—but had caught nothing.

On a second and more lengthy trip which began on August 21, Lady Head accompanied her husband and came to share his pleasure in travel through the New Brunswick wilderness, in spite of flies and mosquitoes and nights camping in the bush. Going up the St. John River to Grand Falls, which they stopped to sketch, they went on into the Madawaska country to Little Falls (Edmundston). Reporting on this expedition to the colonial secretary after his return, Head commented:

[21]Lewis Papers, Head to Lewis, July 2, 1849.
[22]Fredericton *Reporter*, July 14, 1848. This trip was also described in the Halifax *Sun*, July 21, 1848.

. . . the inhabitants . . . are, as your Lordship knows, for the most part French in origin, habits and language.

I think it may be interesting to your Lordship to hear that I was received with the greatest demonstrations of attachment to Her Majesty and to the Government of this province on the part of the priest and the population who were assembled on the Sunday. It is now some years since the Parish of Madawaska was visited by the Lt. Gov͏ʳ of New Brunswick.[23]

Continuing their journey, the party made its way by the portage route through the bush to the Restigouche and down to Dalhousie, thence along the Bay of Chaleur coast to Bathurst and the Miramichi, and back up that river to Fredericton in the second week of September. A fortnight later, Head set off again for a final trip which took him through St. Stephen and St. Andrews to Saint John and then up through the counties of Westmorland, Albert, and Kent, before returning again to Fredericton on October 13.[24] Summers spent in this way were to become a regular feature of the Heads' life in New Brunswick, and one that they both enjoyed to the full.

[23]P.A.C., C.O. 188/204, Head to Grey, September 13, 1848.
[24]Fredericton *Reporter*, September 8, 15, 29, October 6, 1848; Miramichi *Gleaner*, September 12, 1848.

THREE

Economic Stresses and Readjustment

IN addition to watching over the early functioning of Responsible Government, much of Head's attention during 1848 and 1849 had to be devoted to the very serious economic problems with which New Brunswick was faced. These first years of his administration were years of economic as well as political transition. The province was outgrowing its pioneer economy and was having to reorganize its major industries on a more stable footing. This meant rather drastic readjustments not only in individual enterprises but in the whole balance between the hitherto booming lumbering and shipbuilding industries on the one hand and the neglected agriculture and fishing on the other. Hardships were inevitable even under the most favourable circumstances, and in the late 1840's the circumstances were by no means favourable. They were complicated particularly by two factors over which the New Brunswick authorities had little or no control. One was the widespread economic depression of that period which brought to New Brunswick, along with restricted credits and markets, hundreds of pauper immigrants whose sole contributions seemed to be the Asiatic cholera and the potato blight. The second complication was the revolution in Britain's commercial policy resulting in her adoption of free trade. While free trade may in the long run have had little if any adverse effect on New Brunswick's economy, it afforded an excellent opportunity to blame all of the province's troubles on the British government—an opportunity seized eagerly by a large majority of even the most loyal elements in the population. Those whose loyalty was weaker did not hesitate to talk of annexation to the United States. There were, however, other more positive lines along which an alleviation of the situation was gradually being sought. These led in the direction of closer relations with the rest of British North America, especially through the construction of an intercolonial railway; and in the direction of commercial rather than political association with the United States by means of a reciprocity treaty.

Closer relations amongst the British provinces—including even their political union—had been considered many times in the past, and quite recently by Lord Durham, but had always seemed impossible to achieve because of geographic barriers. The subject had been revived nevertheless in 1847 by Grey and Elgin in connection with the commercial and political reorganization of the Empire that was taking place. On the commercial side, it seemed to them that the time when Britain was transferring to the North American colonies their entire customs establishments and was herself adopting free trade was the ideal moment for them to remove internal tariffs and become associated together in a sort of "zollverein."[1] As for the political aspect of the question, Elgin at least became very conscious of the fact, after a visit to Nova Scotia on his way to Canada, that some or all of the colonies might prove too small for the satisfactory functioning of Responsible Government. The political union of British North America might be necessary to "give greater Scope to the energies and talents of the leading men—elevate their aims & bring a more enlightened public opinion to bear on their conduct and motives."[2] The advent of the railway age made such ideas seem feasible for the first time in the 1840's. A railway from Halifax to Quebec could draw the Maritimes and Canada together despite the forests and mountains that lay between; and as early as 1846 a proposal that such a line be built had resulted in Canada, New Brunswick, and Nova Scotia employing a Major William Robinson to conduct a survey and make recommendations. Robinson's *Report* was completed by the end of August, 1848.[3] The intercolonial railway, intercolonial trade, common postal and currency arrangements, and even political union were in consequence matters of wide public discussion during Head's early years in New Brunswick.

At first, until Robinson's *Report* appeared, interest in intercolonial affairs centred around matters of trade. An act passed by the New Brunswick legislature in the 1848 session, before Head's

---

[1]P.R.O., C.O. 42/541, Elgin to Grey, January 23, 1847.
[2]P.R.O., C.O. 42/541, Elgin to Grey, February 18, 1847.
[3]Robinson's *Report*, dated August 31, 1848, is published in an appendix to *N.B. Assembly Journals*, 1849.

arrival, had provided for the free admission of certain products of the other provinces upon like concessions being made by them to New Brunswick.[4] Similar acts having been passed in Canada and Nova Scotia, Head wrote in May to the governors of those provinces and of Prince Edward Island with a view to their taking concerted action to bring about intercolonial free trade. The replies he received varied widely. Prince Edward Island, which had not passed an act on the subject and was little interested in it, remained aloof. Nova Scotia was as anxious as New Brunswick for a wider market, reciprocated gladly, and free trade between the two was promptly established.[5] Canada raised the difficulty that since the tariff level of the Maritimes was lower than that of Canada, foreign goods might be wholly or partially manufactured there and imported into Canada as Maritime products to the detriment of the Canadian revenue and the Canadian manufacturer. Until tariffs were equalized she could not agree to intercolonial barriers being removed.[6]

This stand by Canada called forth from Head not only a public answer to her objections, but also a most interesting private letter to Lord Elgin expressing his views on intercolonial matters in general:

There can be little doubt but that absolute and unrestricted free trade between these Provinces ought to be preceded by an assimilation of the Frontier duties in each. In short that Lord Grey's view of a Zollverein between the British N. American Provinces should be carried out first. This is the theoretical view, but I apprehend that in practice little or no inconvenience could result from the free intercourse contemplated by these Acts of Assembly. The fears of your Inspector for the Canadian Revenue can hardly be well founded. Neither Nova Scotia nor this Province are likely to become manufacturing countries for the supply of Canada. . . . Another subject which interests us all and is really of vital importance is that of the Currency. I can see no prospect of it being placed on a proper footing. What appears to be wanting is a coinage of British N. American silver common to all the provinces. . . . I think it will be more prudent not to advert to the bearing which the questions raised have on the consideration of a federal union or a quasi federal union for specific purposes of these Provinces.[7]

The whole tone of this letter, written so soon after Head's arrival in New Brunswick—and especially the unhesitating reference to

4 11 Vict., c. 9 (N.B.).
5 P.A.C., C.O. 188/204, Head to Grey, June 15, 1848.
6 N.B. *Assembly Journals*, 1849, Appendix, Elgin to Head, May 20, 1848.
7 P.A.C., Head Papers, Head to Elgin, private, May [27–29?], 1848.

"Lord Grey's view of a Zollverein"—suggests that in their preliminary meetings at the Colonial Office, Grey had discussed confidentially with Head, as he had done earlier with Elgin, his views on these larger matters of policy. Indeed, there are many indications that from the beginning Head was brought to a considerable extent into the confidential relationship that existed between Grey and Elgin. For example, writing privately to Elgin in November, 1848, Grey commented regarding an earlier letter on the intercolonial railway: "I have sent t[o] Sir E. Head extracts from my letter to you to explain to him my views, but I have not sufficient confidence in the discretion of Sir J. Harvey."[8] Head's temperament and outlook enabled him to enter easily into such a relationship, and he had his own contribution to make to it as this first important letter shows. He was prepared, as Grey and Elgin were, to consider far-reaching new ideas in a comprehensive way. He was, however, less inclined to be doctrinaire than Grey and was somewhat slower and more cautious than Elgin; and his legal studies,[9] administrative experience, and very considerable reading on matters of government gave him an unusually large fund of knowledge on which to base his judgments.

In early 1849, when Robinson's *Report* had been published and examined, interest and hope throughout the provinces shifted from all other subsidiary topics of intercolonial concern and became firmly centred on the Halifax and Quebec Railway project—the more so since Major Robinson in the course of his survey had himself become an enthusiastic supporter of the railway. He argued its importance in his *Report* with conviction and also with an eloquence not always at the command of engineers:

It concerns the prosperity and welfare of each of the three Provinces, and the honor as well as the interests of the British Empire may be affected by it. It is the *one* great means by which alone the power of the Mother Country can be brought to bear on this side of the Atlantic, and restore the balance of power now fast turning to the side of the United States. . . . the Provinces, therefore, and the Empire having such interest in the

[8]A. G. Doughty (ed.), *The Elgin-Grey Papers*, I, 255, Grey to Elgin, private, November 24, 1848. For an explanation of this reference to Harvey see P.R.O., C.O. 217/209, LeMarchant to Pakington, August 18, 1852, and Colonial Office minute on this: "It has long been apprehended in this office that Sir John Harvey was only a Cypher in the hands of the Provincial Administration of the day."

[9]Cf. Lewis Papers, Head to Lewis, January 24, 1853: "Nothing has done me so much good as the knowledge of law which I picked up before I came out."

formation of the Halifax and Quebec Line, it should be undertaken by them in common as a great public work for the public weal. . . .

In a political and military point of view, the proposed Railway must be regarded as becoming a *work of necessity.* . . . *Weakness invites aggression.* . . . The expenses of one year's war would pay for the Railway two or three times over. . . . And if for great political objects it were to become necessary or advisable to unite all the British Provinces under one Legislative Government, then there will be formed on this side of the Atlantic one powerful British state, which, supported by the Imperial power of the Mother Country, may bid defiance to all the United States of America.

The means to the end, the first great step to its accomplishment, is the construction of the Halifax and Quebec Railway.

The British Board of Railway Commissioners to whom Robinson's *Report* was submitted gave it a considerably cooler reception than it was receiving in the provinces. They agreed that the route Robinson suggested along the north shore of New Brunswick was the best, but they questioned his financial conclusions on more than one point. They thought the railway might well cost more than the £5,000,000 he estimated and were extremely doubtful whether it would ever prove a commercial success.[10]

Grey, on the other hand, was delighted and outlined privately to Elgin and Head a very ingenious scheme for overcoming the obvious financial difficulties. He suggested that when the colonial preference on timber was abolished—a free-trade measure which the Government intended to carry into effect shortly in any case— the duty on colonial timber should be raised instead of that on the foreign product being lowered as was the normal practice. The extra revenue this would bring into the British Treasury should then be allocated to meeting the interest charges on a loan for building the railway. To minimize the criticisms sure to be raised in England to the imposition of such an added burden on the British public, Grey went on to propose that the initiative in putting forward such a scheme should be taken by the colonies. "This," he added, in his letter to Elgin, "is a question for your consideration & that of Sir E. Head."[11]

[10]*N.B. Assembly Journals,* 1849, p. 185, Railway Commissioners to Merivale, January 12, 1849. Commenting on this letter to the Railway Commissioners, Head drew attention to its limited viewpoint: " . . . it does little more than state economical results of the justness of which there can be much doubt but which do not themselves conclude the question either as regards Great Britain or the Colonies" (P.A.C., C.O. 188/204, Head to Grey, March 31, 1849).

[11]Doughty, *The Elgin-Grey Papers,* I, 253, Grey to Elgin, private, November 16, 1848.

The method Head and Elgin adopted to meet this suggestion was one frequently used by the latter with good results. Francis Hincks, the Canadian inspector general and Elgin's most confidential adviser, drew up a memorandum embodying Grey's plan and urging most strongly that the railway was of Imperial as well as provincial concern, and that the type of financial assistance asked for was only due compensation to the colonies for injury to their trade resulting from the abolition of their preferences on the British market. In due course, Hincks's memorandum was approved by the Canadian executive council and forwarded to Nova Scotia and New Brunswick.[12] Since Nova Scotia was not vitally interested in the timber question, it was the decision of New Brunswick that would be critical. Head was aware of the strong objections there would be to any scheme likely to affect adversely the province's most important export.[13] No doubt he took care to draw to the attention of his councillors, individually, the facts of the situation—the almost certain abolition anyhow of the timber preference, and, on the other hand, the possibility of aid for the railway, so much of which would lie in New Brunswick. On January 6, 1849, he was able to forward to the Colonial Office an executive council minute giving New Brunswick's support for the Canadian proposals.[14]

When this minute reached London, it became immediately apparent that Grey had greatly underestimated the extreme reluctance of the British government to spend money, especially in colonies which many public men in England thought it was no longer desirable to have. One of his own permanent officials at the Colonial Office, clearly ignorant of the scheme's real originator, minuted his belief that it was "scarcely possible to admit" such a plan which would throw the whole burden of the railway on Britain. Nor were Grey's colleagues in the cabinet more favourably disposed when he brought the subject to their attention. So decided was the opposition that Grey had to admit failure at once. He wrote to Head privately before the end of January: "The state of our own finances and the great indisposition both on the part of the public and of the House of Com-

[12]N.B. *Assembly Journals*, 1849, Appendix, Elgin to Grey, December 20, 1848, enclosing Hincks's memorandum of December 18 and the Canadian executive council minute of December 20.
[13]Cf. Doughty, *The Elgin-Grey Papers*, I, 278, Grey to Elgin, private, January 12, 1848.
[14]P.R.O., C.O. 188/108, Head to Grey, January 6, 1849.

mons to listen to any proposition for incurring expense in the colonies renders it hardly possible at this moment to bring forward such a measure."[15] To Elgin he had added the personal comment: "I cannot say how much it mortifies me to find that with all the advantages wh. this spirited offer from the Colonies affords for bringing forward the Railway scheme we are not in a situation to do so."[16]

In spite of their disappointment, the colonies made one more attempt to salvage the railway scheme on which they had now set their hopes. Their new plan still required the loan for the railway to be raised by the Imperial government, but this time, instead of the interest being paid by means of a timber duty, it would be guaranteed by the three provinces to the extent of £20,000 a year each. While the New Brunswick legislature was still debating whether to participate in this fresh effort, Head wrote a private letter which reveals the method by which, from time to time, he tried to influence such important decisions. It was addressed to J. R. Partelow, the provincial secretary, as follows:

I understand that the legislature of Nova Scotia has passed some definite resolutions as to what they will do in aid of the Great Trunk Line. I do sincerely hope that our legislature will not fail to adopt some proposition of this kind also, stating the amount of interest they would guarantee. The chance of this line is not in my opinion so desperate as may be supposed, but if it is desperate no harm will be done by such a pledge. I still entertain strong hopes and I should be very sorry if we were to lag behind the sister Provinces. Pray show this to Mr. Wilmot.[17]

The New Brunswick legislature eventually passed the resolutions and the address to Her Majesty that Head desired, but in course of the debates and in reports of the railway committees of the two Houses, somewhat disturbing language was used. Blame for the economic distress from which the province was suffering was placed squarely on the changes that had taken place in British commercial policy, and the building of the railway was asked for by way of alleviation.

We think that the plain broad question on this subject is—*Do the People of England wish to retain the North American Colonies or not?* If they do the

[15]W. P. Morrell, *British Colonial Policy in the Age of Peel and Russell*, p. 438, Grey to Head, private, January 29, 1849.

[16]Doughty, *The Elgin-Grey Papers*, I, 286, Grey to Elgin, private, January 25, 1849.

[17]P.A.C., Head Papers, Head to Partelow, private, March 22, 1849.

Trunk Railway is indispensable . . . if on the other hand there be a pre-vailing disposition at Home to throw us off, it will be far better to do so at once, and not leave us as at present, depending upon hopes never to be realized and looking for aid from whence it can never be derived.[18]

Questions of this sort were being asked frequently in all of the North American colonies in 1849, and threats, not always as veiled as this, were being made with the object of obtaining British sympathy and help in connection not only with the rail-way but with reciprocity and other matters as well. On this oc-casion, the language of the legislature called forth from Head one of the first of the long and very able despatches that it be-came his habit to write, analysing practical problems in a practical way, but going on in addition to draw particular attention to the psychological and other reasons underlying them:

The language of the reports of the Committees may appear to your Lord-ship to be somewhat strong but I think I can conscientiously assure you that the persons composing the committees are deeply attached to Her Majesty's Government, and, if they have erred in the manner of expressing what they meant, it has been from their anxiety on the subject to which the reports related. . . .

I would observe that the tone of feeling in this colony at the present time is somewhat peculiar, and is by no means understood in England though it is easily accounted for. The principal inhabitants of New Brunswick have been, and are by descent and by inclination loyal in their feelings and strongly attached to the British Crown. They have felt a pride in forming an integral part of a mighty Empire and the sense of self importance con-nected with this feeling receives a shock from every expression or every fact which appears to impair this Unity. In addition therefore to the im-mediate effect on their material interests produced by the withdrawal of full protection to their timber trade, their sympathies at the same time received what may be called a moral blow. . . .

This depression of our material interests and the want of importance implied in a diminished consciousness of identity with the Mother Country have naturally directed the eyes of stirring and intelligent men to some source of colonial importance which may compensate for these losses, and thus it is that the notion of an union of the British North American Colonies has embodied itself in the enclosed reports of the Committees. The mass of our population here have probably conceived no definite idea of the kind, but reflecting minds cannot but feel painfully conscious of the want of common interest between the adjacent members of the same Empire. We know little of Canada except as rejecting all attempt to establish free trade,

[18]*N.B. Assembly Journals,* 1849, p. 199, Report of Railway Committee, March 17, 1849.

and as the party to a sort of lawsuit now pending with reference to our common boundary.[19]

The railway, then, in Head's view, would not merely assist the provinces economically and materially. It would, by strengthening their "common interest," help compensate them for their loss of a "sense of self importance" consequent on the loosening of their ties with the mother country. This latter point was a basic one in Head's analysis of British North American affairs. He would return to it frequently in discussing not only the economic effect of free trade on the ties of Empire, but also the political effect of Responsible Government, and it was a main reason for his becoming himself one of those "stirring and intelligent men" with thoughts of union.

In the meantime, there were, in Head's opinion, two other especially important advantages that would accrue to the Empire and the province from the railway, and in the later part of his despatch he dealt with these at some length. One was that its building, and the employment thus provided, would hold out "the cheapest and best opportunity for promoting Emigration from the United Kingdom." Head went into this matter carefully and gave much exact detail, knowing the appeal of planned emigration to Grey and to most of those in England who were interested at all in colonies. The other advantage was of more local significance. It related to the peculiar geography of the province and the special political problems created by it—problems that affected every phase of Head's administration and of which he was always conscious.

In order fully to understand the view likely to be taken by the Assembly here of any definite railroad scheme to be determined on by themselves, I must ask Your Lordship to take up a map of New Brunswick. You will find that the province is divided into certain long lines of settlement and population with tracts of wilderness between them, traversed in one or two points only by roads leading from one line of settlement to another. . . .

To go from one of these lines of settlement to the others, except at very distant points where the intermediate country is traversed by roads, is all but impossible. . . . In the course of last summer, I passed myself from the Valley of the Saint John to the Bay of Chaleur but I was obliged to make the journey in canoes, and had to sleep five nights in the woods.

Now the result of this disjointed conformation of the country is naturally that local interests predominate over Provincial interests and I believe that this fact has been made peculiarly manifest in the very lengthened debate

[19]P.R.O., C.O. 188/108, Head to Grey, March 31, 1849.

in the House of Assembly on the subject of Railroads. . . . The result of
these incompatible interests is a species of equilibrium from opposing
forces, which would necessarily render any merely Provincial action on a
specific line almost impossible.

But it will be equally clear that these very difficulties shew a state of
things eminently requiring such an improvement in our communications
as may substitute a Provincial interest for these narrow local sympathies,
and a railroad for which the line was selected by the Imperial Government,
and the funds supplied by the agency or the guarantee of that Government,
would do much to break down these noxious feelings.

For the time being these arguments were wasted. The British
cabinet still refused to contemplate any proposal that would
place the main burden of the railway on their shoulders. A few
days before Head's despatch reached the Colonial Office, Grey
had been obliged to write, on April 5, informing him officially
that "for the present at least, it has been found impractical to
overcome the difficulties which have stood in the way of every
plan which has hitherto been suggested for providing for the
cost of a work of such magnitude as the proposed railway."[20]
Head's prematurely obsolete despatch was filed and forgotten
among the mass of other railway papers.[21] With it was shelved
for almost two years the intercolonial railway project and any
prospect of a union of the colonies.

Disappointment at this outcome of their hopes for the railway,
and the continuance of their economic hardships, were the factors
that caused the colonies, as 1849 went on, to turn their thoughts
more and more to reciprocity—and in some quarters even to
annexation. In her interest in reciprocity, New Brunswick lagged
very little behind Canada. A year earlier, within a fortnight of the
formation of his first "responsible" government, Head had had
drawn vigorously to his attention this solution for the province's

[20]P.R.O., C.O. 42/552, Grey to Head, April 5, 1849.

[21]Minutes on this despatch record its fate at the Colonial Office. On May 1,
1849, A. J. Blackwood, senior clerk for the North American department, wrote
that an answer would be necessary but that Grey's despatch of April 5 would
enable the colony "to conjecture with tolerable accuracy" what that answer would
be. Almost a year later, he noted that Head's despatch had got in with other
railway papers and never been answered. After some indications of embarrassment on the part of various officials, it was decided that a belated answer would
only serve to revive an issue best forgotten and therefore none was ever sent.
When another year had passed, however, and the railway was again in the
public eye, this despatch along with others was printed for parliament (April,
1851).

economic problems. Since then he had become increasingly concerned with developments along these lines which were to reach an important turning-point in the fall of 1849.

The beginning, so far as Head was concerned, was on May 31, 1848, when a meeting of Saint John merchants passed a series of resolutions denouncing Britain's withdrawal of protection from colonial goods and requesting his aid, as lieutenant governor, in seeking a new trade outlet by having New Brunswick included in Canadian negotiations for a reciprocal free-trade agreement with the United States. The merchants, with a determination characteristic of the commercial, if not always of the political, community in New Brunswick, voted also to have their resolutions engrossed, sent to important congressmen in the United States, and widely distributed throughout the province. In addition, their chairman was instructed to try to arrange meetings for a like purpose in other parts of New Brunswick in the near future.[22] In fact, agitation did grow during the summer, spurred by the fact that trade remained in "a most depressed state" and also by the apparently brightening prospects for success of the Canadian efforts.[23] Canada, affected earlier by the changes in British trade policy, had been striving for an agreement with the United States since 1846, and in July, 1848, rejoiced at the first sign of progress, the passage of a reciprocity bill through the House of Representatives. The bill did not come to a vote in the Senate before the session ended, but nevertheless a wave of optimism spread through Canada and across into New Brunswick as well. In October, the New Brunswick executive council began to contemplate the introduction in the next session of a bill "allowing the importation into New Brunswick of certain Articles, the growth or production of the United States of America Free, on the United States Congress granting the same privilege to this Province."[24] The following January, before the session began, the Saint John merchants held another meeting and passed another series of resolutions culminating this time with the request that Head appoint a commission "to proceed without unnecessary delay, to Washington, fully empowered" to negotiate a reciprocity treaty.[25]

[22]P.R.O., C.O. 188/106, Head to Grey, July 3, 1848, enclosure.
[23]P.R.O., C.O. 188/105, Head to Grey, June 29, 1848.
[24]P.R.O., C.O. 188/106, Head to Grey, October 27, 1848.
[25]P.R.O., C.O. 188/108, Head to Grey, January 8, 1849.

Up to this stage, Head's role had been a passive one. He had transmitted information as to the state of the province's economy and the wishes of its merchants and council to the Colonial Office with little in the way of personal comment. There was as yet no need for him to do more, and he knew well the fundamental differences of opinion about economic theory that existed between Grey, the doctrinaire free trader, and the New Brunswick legislature, which had already earned his severe displeasure on several recent occasions by offering a hemp bounty and imposing differential duties. In the case of this latest petition from the merchants he followed the same course: he answered them simply that the colonial government had no authority to treat directly with a foreign power, but he forwarded their request to the Colonial Office.

Grey's view on reciprocity, under the influence of Canadian pressure, was for him unusually liberal. Regarding the New Brunswick proposal for a reciprocity bill, he merely advised strongly the repeal of the duties in question without waiting for reciprocal action on the part of the United States. But in default of this, he would agree to the New Brunswick measure provided it contained nothing savouring of differential duties—that is, it would have to be understood that when the United States reciprocated, the duties would be removed on all goods regardless of their place of origin. There would also have to be a suspending clause, in order not to infringe in any way upon the right of Her Majesty's Government to control the foreign relations of the whole Empire. Even the further request that a "fully empowered" commission be sent to Washington, while it caused some slight stir at the Colonial Office, was not viewed with any alarm. It could not be granted, of course, as Head had already made clear to the merchants, but the request itself was not looked upon as altogether surprising because Canada was known to have at the moment a representative in Washington in the person of its enterprising president of council, W. H. Merritt, although what he was doing, or how official was his capacity, was not clear. After some consideration, Grey decided on the important step of having instructions sent to the British minister at Washington "to use his best endeavours to effect the arrangement desired by the Exec. Council of N. Brunswick." To save time in keeping the minister informed of the colonial viewpoint, Head should be allowed to correspond with him directly. If necessary, he might even send someone to Washington, not to negotiate with the American government, but to give additional verbal information to the minister.[26]

Head took full advantage of this opportunity and throughout the spring and summer of 1849 he, as well as Elgin, kept in close touch with J. F. T. Crampton, the British *chargé d'affaires*, on the subject of reciprocity.[27] There seemed at first little possibility of success, the United States administration being avowedly protectionist. The prospect of other colonies besides Canada being interested, however, soon began to change the outlook of J. M. Clayton, the American secretary of state, and by July he hinted that an arrangement embracing "not only Canada and New Brunswick, but all the other British possessions on the northern frontier, more particularly those which enjoy any exclusive rights with regard to the cod fisheries" would be carefully considered. In fact, he let it be understood that the abrogation of their fishing rights by the British colonies would be an indispensable condition for the continuance of the discussions.[28]

At last a firm basis for negotiation had been reached. The fishery question was becoming one of considerable importance in the domestic politics of the United States. American cod fishermen had been receiving a bounty in compensation for their handicap in not being legally able to enjoy the rich fisheries off the coasts of British North America. It was estimated that in the previous four years the bounty had totalled more than a million dollars and that in 1848 it had amounted to more than one-quarter of the value of the catch. Admission to the fisheries on terms which would make possible the withdrawal of the bounty would be a popular measure. It would be worth certain trading concessions to the British provinces.[29]

By midsummer, 1849, therefore, when the annexation movement was approaching its peak, the substitute of reciprocity was becoming a real possibility provided Canada and New Brunswick could persuade Nova Scotia, whose fisheries were the most important to the United States, to join in the negotiations. At this stage the initiative passed, on the suggestion of the ubiquitous Merritt, to New Brunswick, whose interests like her geographic

[26]Minutes and draft replies on Head's despatches of October 27 and January 8.
[27]P.A.C., Head Papers, Head to Crampton, February 26 and March 23, 1849.
[28]P.R.O., F.O. 5/500, Crampton to Palmerston, July 9, 1849.
[29]*Ibid.*

position made her a natural link between her neighbours. More interested in the fisheries than Canada, but less than Nova Scotia, New Brunswick was intermediate also with respect to her desire for a trade agreement with the United States. It seemed appropriate, therefore, that the New Brunswick executive council should in July propose a British North American conference to discuss reciprocity, stating at the same time its own willingness to "consent to such modification of the existing Treaties relating to the Fisheries, as would admit the United States to a full participation therein." The place suggested for the conference was Halifax in the obvious hope of influencing opinion there.[30]

The conference which met at the beginning of September with delegates from all of the provinces except Newfoundland in attendance, was not entirely successful in achieving its main objective. In spite of every effort of the New Brunswick and Canadian delegates it was not possible to secure the passage of a resolution in favour of the surrender of the fishing rights, although all agreed on the desirability of reciprocity. Nevertheless, this Halifax conference of 1849 was a major turning-point. By means of it, all of the provinces except Newfoundland were drawn into the reciprocity negotiations and a realization of their common interest was created which prepared the way for common action in the future. And although the final resolutions passed over the fisheries proposal in silence, it had been given a place in the forefront of the discussions and was not to be forgotten.[31]

As a commentary on the report of its conference delegates, the New Brunswick executive council passed, in the middle of September, a strongly worded minute dealing with the situation as a whole. In their view the commercial depression had been "chiefly brought about by the withdrawal of British protection." But, they added:

We see not the only remedy for our present difficulties in the forfeiture of our allegiance and the alienation of our affections and our Territory from the British Sovereign. . . . Deprived of adequate protection at Home we now only ask a market abroad. Free access to the markets of the United States . . . will not only give prosperity to the Colony but greatly add to the power and secure the permanency of the British Empire. To obtain such access we must depend on Imperial influence. . . . But if with that influence on our behalf we should fail in the accomplishment of our present purpose, a stern necessity will ere long impel the Public mind to seek for relief by an in-

30P.R.O., C.O. 217/202, Harvey to Grey, August 10, 1849, enclosure.
31P.R.O., C.O. 188/110, Head to Grey, September 15, 1849, and enclosures.

corporation with the neighbouring Republic. . . . In common with the People whom we represent we are devotedly attached to the British Institutions. . . . But at the present crisis there is danger and a sense of duty compels us to distinctly point out what we conceive to be the only immediate and efficient remedy.[32]

Unlike the Annexation Manifesto that was to appear in Montreal the following month, this was an official expression of the views of a colonial ministry and, in spite of the protestations of loyalty it contains, its threat to the British connection is apparent. In forwarding it to the Colonial Office, Head expressed for the first time in a brief but comprehensive way his own views on the subject. His part hitherto had been that of intermediary between New Brunswick and outside authorities such as the Colonial Office, the governor general, and the British minister in Washington. In his typically careful and scholarly fashion, however, he had been assessing the various elements in the situation, and now when the crisis in the agitation for annexation and in the negotiations for reciprocity was upon him, he was prepared to give a balanced judgment for the guidance of the colonial secretary, writing:

I concur with the members of my Council, in thinking that the object in view is one of the utmost importance & I also believe that it would be advantageous to us to obtain that object at the cost even of our exclusive rights of sea fishery—which are as your Lordship knows most valuable.

I can only recommend this subject to the serious consideration of Her Majesty's Government since the uneasy feeling arising from a cramped trade & a notion that they are neglected by England is fermenting in this province as it is in Canada, though I am happy to say in a less degree.

The words 'annexation' or 'independence' are heard as subjects for discussion in the mouths of persons whose loyalty was their peculiar pride. I attach however little value to talk of this character. 'Annexation' for the most part represents nothing but the desire of access to the markets of the United States & 'independence' expresses a feeling that they are neglected by Great Britain & a conviction that the connection is not valued by the Mother Country.

I believe myself that the value attached to English institutions & the true affection for Her Majesty as their Sovereign is yet unimpaired in the great majority of the people of this Colony.[33]

The arrival of this despatch with its enclosures, particularly the report of the Halifax conference, was considered most opportune by the Colonial Office. It was forwarded at once to

32P.R.O., C.O. 188/110, N.B. executive council minute, September 13, 1849.
33P.R.O., C.O. 188/110, Head to Grey, September 15, 1849.

the Foreign Office and the Board of Trade and by autumn a firm policy had been decided upon. Sir Henry Bulwer, now the British minister at Washington, was ordered to press definitely for a reciprocity agreement between the United States and all of the British North American provinces. The views of the latter were to be forwarded to him through Lord Elgin alone so that there might be no lack of co-ordination. The beginning of negotiations on a realistic basis was now possible.

In his study of the provincial economy Head had been greatly impressed with the need to stimulate its agriculture. He was convinced that the rapid and wasteful exploitation of the forests previously encouraged by the protective system not only had been harmful in itself but had been quite largely responsible for the serious neglect of agriculture. The balance must now be readjusted. In a despatch of June 27, 1849, accompanying the annual Blue Book of the province, he drew special attention to this matter and criticized the continued reliance of many New Brunswick leaders on protection:

New Brunswick with a fertile soil cannot at the present moment grow its own food and staggers under the reaction consequent on the mere withdrawal of the artificial stimulus which caused its apparent prosperity. It is, I venture to think, a mistake to suppose as many men in this province now do, that the Legislature here can advantageously encourage native manufactures by protective duties. The one manufacture to which we ought to look is that of food. We have the machinery to produce it in unlimited abundance, and in no other way can the little capital which the Colony possesses be turned to so good an account as in working this machinery.[34]

Head made a real personal effort to direct provincial thought along these lines. Early in 1849, for example, he wrote to Grey and to the registrar of King's College, Fredericton, saying: "I am extremely desirous that a course of lectures in Agricultural Chemistry should be delivered at Fredericton during the sitting of the Assembly. . . . I look upon the diffusion of scientific information relating to Agriculture as a most important object to this Province." To pay for the lectures which would be given by Dr. Robb of the college, Head suggested the allocation of part of the revenue from a vacant professorship. Grey agreed that this would be a justifiable diversion of college funds but the college council refused, and Head eventually paid for the lectures

[34]P.R.O., C.O. 188/109, Head to Grey, June 27, 1849.

out of his own pocket.[35] When they proved a success, he suggested to Robb that he repeat them at Saint John, "either gratuitously or at a small admission fee."[36] In consenting at about the same time to act as patron of the Fredericton Agricultural Society, Head promised that he would "not fail to be present at their meetings unless absent from Fredericton."[37]

One further instance of Head's efforts for the improvement of agriculture is worthy of brief mention. An important survey of New Brunswick's agricultural capabilities was made in the summer and fall of 1849 at the expense of the provincial government by Professor J. F. W. Johnston, the well-known authority from the University of Durham. Head had been largely responsible for the invitation to Johnston in the first place, welcomed him at Government House during his six weeks in Fredericton while he was writing his *Report*, read this latter with interest and approval, and arranged for it to be printed in the colony and also in England. When Johnston wrote his two-volume *Notes on North America* a year later he dedicated it to Head "chiefly as a mode of testifying the respect and regard I entertain for yourself and your family, and as affording me an opportunity of expressing my sense of the many acts of kindness I experienced during a prolonged stay at Fredericton, under your hospitable roof."[38]

By 1849, Head had had an opportunity to settle in to the life of the province and to learn something of the special characteristics of its society. Typically, Orange activity early forced itself on his attention. Serious Twelfth-of-July rioting had occurred at Woodstock in 1847. Over a year later the ringleaders were still seeking further postponement of their trial by an appeal to the lieutenant governor. Head rejected this on the ground that "where party feeling of this kind is involved all interference of the Executive Government with the regular & ordinary course of Justice is to be avoided if possible." He was not swayed from this course by being conscious that he "acted rather against, then in accordance with, the opinions of the majority of my Council

---

[35]P.A.C., C.O. 188/204, Head to Grey, January 16, 1849; Head Papers, Pennefather to Registrar of King's College, July [January ?] 12, 1849; Head to Chief Justice, March 19, 1849.

[36]P.A.C., Head Papers, Pennefather to Robb, n.d.

[37]P.A.C., Head Papers, Head to Odell, May 16, 1849.

[38]See also Lewis Papers, Head to Lewis, January 22, 1850.

though they acquiesced to the course which I considered as the proper one."[39] Again on July 13, 1849, when Head learned that Orange riots at Saint John the day before had been unusually violent, resulting in a number of deaths, he set off himself with the attorney general by the night boat from Fredericton and at an early hour on July 14, heedless of warnings, he proceeded through the most troubled districts on foot before conferring with civic officials and insisting on "the absolute necessity for prompt & impartial action in following up the legal proceedings to be instituted." He discovered accidentally as a result of this personal intervention that a number of Orangemen had been imported from Fredericton for the occasion and that one, a painter currently working on the roof of Government House, was lying hidden with a gunshot wound in his leg.[40]

That Head took a keen interest in such incidents of colonial life is revealed in his letters to Lewis, for example, in one written earlier in that same month of July, 1849:

The State of Society here is curious: There are not as you may suppose a great many people: we have been here a year & in that time two grand quarrels have occurred. In the first the Bishop denounced one man from the pulpit, which as that man was in the main on the right this rather tended to excite fresh sympathy with him. His Ecclesiastical offence was that after having fought a duel he refused to confess his sinfulness to the Bishop. . . . The other party who was originally in the wrong owned his error & was dealt with leniently. . . . However, this quarrel has subsided a little & now comes another—a . . . brother in law of one of the Judges went drunk on a public night to the mess of a Regiment here & knocked over the chandelier. This produced a correspondence very badly managed on the part of the regiment & mainly taken up by the Judge. The whole is now published & the result it appears to me is that the Judge & his brother have the best of it *on the pleadings* but any jury would find a verdict *'served him right'*.

These little squabbles do not affect me much except that I tell people I must make my secretary keep a book with a column for every quarrel & a statement opposite each person's name setting out to whom they will speak & to whom they won't. Is not all this thoroughly colonial & 'kleinstädterisch'? It is amazingly amusing to look on it. . . .

I intend shortly to make an excursion across to the Eastern Coast up the Tobique River which is a tributary of the St. John about 100 miles above this. The whole country is perfectly wild forest & I shall have to camp in the woods for at least a week. The person who will probably [be] going with me is a Mr. Grant of the Crown Land Office here who nearly lost his life in that district when out on a railway survey. He lost himself & after

[39]P.A.C., C.O. 188/204, Head to Grey, July 26, 1848.
[40]P.R.O., C.O. 188/110, Head to Grey, July 15, 1849.

walking till he dropped from exhaustion on the bank of a stream lay unable to move. His feet were frozen but luckily he had tied a handkerchief to the bough over his head before he fell down. He saw a boat with provisions for lumberers come up & land their cargo just below him but he was too weak to call out so as to be heard. The boat went away & he then gave himself up for lost but something brought them back again—he made another effort—the men heard him but thought it was some beast, however one of them saw the handkerchief & they then came & looked. In this way he was saved. He is a clever fellow & a good surveyor.[41]

As stories such as these of persons and events in New Brunswick would indicate—and his letters are full of them—Head's early years in that colony were in many ways as active and happy as any of his whole life. His health was excellent, his work stimulating and varied, and his opportunities for vigorous out-of-doors recreation, in which he delighted, were abundant. He still found, however, his greatest pleasure in scholarship and occasionally, as for example in a letter to Lewis written in the gloom of midwinter in 1850, his nostalgia for the intellectual companionship he had enjoyed so fully in London becomes rather pathetically evident:

I have never said much to you about Pennefather, my private secretary. . . . He is young—about 21—well informed & a gentleman—but I cannot say that he is particularly agreeable to me. I tried at first to get intimate with him & read some of the Agamemnon with him, but I soon found that he was so shy & reserved that I could do nothing. He is trustworthy & not likely to tell anything—which is a great matter in a Colony—but except in this particular a good clerk would answer my purpose as well. He has now been foolish enough to set about getting married to a young lady here. . . . The people are very respectable in every way & I dare say *he* thinks her pretty—which I do not. His ceasing to live in the house with me will be a relief to me rather than otherwise for I scarcely open my lips to him except on business. . . .

The result of all this has been that I live a good deal by myself & walk alone for the most part—but I don't know that I dislike it—I have no lack of books & at large parties I always get small talk which savors a deal of convention.[42]

[41]Lewis Papers, Head to Lewis, July 2, 1849.

[42]Lewis Papers, Head to Lewis, January 22, 1850. Pennefather remained as Head's private secretary except for one brief interval until toward the end of his Canadian administration and was the subject of the story told by E. W. Watkin in *Canada and the United States* (p. 502): ". . . when, during the visit of the Prince of Wales, one of the Governor's aides-de-camp [actually, private secretary] was pushed over from the steamer at Detroit by the press of the crowd, and fell into the water, Colonel Irving [Irvine] said:—'Ah! there was no danger whatever to ——'s life. The Governor-General has blown him up so much that he could never sink.'" See also G. D. Engleheart, *Journal of the Progress of H.R.H. the Prince of Wales*, p. 68.

FOUR

The Political Crisis of 1850-51

IN the years 1850 and 1851 the major political crisis of Head's term in New Brunswick occurred. Centring around the general election of the summer of 1850 and the resignation of the chief justice at about the same time, it had its beginnings in the preceding session of the legislature and it did not end until the executive council had been largely reconstructed and had been sustained through the session of 1851 and in an important by-election at Saint John during the following summer. The events of this period, in which Head played a leading part, made it clear beyond any doubt that the acceptance of the principle of Responsible Government in 1848 had been a first step, rather than the last, on the road toward its effective introduction in the province. They showed in particular that further reforms of an administrative nature were essential, the most important being the inclusion in the executive council of a larger number of heads of government departments, the surrender to the executive council of the initiative regarding money votes, and the establishment of elective municipal institutions. By bringing these three issues to the fore, the crisis served to educate political leaders and the general public and to win wider support for the necessary changes. In the meantime, it also demonstrated the need for a step back to firm control by the governor before further progress toward parliamentary government could take place. It thus obliged Head to abandon, to some extent at least, his role of dependence on the advice of a "responsible" ministry and to become for a while virtually his own prime minister. This necessity, uncomfortable enough for the governors of Canada in the 1840's, was worse for Head in the 1850's when the new system was already more advanced in some of the sister colonies. The skilful manner in which he dealt with the difficulties and dangers of this time brought congratulations from Lord Grey and did much in the long run to smooth the way for the development of true Responsible Government in the province.

Head was fully conscious of the troubled political waters that lay ahead—indeed he was looking forward to good fishing in them—when, in his Speech from the Throne opening the last session of the provincial legislature on February 7, 1850, he took the unusual step of adding to the formal declaration of government policy which it contained a further statement of his own:

. . . I cannot conclude this Speech without expressing to you distinctly my own convictions on one or two Constitutional matters of the highest importance.

I believe, in the first place, that it is most desirable to define more accurately the responsibility attaching to the initiation of money votes. This can only be done by throwing such responsibility on the Executive Government.

The undisputed right to originate money votes is vested in the House of Assembly; and the Members of the Executive Council, it is now understood, practically retain their seats only so long as they are presumed to enjoy the confidence of the people, expressed in the Legislature.

To the people therefore through their Representatives, as well as to the Crown, they are strictly responsible, and although the burthen of being answerable for the introduction of money votes would be a heavy one, that burthen might be lightened by leaving to local controul such local charges as no central Government can by any amount of vigilance efficiently check. Local controul over local charges, presents moreover advantages of its own with which every man of English race is sufficiently familiar. Economy would be promoted—habits of self reliance and self government would be fostered—and the elements of true political freedom would be developed by the management of the affairs of each separate district. . . .

It implies no mistrust of the people or the Legislature of this Province to advocate principles and measures practically a part of the Constitution of England, and of the Constitution of other Colonies, where free and Responsible Government is acknowledged as completely as in New Brunswick. . . .

I could not properly meet you in this, the last Session of the present Assembly, without imparting frankly my hope, that in the course of your deliberations you may, at any rate, pave the way for measures such as these to which I have adverted. . . .

In thus drawing attention to the need for reforms with respect to money votes and municipal institutions, Head was not breaking new ground. Changes along these lines had been repeatedly urged by his predecessor, Sir William Colebrooke, and they had been widely discussed in the province. He was, however, beginning to play what he later confessed was "a more or less hazardous game."[1] He was entering personally and openly into a field of bitter political controversy. He would have to "tempor-

[1]Lewis Papers, Head to Lewis, March 31, 1851. The further brief phrases quoted in this paragraph are also from Head's account in this letter.

ize & resist as occasion offered," but he might hope for some progress in the right direction. "I am satisfied," he explained to Grey, "that there exists in the Colony a growing feeling in favor of changes such as these recommended by me & approved by your Lordship, and I am desirious of letting the questions connected with them be fairly brought before the public on the eve of a general election."[2]

There can be little doubt that these measures were important enough to justify the risks Head ran in sponsoring them himself for discussion on the hustings. Their lack in New Brunswick had resulted in financial chaos and in the conversion of a surplus of £150,000 into a large deficit in the few years since 1837, when the province had taken over from the Imperial government control of its whole revenue in return for a civil-list settlement. A vivid and not inaccurate account of the situation as it still remained in Head's time was given by a correspondent of the Saint John *Morning News* in 1842:

Every member has a different sum fixed upon, as the real debt of the Province; and there has been no labour spared to conceal the actual state of the country from its inhabitants. One Hon. gentleman says it is only £30,000; another £50,000; a third £80,000; and one of the Executive Councillors, during debate, stated the sum to be at least £100,000. Those who insist on the smaller amount, take into account sums that are due, but cannot be collected; and, like many other silly swaggerers, in reckoning upon their future, embrace all they have ever lost. But from all I have been able to collect from the Journals and Debates, the real debt of New Brunswick is at least £100,000!! And this grand discovery was never made known to the people until the last shilling was gone from the Treasury, and the Banks refused to pay the cash for warrants upon it. Now what effect has this discovery had upon the conduct of the majority of the members of the House of Assembly? Why, it appears to have driven them to desperation; for they have within a few days actually granted away £90,000 more, without providing any certain means of meeting one half of the amount.[3]

Apart from the fact that there was real need for heavy capital expenditure in opening up a new country, the reason for this extravagance clearly lay in the "log-rolling" that went on in connection with votes for roads, bridges, schools, poor relief, and numerous other items, many of a purely local nature. "This was the system throughout, 'help me and I'll help you'"[4]—the in-

[2]P.A.C., C.O. 188/205, Head to Grey, February 15, 1850.
[3]G. E. Fenety, *Political Notes*, I, 33.
[4]*Ibid.*, p. 38.

evitable result of strongly centralized but inefficient government in a province divided into a number of almost separate geographic regions and not having therefore any strong sense of community of interest. The two reforms advocated by Head and others would undoubtedly help to end this evil. By transferring to the executive council the right to initiate money votes, a balancing of revenue and expenditure could be procured in a businesslike way. By setting up elective municipal institutions obliged to raise the money they spent, it would become possible to meet local requirements economically and efficiently.

In so far as there had been any valid objection to these changes, it no longer existed. The assembly had in the past, quite rightly, been unwilling to surrender any part of its power of the purse to a ministry over which it had no control. But the principles of Responsible Government having been accepted, the assembly would be simply delegating—not diminishing—its authority by giving a "responsible" ministry sole right to initiate money votes. So far as elective municipal institutions were concerned, their absence in the past seems to have been due originally to Britain's reaction against democratic tendencies in the colonies following the American Revolution. Townships on the New England pattern, organized by early English-speaking arrivals, had been abolished in 1784 when New Brunswick became a separate province. They had been replaced by counties and parishes whose purse-strings and patronage were retained firmly in the hands of the government at Fredericton.[5] To change this after so long a time was difficult because members of the assembly were reluctant to abandon their custom of influencing local appointments and of raiding the provincial Treasury on behalf of the local needs of their constituents.

To the argument that reform was essential in the interests of economy, those who opposed it had a stock answer which they had used ever since the civil-list settlement in 1837: for economy, reduce official salaries and transfer the resulting civil-list surplus to the provincial Treasury. This answer was a red herring, but it had a redolence that remained distracting through the years because of the fact that some salaries really were too high for a small and rather impecunious province. Salaries of £1200 paid to the surveyor general, £1090 to the chief justice, and £750 to the other supreme court justices were high as compared with

[5]A. Shortt and A. G. Doughty (eds.), *Canada and its Provinces*, XIII, 130.

the general level of incomes in New Brunswick or even with the salaries of the heads of government departments, which ranged from £600 for the attorney general and the provincial secretary to only £230 for the solicitor general. What was not mentioned, of course, was that even if some salaries were reduced and the surplus turned back to general revenue, its amount would be so small as to be of almost no significance. Whatever the validity of arguments favouring the reduction of salaries *per se*, those who urged this as a solution of the province's financial difficulties were deluding themselves—or trying to deceive others.

Understandably this fallacy did not prevent the session of 1850, after Head's Speech from the Throne advocating reforms, from following the normal pattern in which members turned instead to the discussion of official salaries. As pre-election excitement grew, Attorney General Wilmot, the leader in the House, came under increasing pressure in this regard and, fearful of being underbid by the Opposition, he brought the matter before a meeting of the council. After much tense debate in which it became obvious that to make any decision would cause a disastrous split in the Government, it was agreed to postpone action until the House went into committee on the state of the province and then allow Wilmot on his own initiative to sponsor whatever measures might seem to him politically necessary.[6]

Head watched these developments carefully. The one thing he was not prepared to sanction was reduction of the salaries of individuals then in office. Any such measure would, he believed, "imply a breach of the compact with the Crown in the matter of the Civil List voted in perpetuity, . . . [be] inconsistent with the good faith of the Crown as pledged to individuals . . . [and, in the case of the judges,] violate the great principle of the independence of the Judicial Bench."[7] Other than this, however, Head was willing to let the council make what compromise it could. And even when Wilmot felt himself obliged for the survival of the Government to go beyond this limit and introduce bills for the immediate reduction of various salaries including those of the judges, Head temporarily refrained from protesting.

For a time, the situation seemed most dangerous. The language

[6]P.A.C., N.B. Executive Council Minutes, March 26, 1850. See also P.R.O., C.O. 188/112, Head to Grey, separate and confidential, May 2, 1850.
[7]P.A.C., N.B. Executive Council Minutes, "Lt. Governor's Memo. relating to Resolutions for reducing the Judges' Salaries &c," April 26, 1850.

used in the committee on the state of the province was frequently intemperate: reference was even made to "such feelings of dissatisfaction as must inevitably lead to a separation from the Mother Country."[8] While not unduly alarmed, Head felt it necessary to proceed with the utmost caution:

... the tone assumed & the unscrupulous manner in which it is evidently proposed to throw over pre-existing engagements with the Crown, are in a great degree due to the notions afloat, with reference to 'annexation' and to the loose talk consequent on the troubles in Canada. The proceedings too of the reform party in Nova Scotia have had this influence. There seems to be an idea that under a covert threat of dissatisfaction any terms may be extorted.[9]

In such a political atmosphere, to force a stand that would likely lead to the fall of the Government in the midst of the session and on the eve of an election might be disastrous.

I thought it better ... to let the session go on—to get the supplies voted, and when all was safe for the year, express my own views decidedly to the Council. ... I thought it probable that what has happened, would happen; that is to say, that partly from the insincerity of some of their supporters, and partly from the pressure of business, any measures would be sent up so late as either to be thrown out by the Legislative Council, or to drop of themselves. This last ... was the case.

The memorandum in which Head expressed his views to the council at the end of the session was a long and strongly worded protest against the measures sponsored by Wilmot. "If the Attorney General choose to resign, because he is offended by the expression of my opinion ... ," Head wrote to Grey at this time, "he must do so ... and if he were to resign before the election on the professed ground of reducing salaries, there is no doubt he might raise a popular cry. I very much question his intention of doing so." In fact Head was fully "sensible of the awkward position" in which Wilmot found himself, and the tone of his memorandum was not recriminatory. Rather, its intention was to bring about a return to sound ways of thinking about reform on the part of the council as soon as possible. For this, resolute firmness combined with sympathetic understanding seemed essential. In two long and carefully written despatches to Grey, one marked "separate & confidential," Head explained the whole

[8]*N.B. Assembly Journals*, 1850, p. 339.
[9]P.R.O., C.O. 188/112, Head to Grey, separate and confidential, May 2, 1850. The remainder of this account of the session of 1850 is taken from this despatch or from Head to Grey, May 1, 1850, in the same volume.

situation most thoroughly and gave in detail his recommendations for handling it. He summed up:

In my opinion . . . , the proper mode of meeting demands such as those which are implied by the resolutions of the House & by the introduction of these two most objectionable bills, is to profess on the part of Her Majesty's Government a readiness to redress all real grievances . . . with an evident intention of resisting all claims contrary to good faith & sound principle. The more decided the manner in which this determination is announced the less will be the agitation on the subject.

These despatches were received with approval in the Colonial Office. Grey minuted: "I agree with Mr. Merivale that the Lt. Govʳˢ own despatches (the public & the confidential one) supply the means of framing a suitable answer. I entirely concur in Sir E. Head's views." Subsequent events, in which these views were put to the test, proved them in the main correct. The election which took place during the summer was indecisive in its results but "the subject of the 'initiation' has been loudly discussed . . . and generally in the right sense."[10] Excitement thereafter soon tended to die down and the wild language that had been used during the spring session regarding annexation began to be forgotten. The state of the province was sufficiently quiet by autumn for Head to leave it in order to visit Lord Elgin in Canada.

The purpose of Head's trip to Canada in the fall of 1850 was to confer with Elgin and the Canadian government regarding a long-standing dispute between New Brunswick and Canada as to the exact location of their common boundary. This was a matter of increasing importance to New Brunswick, in particular, because of the timber cutting that was beginning in the disputed area, and as early as December, 1848, Head had offered to go to Canada to try if amicable discussion could not produce a more speedy settlement than formal correspondence.[11] In March, 1850, when there had still been no progress toward an agreement, he repeated this offer privately to Merivale, arguing: "I have no doubt that on the spot some middle course might be hit on which would be acquiesced in by both parties. . . . [The] information I should acquire on administrative matters both in going & returning by the north of this province & by the Northern States would be of great service to me hereafter."[12] This led to the

10P.R.O., C.O. 188/113, Head to Grey, private, August 26, 1850.
11P.R.O., C.O. 188/106, Head to Grey, October 26, 1848.
12P.R.O., C.O. 188/112, Head to Merivale, private, March 18, 1850.

desired result, and it was arranged that Head and his attorney general, L. A. Wilmot, should meet in Toronto toward the end of September with Lord Elgin and members of the Canadian executive council.

The journey to Canada, on which he was accompanied by Lady Head, was itself a most interesting experience for Head who had not been outside of New Brunswick for over two years and who had never before visited the great new republic, the land of his father's birth and of his grandfather's explusion. Travelling from Saint John to Boston by steamer, the Heads first spent almost a week in that "English country town multiplied by 20," meeting George Ticknor and other literary friends and also Sir Henry Bulwer, the British minister to Washington.[13] "The latter suffers much from nervous headaches & is evidently much 'used up'. Lady Bulwer is amusing. She dislikes Washington immensely & expatiated to Lady Head on her grievances." From Boston to Burlington and by Lake Champlain to Montreal the trip was impressive for its scenery, particularly "that mountain nest in which Burgoyne entangled his army." With Montreal the Heads were

most agreeably disappointed. It is magnificiently situated & is really a fine City—but what strikes one as so odd is that here & at Quebec whole streets & sides of streets appear like a French country town. From Montreal we ran down to Quebec & staid there two days. . . . I have never seen above 3 or 4 cities which I should call so picturesque as Quebec. Geneva, Naples & Edinburgh are the only ones which occur to me as equal to it. The shipping lying right under the great mass of the citadel with its fortifications & the town glittering on steps all the way up the hill form a whole of the greatest beauty.

Returning to Montreal, the Heads went on to Toronto by steamer, a 48-hour trip. To Head's delight, the captain of the boat was "the very man who had taken Sir Francis Head & landed him in the U.S. when he made his wonderful gallop through the State of New York." Having always doubted the necessity for Sir Francis's thus risking capture and "a violation of the law of nations by the Americans which might have involved both countries in war," he questioned the captain carefully and received the answer: " 'Oh no Sir, there was nothing to apprehend

[13]Lewis Papers, Head to Lewis, October 17, 1850. Except where otherwise noted the remainder of the account of Head's visit to Canada is also taken from this long letter which he wrote immediately after his return.

on the road to Quebec & I told him that the Yankees would certainly try to waylay him—but he would go.' "

The meeting with Elgin was one that both men had anticipated
with real pleasure and with special interest in remembering, as
Elgin put it, that "the last time we met he examined me for a
Fellowship at Merton Coll. Oxford!"[14] After it was over, and had
been prolonged by the Elgins going on with their visitors for
several days at Niagara Falls, both were conscious of the growth
of a genuine friendship and of mutual esteem. "We have
accompanied the Heads thus far on their way homewards," Elgin
wrote to Grey from Niagara Falls. "I have been very glad to
renew my acquaintance with him as he is an old friend and a very
clever & well informed one. Mary has got on swimmingly with
Lady Head."[15] Head's account to Lewis was equally glowing:

Lord Elgin received me like an old friend & most fortunately Lady Head
& Lady Elgin started up a wonderful friendship. She (Lady Elgin) is a
charming person—she has bad health but I never met anyone more completely sensible & unaffected. . . . I enjoyed myself at Toronto, partly
because I like Lord Elgin personally, & partly because I felt the pleasure
of being able to talk freely & unreservedly on matters of Government &
general policy after 2½ years of comparative restraint. I don't know whether
Lord Elgin felt the same but we got on very well.

Few single events were more important in helping develop
Head's insight on colonial problems than these talks with Elgin
and the experience of finding himself "in amicable discussion at
Lord Elgin's Council Board, with Lafontaine & Baldwin & the
'rebels' of Sir Francis Head." In particular, they gave him a truer
picture of the Canadian situation.

I really believe that Canadian politics are now in a sound state. The French
party believe for the first time that the Government means to act honestly
by them & Papineau is thus left in a minority altogether. In fact the system
is in a transition state & in my opinion Lord Elgin deserves great credit
for the courage with which he took on himself the odium & risk of the bill
of the session of 1849. Nothing could have been easier for him than to have
thrown the difficulty on the Home Government. Annexation is at a dis-
count—in fact it never existed except at Montreal in any force. . . . I have
same satisfaction in thinking that my own views agree very well with those
which are now being acted on in Canada. My journey therefore has given
me confidence & I have learnt a great deal that is material to me.

[14]A. G. Doughty (ed.), *The Elgin-Grey Papers*, II, 714, Elgin to Grey,
September 27, 1850.
[15]*Ibid.*, p. 720, Elgin to Grey, October 6, 1850.

An equally satisfactory conclusion was reached regarding the boundary question. A New Brunswick executive council minute of September 5 was used as the basis for discussion, and after three days of meetings the terms under which arbitration would take place in London were agreed upon.[16]

The trip home, going through New York this time as well as Boston, gave Head a further opportunity to learn something of the American way of life:

> No two things can be conceived more unlike the same country than New York & Boston. The former is like the Metropolis not only of the U.S. but of S. America, California & the West Indies. I had not been in a large town for so long that I expected to be run over. The stream of population in the Broadway & the forest of shipping in the Port are most surprising. We only stayed 3 days & with difficulty got away from Mr. Bancroft & his wife who overwhelmed us with civilities.
>
> One of the phenomena at New York & a very important one to my mind is the rise of a monied aristocracy showing all the outward signs of wealth. Homes [are] furnished in a style scarcely dreamed of by people of moderate means in Europe—I ceased to wonder why Sèvres China had risen in price at Paris & in London after seeing the home of a Mr. Height who made his fortune as a hatter. He has a winter garden opening into a drawing room & every door & window is draped with Lyons brocade or Gobelins tapestry. Liveries & arms on carriages are not uncommon. It is a curious problem how long this ostentatious prominence of wealth with no prestige of rank or station or traditional eminence to support it will be borne by the masses. The safety valve of the 'Far West' is the only hope.
>
> I have some reason to think too that republican purity of morals does not exist in any great degree. Divorce is frequent & *it is said* (but I cannot vouch for it on good authority) that the practice of abortion is not infrequent. . . . No doubt with people who board at Hotels children must be a nuisance—don't state this on my authority.
>
> At Boston all is outward correctness & I should think the society very agreeable. . . . A certain spice of the old puritan leaven exists still.

Finally, in mid-October after an absence of some five weeks, the Heads arrived back in Fredericton. "We arrived home last night safely & prosperously after a good voyage & found our children better than when we left them."

On October 17, 1850, the day following Head's return from Canada, Chief Justice Chipman tendered his resignation. Chipman, whose age and infirmities had long made his continuance in office difficult, had informed Head of his intention earlier, in the course of a private conversation in August, but had agreed

16P.R.O., C.O. 188/113, Head to Grey, October 24, 1850.

to do nothing until the visit with Elgin was over when it would be more convenient for Head to deal with what was bound to be an awkward problem.[17] It was obvious that the disposal of this most tempting plum of patronage within the province—the event eagerly anticipated by lawyer-politicians for some years—would complicate still further the delicate political situation resulting from the excitement of the past session and from the rather indecisive election. "I expect My Government here to break up in a scramble for the Chief Justiceship," Head wrote to Lewis on the day that he received Chipman's letter.[18]

Head's expectation was very nearly realized in the course of the stormy sessions of the executive council which took place the following week. Meeting first at Government House on Wednesday, October 23, the council was given by Head, in a sealed envelope, a copy of Chipman's resignation together with a memorandum in which Head asked their advice with regard to a successor, and in which he himself pointed out certain advantages there might be in promoting one of the puisne judges. It was the final sentence of Head's memorandum, however, that attracted the particular attention of the council when they withdrew, as was customary, to the provincial secretary's office to continue their discussions. This stated that His Excellency "reserves of course to himself the liberty of making such recommendations to the Sec^y of State as may seem to him expedient for guiding the ultimate decision of H.M. Govt." Upon asking Head to clarify the meaning of this, they were informed

that he conceives it to be his duty to ask the advice of his Council on such a matter as the appointment of the Chief Justice.

In this, however, as in many other matters, the recommendations which H: E: may ultimately make to H: M: Secretary of State are made on his own responsibility and not necessarily on that of his Council. If those recommendations are at variance with the advice of the Ex. Council it is open to the members of that body to take their own course.[19]

With this firm and rather challenging reply the executive council had to be content, and throughout Wednesday and Thursday and on Friday morning they debated what advice they should give. Their problem was most complex. A coalition brought together several years before by Head, they lacked the

[17]P.R.O., C.O. 188/113, Head to Grey, private, August 26, 1850.
[18]Lewis Papers, Head to Lewis, October 17, 1850.
[19]P.A.C., C.O. 188/205, Head to Grey, February 15, 1851, and enclosure.

strength of party unity, their support in the spring session had been feeble, and their standing in the new House was as yet uncertain. If one of their number were to accept the vacancy on the Bench, might the rest not be left too weak to carry on? Or if this risk were accepted which individual should be given the opportunity to ascend to the peace and security of judicial office? Wilmot's claim as attorney general was good but Chandler had received certain pledges back in 1848 when the Government was originally formed. If either of these were appointed, however, might the balance in the council not be shifted to the right or to the left in such a way as to affect unfavourably some or other of its members? Unable to find a satisfactory solution along these lines, a majority consisting of six out of the nine councillors finally handed Head a memorandum on Friday afternoon expressing the opinion that it was "not advisable to appoint any person to the vacant office, and that such a revision of the Judiciary should be made by the Legislature as will secure the efficient discharge of the Judicial duties by three Judges of the Supreme Court together with the Master of the Rolls."[20] Solicitor General Kinnear, Fisher, and Rankin were the dissenters from this recommendation. After a brief discussion in which Head showed obvious displeasure and drew particular attention to the council's lack of unanimity, members who lived at a distance hurried away to get home before the week-end.

That evening there occurred an event for which no satisfactory explanation has ever been given. Hardly had his colleagues dispersed when Wilmot sat down and wrote them a letter reopening the question and concluding: "I certainly think we have not acted wisely in the advice given by our minute today, and I am now disposed to retract the opinion therein expressed."[21] The next morning he called at Government House and read this letter to Head.

The circumstances in which Head found himself as a result of this action were most perplexing. Should he assume that the majority, now reduced to five out of nine, would adhere to their same advice in spite of the defection of the attorney general, and should he consider this advice binding? Or should he hold that Wilmot's letter had created a new situation in which the previous advice of the council was not applicable? Head had little difficulty

[20]P.R.O., C.O. 188/113, Head to Grey, November 5, 1850.
[21]*Ibid.*

in deciding to reject the first of these alternatives. From the beginning he had taken the stand that his ultimate recommendation to the colonial secretary would be made "on his own responsibility and not necessarily on that of his Council." What he now had from the council could hardly be called a recommendation at all since it had only the doubtful support of five of its members. Opposed were both of the law officers, the men most concerned, presumably, with the efficient functioning of the judiciary. And regardless of the opinion of the council, Head himself was most unwilling to permit tampering with the judicial system of the province for what seemed obviously to be reasons of political expediency. "According to my ideas of English institutions, one of their most valuable and cherished characteristics is the stability and independence of the Judiciary. To solicit interference with this part of our system, without clear proof of abuse, or evidence of any practical grievance appears to me to be running great risk with little hope of advantage."[22]

An obvious possibility was to call another meeting of the council. This would involve considerable inconvenience to its members and some almost certainly would be unable to attend. But even if the whole council met once again, would it be able to agree any better on a satisfactory course? Head had no reason to think that it would: "My own conviction was and is still, that there exists a hopeless diversity of opinion among the members of the Council on the points at issue." In any case, Head did not believe, as he had already warned the council, that its consent was necessary in an affair of this sort. "I never conceived . . . that the appointment of the Chief Justice and the Judges is a matter on which the ultimate decision can be withdrawn from Her Majesty, & Her Advisers in England although the opinion of the Executive Council of the Province with regard to the persons to be appointed would when tendered be entitled to the highest respect and consideration."[23] Head's decision, therefore, was to follow the bolder course of not recalling the council but instead undertaking a careful survey of the whole situation himself, explaining it all fully to the colonial secretary, and making his own recommendations without further delay.

The more thoroughly he examined the matter, the firmer became Head's conviction that the vacancy on the Bench should

[22]*Ibid.*
[23]P.R.O., C.O. 188/114, Head to Grey, January 10, 1851.

be filled despite the views of some members of the council. A statement which he asked for from the three puisne judges argued strongly that a reduction in the number of the judges might seriously impair their efficient administration of the law. So too did an able paper which Fisher had read to the council-in-committee and which he forwarded to Head after the meetings were over.[24] It seemed clear that the proposal of the council majority had been based more on political than on judicial considerations. Head decided, therefore, to ignore it and recommend an appointment.

So far as the choice among individuals was concerned, which had been the real stumbling-block of the council, Head had no difficulty because he was himself disinterested. From the first he had believed that James Carter, the senior puisne judge, should be promoted to the position of chief justice and he now recommended this to Grey. To fill the place vacated by Carter, E. B. Chandler had a paramount claim due to the understanding reached when he agreed to remain in the executive council without portfolio in 1848. "For a long time I know he desired this promotion," Head explained to Grey on November 5, "but I can now inform Your Lordship, on his own authority, that he would decline it."

Much that is obscure in this whole crisis would be clarified if there were any clue as to the exact nature of the private conversations that must lie behind this sentence. Head had not seen Chandler since the council meetings and there is no evidence of written correspondence. Had Head at some time during the days of the meetings talked privately with Chandler and found out from him that he was less anxious than he had been when Responsible Government was first being introduced to abandon the uncertainties of politics for a secure place on the Bench? Had Wilmot also made this discovery either from Head or from Chandler, and may this have influenced his astonishing *volte-face* on the evening the meetings ended? Chandler having waived his claim, Wilmot as attorney general was next in line for the position, and Wilmot was undoubtedly anxious to obtain it. His political stock had gone down rapidly since he had entered the Government in 1848—a common fate for members of the assembly who became executive councillors at that stage of New Brunswick's political evolution. Wilmot had been returned at the

24P.R.O., C.O. 188/113, Head to Grey, November 5, 1850, enclosures.

foot of the poll in York County in the election of a few months before and his chief lieutenant in the council, Charles Fisher, had been defeated. But whatever the truth as to Wilmot's role and motivation in the events of this crisis, Head's course in the circumstances was clear; and he had no hesitation in recommending that the vacant position on the Bench be offered to Wilmot.[25]

Head has been bitterly accused of high-handedness not only because he recommended the appointments of Wilmot and Carter without, or contrary to, the advice of his executive council, but also because he kept his recommendations secret from the council until the appointments had been approved by the Colonial Office and accepted by the individuals concerned. At a council meeting early in December, he made no mention of the despatch he had written to Grey. And when Grey's reply was received on December 31, he did not wait for the meeting that was to take place a week later, but on that same afternoon wrote to Carter and Wilmot. Not having received a reply from the latter by January 2, he wrote again asking for an immediate decision, and when this was given in the affirmative, drafted in his own handwriting an official notice to be issued in an extra edition of the *Royal Gazette*—all this still with no reference even to members of the council living in Fredericton.[26]

Actually Head's reasons for rushing the appointments through in secrecy without consulting the council can easily be justified. Having once decided on a course which the council had not recommended and having asked for Grey's approval, it would have been folly to inform the council of this before Grey's reply had been received. It would have been equally foolish, and would as well have involved the colonial secretary in an improper manner, to place the latter's decision before the council for further debate instead of taking immediate action. The reason for

[25]See J. W. Lawrence, *The Judges of New Brunswick*, pp. 448 ff. Lawrence's statement that Wilmot had long felt out of his element in the coalition and welcomed the opportunity to retire to the Bench may probably be true. His further assertion that Head opposed Wilmot's retirement until the latter produced an old letter of recommendation from Lord Glenelg seems less credible. Head had not been entirely satisfied with Wilmot's conduct of affairs during the session of 1850, and did not think him irreplaceable. He did not consider Wilmot at first for the vacancy on the Bench because of Chandler's prior claim. When this was waived, Head was quite ready to give Wilmot the second choice to which his position entitled him.

[26]P.A.C., Head Papers, Head to Wilmot, December 31, 1850; Head to Wilmot, January 2, 1851; C.O. 188/205, Head to Grey, February 15, 1851, and enclosures.

haste was that the first session of the newly elected legislature was due to open early in February. The announcement of these appointments, involving as they did the withdrawal of a leading figure from the Government, had to be made as long before the opening as possible if the council were to have any chance of pulling itself together again and preparing to face the House.

Head's later, apparently arbitrary, actions can therefore be seen to have followed necessarily upon his original decision to make these recommendations on his own responsibility. Nor can there be any just criticism of the recommendations themselves. The men appointed were those generally considered the most suitable, and dangerous political interference with the judiciary was avoided. The real question at issue between Head and his critics is in essence twofold: Was Head correct as a "responsible" governor in disregarding the advice, such as it was, of his executive council on this occasion? Was he correct in his further belief that appointments such as these were still subject to the ultimate decision of Her Majesty's advisers in England, the opinion of the local council being entitled only to "the highest respect and consideration"?

Head's own answer to the first of these questions seems unexceptionable. He could not put completely into practice what was vaguely called Responsible Government in the prevailing circumstances in New Brunswick. He could not rely fully on the advice of an executive council which did not itself have real executive authority and did not even have any but an intermittent existence. Five of the nine members of the council lived at least one hundred miles from Fredericton and received no salaries. Meetings accordingly had to be carefully planned to suit all and usually lasted only two days, the unpaid councillors being anxious to get back to their own affairs. There was, therefore, the greatest difficulty in getting full and fair discussion of complicated business.

It is evident enough that in order to imitate in the smallest degree the working of the English system, a certain amount of patronage and power must be in the hands of the Government of the time. It must be worth the while of competent men to attend to the business of the public rather than to their own affairs and to be ready at any moment to assist the Lieutenant Governor with their advice and countenance. These men too must be entrusted with a certain discretion to be exercised under the controul of the Representative Body. . . . An exact counterpart of the English System of Parliamentary Government is perhaps scarcely possible in a community of

74 *Sir Edmund Head*

200,000 people separated by long tracts of wilderness and Forest. The first conditions however for getting nearer to the principle at which we aim are in this Province—

1st Such offices or emoluments in the hands of a majority of the members of a Government as will make it worth their while to act continuously and jealously for the public.

2nd Such a controul over the introduction of money votes as will enable a Government to take the responsibility of proposing to the House of Assembly, or of rejecting, appropriations to be made, and thus making the Executive Council answerable for some correspondence between income and expenditure. . . .

In the mean time, I shall steadily go on as well as I can under existing circumstances, endeavouring always to develop in this Colony as much self government as is compatible with its relation to the Mother Country and with the welfare of the People at large, understood in its widest sense.[27]

As to the second question, whether Head was correct in his assumption that the ultimate decision in connection with such appointments still rested in any case with Her Majesty's advisers in England, an exact answer is more difficult to give. In the gradual and indefinite manner typical of English constitutional developments, Responsible Government was being introduced in British North America without any attempt to specify the separate powers of the local and the Imperial governments. The sole criterion was that the governor govern through an executive council "responsible" to the local legislature. The whole system depended fundamentally on mutual consent rather than on constitutional definition. Head's assumption was correct therefore as long as—but only as long as—it met with the consent of the local executive and legislature.

In this instance, his judgment may be said to have been rendered valid by the events that followed. Clearly he had played a "hazardous game." He had taken a course which might have led to the resignation of the executive council or to its defeat in the assembly. In either case he could probably not have formed another government and so would have been unable to carry on in accordance with the general principle of Responsible Government. His estimate of the circumstances, however, and of the men he was dealing with, was based on sure knowledge and insight. Only one member of the council, Charles Fisher, resigned;[28] the

[27]P.R.O., C.O. 188/113, Head to Grey, separate, November 6, 1850.
[28]Hanington resigned December 24, 1850, before the appointments of Wilmot and Carter were made, and on other grounds. (See Hanington to Head, December 26, 1850, in P.R.O., C.O. 188/114, Head to Grey, January 10, 1851.) Fisher's resignation to uphold "my ideas of Responsible Government," does not

rest protested that Head's action was "at variance with those principles of responsible government understood to be now in force in this Province," but they remained in office.[29] Moreover, after a new attorney general, J. A. Street, was appointed, this council managed, albeit with some difficulty, to retain the confidence of the assembly throughout the succeeding session. As Herman Merivale, at the Colonial Office, commented: "if the affair ends in producing more unity of action & purpose among themselves [the council], good will have been done, even at the expense of some discontent with the Lt. Govr."[30]

The firm hold that Head had been obliged to taken on the reins of government during the chief-justiceship crisis of 1850 was to be relaxed only very gradually during the remaining years of his administration in the province. His responsibilities were perhaps greatest in the early months of 1851, before and during the first session of the new legislature, when his weakened and confused executive council was barely able to maintain its precarious tenure of office. The loss of Wilmot and Fisher, and the circumstances under which this had occurred, greatly reduced its probable support especially among reform elements in the assembly. Possibly its ablest member was E. B. Chandler. Head seems to have had closer associations with him than with any other New Brunswick politician, and was to rely on him during the coming years, particularly in railway and reciprocity negotiations, to such an extent that Chandler came to be generally known as the unofficial prime minister.[31] But Chandler was in the legislative council, not the assembly, and held no portfolio.

On the other hand the most influential member of the assembly, John R. Partelow, the provincial secretary, though he was an expert at political management lacked the breadth of view needed for constructive leadership. Nor was the new attorney general, J. A. Street, yet in a position to lead the Government effectively. Long experience at the Bar and in the assembly had resulted for

afford absolute proof that he was more a man of principle than his colleagues. Having been defeated in the election, he was the only member of the executive council without a seat in the legislature. His retirement before the session opened was therefore almost inevitable in any case.

[29]P.R.O., C.O. 188/114, Head to Grey, January 10, 1851, enclosure.

[30]P.R.O., C.O. 188/114, Head to Grey, January 10, 1851, minutes.

[31]Mrs. Lyell (ed.), *Sir Charles Lyell*, II, 182; P.R.O., C.O. 188/122, Manners Sutton to Sir George Grey, confidential, November 15, 1854.

Street in growing prestige, and his moderate views made him an excellent choice to team with Partelow in a practical middle-of-the-road government. He was in no way outstanding, however, and certainly for the time being was in no position to assume a vigorous initiative. The weakness of the executive council was all the more critical since organized political parties were non-existent and much depended on what impression the Government could create in the early stages of the debate among the large number of new members not yet definitely committed for or against its policies.

Under these circumstances, Head, who was already personally committed in the matter of the judicial appointments and would have found the defeat of his Government on this issue most embarrassing, felt it necessary to step into the breach himself. He was fully prepared to do so. The experience of the past three years and the scholarly thinking he had done on the subject during that time had given him a thorough understanding of what was needed to transform the New Brunswick system into a true form of Responsible Government—if indeed that could be done at all. His conversations with Lord Elgin had also been most useful in this regard and in addition had increased his assurance that his own views were correct. He knew, too, that his administration of New Brunswick affairs thus far had won the approval of Grey and the Colonial Office. "[Your] government seems quite successful," Lewis had written some time before. "I heard Hawes cite you one night as a specimen of one of Lord Grey's appointments."[32] Grey himself, at just this time, when he thought he might be leaving the Colonial Office wrote privately to Head expressing "'his sense of the great obligation he was under to me for having averted very serious difficulties here by my judgment & ability under very trying circumstances.'"[33] Head's connection with the unfortunate and bitterly attacked Poor Law Commission had made him fear with some reason initial distrust by the Colonial Office,[34] and these compliments and the warm

[32]Lewis, *Letters*, p. 201, Lewis to Head, April 5, 1849.

[33]Lewis Papers, Head to Lewis, March 31, 1851. A few months later Head received confirmation of Grey's good opinion from his Colonial Office friend Henry Taylor who wrote: "Lord Grey said to me, some months ago, that your appointment was the best hit he had made since he had been in office. . . . He said last night that you were the best man we had. . . . he gives you credit for a gift in the managing of men." E. Dowden (ed.), *Correspondence of Henry Taylor*, Taylor to Head, November 16, 1851.

[34]D. C. Masters, *The Reciprocity Treaty of 1854*, p. 14.

welcome from Lord Elgin were valuable in building up his confidence in himself. They help explain the vigorous and self-reliant way in which he now placed his ideas on Responsible Government before his executive council and drew up for it a fully thought-out programme of reform with which it could meet the legislature.

Head did this in a long memorandum which, "after maturely weighing the whole subject," he laid before the council prior to the opening of the session.[35] Writing formally, in the third person, but in direct, sometimes tutorial language, he set forth his understanding of Responsible Government.

He is sincerely desirous of carrying out fairly and honestly what is understood in these Colonies by 'departmental' and 'Responsible' Government, which should rather be described as 'Parliamentary' Government.

Whatever the theory of such a system may be, the Lieutenant Governor cannot really act by the advice of his Council unless two conditions are fulfilled.

1st   Unless his Council is composed of men competent to advise upon the several departments of the administration and having the power entrusted to them.

2nd   Unless such Council are at hand to advise him as the necessity for action arises. . . .

It follows . . . that if the Public in the Province wish for what they call 'Responsible Government', and if they desire that the administration should be practically carried on by those whom their Representatives control, they must in some manner pay the men who give up their time to the public service, and advise the Lieutenant Governor. They must do this directly as members of the Executive Council, or they must allow them to hold offices which will make it worth their while to attend to public business instead of their own affairs. If they do neither, the inevitable result will be that many acts must be done by the Lt. Governor or the Colonial Secretary without advice, and consequently without any immediate responsibility to the people of the Colony or to their Representatives. . . . [So] long as the House of Assembly decline to admit the conditions absolutely necessary for 'Responsible' Government they must forego the practical enjoyment of its benefits, and things must go on in their present provisional condition.

Turning from general principles to matters of immediate practical concern, Head continued his memorandum by making a careful analysis of the provincial executive. In addition to the three offices of attorney general, solicitor general, and provincial secretary already held by members of the council, that of the surveyor general was one that he had always believed should be placed on a political tenure. He recommended that this now be

[35]P.R.O., C.O. 188/114, Head to Grey, February 10, 1851, enclosure.

done by giving its present occupant a suitable retiring allowance. Further, he suggested that two new offices of inspector general of schools[36] and commissioner of public works be created and also be made political. On the other hand, the treasurer, auditor general, and postmaster general ought not to be connected with politics, he thought, because theirs were positions requiring technical knowledge and a high degree of impartiality. "It may be observed generally that in a small and economical community the English system of permanent subordinates in all offices well-paid, is hardy admissible, and it follows that some departments which may be held politically under the latter, will not admit of being so dealt with under the former."

Having shown how the council could be satisfactorily re-constituted by the inclusion of at least three more heads of departments, Head went on to insist once again that its powers must be enlarged as well by giving it the sole right to initiate money votes:

All responsibility implies a trust of power—but how is this under the present system with regard to the Executive Council? Can the Government originate improvements? Can they carry out measures for the benefit of the Province? How do they know that there will be a farthing in the Treasury to pay for such improvements or to meet the charges of such measures? They cannot say 'no' when a money vote is introduced. . . . What is the sense of 'responsibility' when no one is responsible for the main condition of all progress—the correspondence of expenditure and income?

At this point Head asked the council bluntly: "Do they concur in these principles? If they do so, are they disposed to do their best to make such principles intelligible to the Legislature, and to endeavour to get the conditions necessary for carrying out these principles fulfilled?"

Acting for the moment on the assumption that both of these questions would be answered in the affirmative, and pointing out that "the real estimate which the people of New Brunswick will form of the value of any Government . . . depends at this time infinitely more on the measures brought forward . . . than on the supposed politics of the individuals," Head outlined the following legislative programme for their consideration:

[36]"If it is the wish of the People to have an efficient system of Common Schools (and nothing is more important) there ought to be some one paid officer always connected with the Government, and probably holding a seat in the Council, in whose charge all matters relating to schools should be placed, perhaps in conjunction with a Board."

i A measure for placing the initiation of money votes on a proper footing.

ii A measure for establishing a proper registration of voters, and perhaps improving the nature of the Elective Franchise.

iii A measure giving a local Body of some sort in each County consisting mainly of Elective members the apportionment and expenditure within the County, of money granted by the Legislature for Bye Roads, or raised for that purpose in the County itself.

iv A measure for introducing with the least disturbance of existing Institutions, an Elective Legislative Council.[37]

v A measure for commuting the Judges' fees, and charging such commutation upon the Civil List.

vi An effective Law for the better regulation of Common Schools.

vii The appointment under an Act of Assembly of a Commission to consider what changes can be made in the procedure of the Courts of Law, and the Court of Chancery so as to afford more ready redress at a less expense to the suitor.

Some such propositions ought to be laid before the Legislature in a complete form with a distinct understanding among the members of the Government itself what portions of them the Government consider as essential to the objects aimed at, and what portions are properly to be treated as open to questions. . . .

The Lieut: Governor, therefore, invites the Council fully to discuss with him the steps necessary for carrying out all or any of these measures. He is prepared to devote to this object any time necessary for assisting to digest into shape the measures above described in concert either with his whole Council or with a Committee of its members, and he would desire to announce in his opening speech that bills for effecting the principal at least of these objects may probably be submitted to the Legislature.

Head's proposals in this very important memorandum were by and large accepted by the council as their legislative platform and most were referred to in the Speech from the Throne. The session, however, as had been expected, was a turbulent one. The Opposition was led by the six members from the city and county of Saint John, most of whom were extremely able and were beginning brilliant careers leading in the case of two of them, by an interesting coincidence, to the very position of lieutenant governor of New Brunswick then held by Head himself.[38] In the

[37]This was a subject of wide discussion in all of the provinces at the time, and involved exactly the sort of complex constitutional problems that interested Head most. P.A.C., G 18/21 contains a long memorandum in his own hand dated September 18, 1851, "on an Elective Legislative Council in New Brunswick with reference to the report of the Comᵗᵗᵉᵉ of Council on the same subject at the Cape."

[38]S. L. Tilley and R. D. Wilmot eventually became lieutenant governors of New Brunswick. W. J. Ritchie became chief justice of Canada, J. H. Gray, a member of the supreme court of British Columbia. The others were Charles Simonds and W. H. Needham.

assembly in 1851 they made a vigorous attack on Head and his Government. In resolutions introduced in the committee on the state of the province they complained that Head made public only extracts from his official correspondence with the colonial secretary, thus failing to keep the legislature informed of much that was taking place. They protested in particular the manner in which Carter and Wilmot had been elevated to the Bench. They returned too to a demand for the reduction of official salaries. They worded their resolutions in such a way as to associate the Government with the policies which they criticized, their main object clearly being its defeat. Only by skilful amendments, and by joining in the attack on Head and the colonial secretary, was the Government able to escape. "To this we must submit and, I apprehend, notwithstanding the violence of the language, the 'Resolutions' in question will have very little practical effect," Head wrote to Grey. "They will not change my conduct in any way."[39]

In looking back over the session of 1851 after it had finally ended, Head was able to report himself "not on the whole dissatisfied." Much had been accomplished. A bill providing for the introduction of municipal institutions in counties where the people desired them had been passed. Executive control over money votes had very nearly been accepted as well, a resolution favouring this actually being approved by a majority of one only to be rescinded at a later sitting. At least some progress had been made therefore along these two most important lines. Moreover, although the language of the resolutions had been violent, no effective measures for the reduction of salaries had resulted. The Government had held its ground only by very narrow margins, but it had survived.

One act of the legislature which was to give Head a most remarkable opportunity to strengthen his position had been the granting of a retiring allowance to Baillie, the surveyor general, to enable his office to be made political. By offering the surveyor-generalship to R. D. Wilmot, one of the six Saint John members, Head was able to persuade him and another of his colleagues, J. H. Gray, to enter the council. This provoked an outraged protest from the four remaining Saint John members, and when Wilmot on accepting office had to return to that city for re-

[39]P.R.O., C.O. 188/114, Head to Grey, separate and confidential, May 10, 1851.

election, they declared publicly that it was impossible for themselves and the "traitors" to represent the same constituency. Wilmot, nevertheless, was victorious over their candidate by a large majority. Three of them had the integrity to resign.[40] "The result as far as I am concerned," Head noted with some mild complacence, "is that I have not only re-constructed the Ex. Council but the H. of Assembly, without a general Election. The leaders of the opposition have done the work themselves & if all things go right I shall have less trouble in the next Session than in any which I have yet gone through."[41]

Just in case this prediction proved too optimistic Head summed up his opinions on Responsible Government in a despatch to the colonial secretary early the following year. He did so in order to put on record in clear and definite terms the principles on which he had based his actions of the past few years and by which he proposed to continue to be guided. With this despatch, and the expression of approval which he rightly believed it would elicit from the Colonial Office, he would be fully armed to meet attacks such as those made by the Opposition in the session of 1851. He wrote to Grey:

I am satisfied by experience that a good deal of irritation and difficulty have from time to time arisen in this Colony in consequence of a misconception on one side or the other of the true nature and conditions of the system of Government established in British North America under the popular name of 'Responsible Government'. I say in 'British North America' for I disclaim all idea of the system in this Province being different from that pursued in Nova Scotia or Canada, although the imperfect organization of departments here may for the moment increase the difficulties of the Lieut: Governor. . . .

According to my views then—
1. The Executive Council (if they remain in office) are 'responsible' to the Colonial Legislature for the acts of the Lieut: Governor as administrator of the Colonial Government whether such acts are done with or without their express advice or whether done by the direction of the Secretary of State or not. Of this 'responsibility' they can at any moment relieve themselves when an obnoxious act is done. The Lieut: Governor may then swear in another Council (provisionally) or he may have to appeal to the people of the Colony by dissolving the Assembly.
2. The Lieut: Governor is 'responsible' to no authority in the Colony, but he is 'responsible' to the Law of England and the Crown and Parliament of England for all his acts and all his despatches.
3. The Executive Council are in no sense or degree 'responsible' for the

40The exception was W. H. Needham.
41Lewis Papers, Head to Lewis, November 4, 1851.

despatches addressed by the Lieut: Governor to Her Majesty's Secretary of State, except so far as such despatches expressly convey their opinion and advice. . . . The Executive Council are not 'responsible' for the Lieut: Governor in his relation to the Queen's Government but in his relation to the people of the Colony. His responsibility in England in the former capacity is complete and undivided. It could not be if he were bound to sign as his own the opinion of others. . . .

4. If the Executive Council desire at any time to place their opinions before the Queen's Advisers in England, it is the duty of the Lieut: Governor at once to forward their representations to the Secretary of State; and he is bound to inform the Secretary of State when the Council differ from himself on important points. . . .

The Executive Council thus stand with regard to the ordinary administration in the same constitutional relation to the Colonial Parliament as Her Majesty's Ministers occupy with reference to the Imperial Parliament. The exceptions and anomalies, such as they are, are implied by the fact that the Government is that of a Colony—not of the Empire.[42]

In fact, by the time this despatch was written, the political crisis that had lasted through the previous two years was over and a period of relatively stable government in New Brunswick that would endure until the end of Head's administration was beginning. There would be few changes from then on in the personnel of the executive council and no serious threat to its continuance in power. Head's own position and his view of Responsible Government would remain almost unchallenged, as is indicated by a note he made on the margin of this despatch itself when going through his papers before leaving for Canada in 1854: "This despatch and its answer have never been laid before the Executive Council." He had had no need to use them. It did not follow of course, on the more positive side, that the reforms he had advocated could be quickly brought about. A long and persistent process of education was necessary before political leaders and the public generally could be brought to see the complete implications of Responsible Government.

[42]P.R.O., C.O. 188/116, Head to Grey, separate, February 28, 1852. Merivale, whose experience as professor of political economy at Oxford as well as colonial under-secretary gives his judgment unusual weight, minuted on this despatch: 'I believe the Lt. Gov. has very accurately stated the principles of the system called 'responsible government' in colonial administration. But his own statement shews in what respect it is, and must be, anomalous. The Ex^r Gov^t of an independent community may be responsible to the Legislature only. The Executive Government of a dependency has a double responsibility: that of the Governor's Council toward the Legislature: that of the Governor himself toward the Home Government: and it is the difficulty of reconciling this double obligation which produces most of the temporary differences & *hitches* in colonial government as at present organized in the N. Am^n provinces."

FIVE

British North American Union and Reciprocity

IT was probably late in 1850 or early in 1851, in the midst of the political crisis that followed the resignation of Chief Justice Chipman, that Head despatched privately to Grey an important memorandum which he had prepared on the union of British North America.[1] The subject was one that, for a variety of reasons—some general, some specific—had come to occupy his thoughts more and more in the years since it had been raised in his initial conversations with Grey at the Colonial Office. Even the failure of the scheme for building the Halifax and Quebec Railway, in 1849, which made union impracticable for the time being, did not cause Head to abandon his studies and speculations regarding it.

Theories concerning federalism as a form of government were almost certain, in any case, to attract the interest of a man of Head's mentality in the middle years of the nineteenth century. On the one hand, certain groups of states such as those in Germany and Italy were advancing steadily and perceptibly toward some form of union. On the other, in addition to the evidences of disintegration in Austria, there had recently been civil war in Switzerland, the model of all confederacies, and there appeared to be an inexorable approach of it in the United States, the greatest. Was there any stage between complete separation and complete unity at which neighbouring states might enjoy the advantages of both and find a just equilibrium in their association with one another? It was for this question, both in its abstract form and in its application to British North America, that Head was beginning to seek an answer.

Revealing glimpses of the way his mind was ranging in 1850

[1]Chester Martin, "Sir Edmund Head's First Project of Federation, 1851," *Canadian Historical Association Report*, 1928, pp. 14–26; D. G. G. Kerr, "The New Brunswick Background of Sir Edmund Head's Views on Confederation," *ibid.*, 1949, pp. 7–13.

and 1851 over the question's various ramifications may be obtained from his letters to Lewis. In March, 1850, for example, he noted in connection with Joseph Story's *Commentaries on the Conflict of Laws*, from which he was to quote later in the memorandum to Grey: "It illustrates well the difficulties occurring in a Federal Country with Laws of different characters prevailing in neighbouring states."[2] Discussing the Fugitive Slave Law in another letter, he remarked: "Its enactment shows that the intimate federal union of States with such different institutions is fraught with danger & difficulty."[3] Even the project Head had in mind of translating Aristotle's *Politics* led him to comment: "Almost all the topics of the day such as slavery, federal governments, &c &c could be touched on in notes."[4] And turning from America to Europe, he wrote: "The German States seem more hopeless than ever. Will they ever see clearly what the real difficulty of a federation really is?"[5]

Specific problems connected with his New Brunswick administration were also directing Head's thoughts toward the subject of federation at this time. The practical difficulties involved in trying to duplicate the British parliamentary system in a small province with a scattered population of some 200,000 were, as we have seen, vivid in Head's mind in 1850 and 1851. So too were memories of the annexation movement and the continuing repercussions of it that were still being felt in England as well as the colonies. He wrote Lewis early in 1850:

I am very anxious to see the policy of the [Imperial] Govt in regards Canada. Notwithstanding all reports & all conjectures I cannot bring myself to believe that a minister will be found who will venture to propose to give it up. Nor do I see where the 'giving up' is to end. India pays us nothing—nor Australia—certainly not the Cape or the W. Indies. Is the pride of the people of England likely to be content with renouncing their boasted universal dominion? I think now *temper* & not pecuniary interest will decide the question some day in spite of Cobden & Co.[6]

[2]Lewis Papers, Head to Lewis, March 2, 1850. It seems almost certain that this was the sentence that called forth from Lewis the rather inconsequent answer: "I quite agree with you in thinking that a federation of the North American provinces is not a likely event." (Lewis, *Letters*, pp. 221–24.) This probability makes somewhat doubtful the conclusion which Dr. W. M. Whitelaw draws from Lewis's letter that Head was definitely opposed to confederation until after his visit with Elgin (*The Maritimes and Canada*, pp. 113–14).
[3]Lewis Papers, Head to Lewis, October 17, 1850.
[4]*Ibid.*, Head to Lewis, March 31, 1851.
[5]*Ibid.*
[6]*Ibid.*, Head to Lewis, January 22, 1850.

The memorandum to Grey itself makes clear that his concern with the evident loosening of Imperial ties and the resulting danger that the colonies would be absorbed into the United States was the main reason for Head's interest in union in the early 1850's:

> It is impossible for any man of common intelligence and education to be familiar with the details of gov^t in the British provinces of North America without feeling that the present state of things is more or less provisional. . . .
>
> These Colonies may ultimately continue in allegiance to the British Crown or they may not. If they remain British dependencies they may hold that character as separate states or as one state of which the several parts should be more or less closely united by something in the nature of a federal tie. I confess I doubt how far their separate existence as single Colonies dependent on Gt. Britain can be secured if the present condition of things continues very long. If they cease to bear allegiance to England then they must be merged in the American Union or they must become independent. That they should maintain their independence singly is hardly conceivable; that they should do so if formed into one compact and United body does not seem absurd especially when the natural and internal sources of division between the north and south of the U.S. are taken into account.

The feeling that the state of things was provisional in British North America was due to the revolution that was taking place simultaneously in both the economic and the political relationships of the Empire. Responsible Government was weakening the political ties that had formerly bound the Empire together; free trade weakened its economic ties. Both of these changes were necessary and good in themselves, but for the time being they left the colonies "in a constant feeling of impending change & in a sence of uncertainty." Head asked therefore: "Is it then possible to devise any system which could employ the common allegiance borne by the Colonies to Great Britain in such a way as to bind them together one to the other until as time advanced and their powers of self gov^t were matured they might if they did separate be ready to assume as a whole, the bearing of a powerful and independent State?" Although he phrased the question in this form, Head made clear that he did not think separation inevitable. "I for one by no means consider it impossible that the connection should be maintained for an indefinite period." In short, Head's argument ran: the logic of Responsible Government and free trade was union—or annexation. Union might preserve the Imperial connection indefinitely, or if it did not, would at least give British North America the opportunity of becoming a powerful independent state.

To explain in a general way Head's reasons for believing the union of the colonies desirable is easier than to say exactly when or why he drew up this particular memorandum and sent it to Grey. It is tempting and may be correct to associate the memorandum with the remarkable developments that occurred early in 1851 in connection with the Halifax and Quebec Railway project. The railway was again coming into the limelight at that time owing to the strenuous, and almost single-handed, efforts of Joseph Howe. After the various earlier proposals had failed in 1849, each province had turned for a while to local railway undertakings but without much enthusiasm or hope. Then in August, 1850, at a convention in Portland, Maine, there had been launched amid great conviviality and speech-making a plan for building the European and North American Railway to link Halifax and Saint John with Portland, and so with the railway systems of the United States and Canada. Howe had not attended the convention, and he was not long in announcing his opposition to its proposals on the ground that they depended so largely for their success on the sponsorship of American financial interests. So far as Nova Scotia's share of the project was concerned, he put it up to the government: "whether they would stand aloof from this movement, and allow a great Highway, which in Peace would be a thorough-fare of Nations and in War might be of vast importance, to be constructed and controlled by Foreign Capitalists, or should at once grasp the enterprise and by the aid of Public Funds and Credit discharge towards the Country the highest and most legitimate functions of a vigorous Executive."[7] By sheer force of personality Howe secured the adoption of the latter alternative, and then he turned to Britain for assistance in obtaining the "Public Funds and Credit" required. Refusing to be discouraged by Grey's first expression of inability to help, he went to England himself and spent five months in persistent negotiations at the Colonial Office.

During this time, probably in the first weeks of 1851, the

[7]P.R.O., C.O. 217/204, Harvey to Grey, August 25, 1850. The signature at the end of this despatch is Harvey's but the rhetoric surely is that of Howe. The despatch also encloses a full account of the Portland convention. See as well J. A. Chisholm (ed.), *Speeches and Public Letters of Joseph Howe*, II, 75 ff.; a full account of the Colonial Office negotiations is also given here.

emphasis in Howe's discussions with Grey began to shift. Instead of the European and North American Railway, it began to centre on the Halifax and Quebec for which the expenditure of Imperial funds could be more easily justified. May it be that Head's memorandum was associated in some way with this stage of Howe's negotiations? Head's insistence that union would preserve the connection of the North American colonies with the Empire—or at least help prevent their annexation to the United States—was undoubtedly a strong argument in favour of Imperial support for the railway which would be of primary importance in drawing the colonies more closely together. Did Head send his memorandum on union to Grey early in 1851, either on his own initiative or at Grey's request, when the latter was gathering material in favour of the railway to put before his colleagues in the cabinet?

A number of reasons suggest this may have been the case though no certain answer can be given. The only evidence of time of composition now known to exist is found on a copy of the memorandum itself in Head's handwriting among the Head Papers in the Public Archives of Canada. There is no covering letter but the memorandum bears Head's endorsation: "This is the Draft of a Mem^m on the Gov^t of the N.A.C. sent privately to Lord Grey, 1851, E. H." The "1" in the date is superimposed on the beginning of what was apparently to be a "0." This may be the error commonly made in the first days of a new year and if so it would tend to confirm the sending of the memorandum at this crucial stage of the railway negotiations. Another possibility, however, is that Head endorsed the memorandum at a later date, at the time of his departure from the province. Unlike some statesmen of the following century, Head appears not to have carried away with him when he left office semi-private papers of this sort but to have looked through them and his regular despatches adding comments for the benefit of his successor. If such is the explanation of this note made on the back of the first page of the memorandum, the hesitancy regarding the "1" might mean momentary doubt as to the correct year—but again this would indicate that the memorandum was sent very early in 1851, or possibly late in 1850.

On the whole, what seems most likely is that Head began to put down his ideas on union some time in the latter part of 1850, probably after his talks with Elgin in Toronto and after the

political crisis that occurred on his return to New Brunswick.
The paper on which he wrote is watermarked "1849" and his
emphasis is on union as the answer to problems arising out of
the introduction of Responsible Government and the growth
of annexationist sentiment, subjects of much greater concern to
him in 1850 than in 1851. The only reference to the railway is:
"Physical obstacles [to union] no doubt exist which perhaps
would only be removed by the construction of such a work as
the Halifax and Quebec railway, though I doubt if these difficulties wd be even now insurmountable." Head could hardly
have expressed himself in this way at a time when there was
any immediate prospect of the railway being built. But having
written part at least of the memorandum, he may have hurriedly
completed it and sent it to Grey early in 1851, knowing that if
it arrived in time its arguments as to the need for union might
help turn the scale in favour of an Imperial guarantee to the
railway which would be such a large factor in making union
possible. The final paragraph is perhaps suggestive of this: "The
views set forth in this memorandum are professedly crude &
undigested. They may appear to more experienced statesmen to
be utterly impracticable & visionary. I have put them on paper
with the utmost mistrust of my own competency to discuss such
a question & with no pretention to do more than suggest them
for the consideration of others."

The type of federation that Head visualized at this time was
in its general outlines not unlike the one that eventually came
into existence a quarter of a century later, although there were
many differences in detail. The new country, to be known as
"British North America," would have five provinces, Upper and
Lower Canada, Prince Edward Island, New Brunswick, and
Nova Scotia, with a capital centrally situated at Quebec City. It
would be important that a feeling of united interest be studiously
fostered by such means as the adoption of a common currency
bearing the Queen's head, and a common flag—"the Union Jack
with a difference of some kind." There would be a governor
general and five lieutenant governors. The federal legislature
would be bi-cameral, the upper house being modelled by and
large on the American Senate. Local legislatures might need
only one house.

The problems of a written constitution and of the separation
of powers among the Imperial, federal, and provincial govern-

ments were, Head realized, fundamental ones, and a very large part of his memorandum dealt with them. But he believed, rather over-optimistically, that differences of theory such as had arisen in the United States in this regard, and arguments as to whether the federation were a complete union or simply a league or compact, might be avoided.

> The Sovereignty of the Queen of England is acknowledged: a written Constitution uniting for certain purposes these Colonies would be in the nature of a Charter and might be established by act of the Imperial Parliament. Any court duly authorized could decide what questions belonged to the competency of the Imperial Gov^t, the 'Federal' Gov^t or the Gov^t of the several States or Colonies. In this respect therefore we have in our hand an 'a priori' mode of solving theoretical difficulties which yet exist in the Constitution of the United States of America.

The problem of what court could act as "the living interpreter" of the constitution was in Head's opinion "the chief difficulty," and he spent much time considering it. The suggestion that the Judicial Committee of the Privy Council would be suitable he rejected on the ground that it sat in England. He prefered a "High Court" of three or five persons located at the Canadian capital but paid and appointed by the Imperial government. They would hold office as judges during good behaviour and in association with the chief justices of the several colonies might also serve as a court of appeal.

Although the constitution would take the form of an Imperial act, Head made it clear that the preliminary assent of the colonies would be needed. He concluded by suggesting how this might be obtained, and by outlining what he thought were the basic propositions to which the colonies should be asked to agree.

> Probably the most feasible scheme would be to submit to the Local Legislatures as now constituted some four or five propositions enunciating the principal features of such a scheme—asking them to consider these principles & if they assented to their general tenor to appoint two delegates from each branch of their Legislatures who should confer with one another & with a Royal Commission empowered to frame with their assistance the draft of an act of Parl^t. to be considered by the Imperial Legislature.
> The principles wh. it would be essential to lay down wd. be—
>
> 1. That the army & navy & diplomacy shd. be in H.M. hands and shd. be paid by England.
> 2. That the general principles of Commercial Legislation as affecting foreign powers shd. be subject to Imperial control.

3. That certain matters of common interest to all the Colonies shd. be regulated by a 'Federal' Govt.
4. That all powers not reserved as above shd. remain in the Local Legislatures of each separate Colony, the form of which shd. be definitely settled by the Constitution and subject to amendment only on an address from the Colony & the Federal Legislature.
5. That a Court shd. be created competent to decide on the constitutional or unconstitutional character of all acts whether federal or local.
6. That the Federal Constitution when so framed & sanctioned by the British Parl^t shd. not be altered or amended (say) for 10 years & then only on address from a majority of the Colonies & by a delegation & commission as before.

Whatever the exact date and circumstances of Head's memorandum on union, Howe's negotiations in England proceeded to a successful conclusion during February and March of 1851. He had seen no reason, from the point of view of Nova Scotia, to object to the shift from the European and North American Railway to the Halifax and Quebec because the routes of both through Nova Scotia would be exactly the same. He had been most conscious however of the fact that the change would seriously affect New Brunswick interests. Abandonment of the European and North American would be strongly opposed there as that line would pass through Saint John and some of the most thickly settled parts of the province while the other probably would not. It was with real satisfaction therefore that Howe received on March 10, 1851, an official letter from the Colonial Office which he believed, or professed to believe, held forth a promise to guarantee loans covering the cost of not one but both of these railways. Benjamin Hawes, Grey's parliamentary undersecretary, wrote in this much disputed letter:

I am directed to inform you that Her Majesty's Government are prepared to recommend to Parliament that this guarantee should be granted . . . on the conditions which I will now proceed to state.

In the first place . . . it must be distinctly understood that the work is not to be commenced, nor is any part of the loan . . . to be raised, until arrangements are made with the Provinces of Canada and New Brunswick, by which the construction of the line of railway passing wholly through British territory from Halifax to Quebec or Montreal, shall be provided for to the satisfaction of Her Majesty's Government. . . . [The] line is to pass entirely through British territory, but Her Majesty's Government do not require that the line shall necessarily be that recommended by Major Robinson and Captain Henderson. . . . It is also to be understood that Her

Majesty's Government will, by no means, object to its forming part of the plan which may be determined upon that it should include a provision for establishing a communication between the projected railway and the railways of the United States. Any deviation from the line recommended by Major Robinson and Captain Henderson must, however, be subject to the approval of Her Majesty's Government.[8]

The ambiguity of these last sentences enabled Howe to take the view that the European and North American Railway, branching off to Portland, could be considered "part of the plan" and that his mission therefore had been successfully accomplished.

In New Brunswick, this interpretation was not at first placed on the Colonial Office letter. Head nevertheless welcomed the re-opening of the Halifax and Quebec project. "A very important despatch arrived by the last mail," he commented to Lewis, "which opens entirely new views as to these colonies. The difficulty & importance of the problems to be solved cannot be well understood without being on this side of the Atlantic. I believe however that Lord Elgin & Lord Grey both understand them."[9]

New Brunswick opinion generally was less pleased with the results of Howe's efforts. "Succeeded in his mission, has he?" the Saint John *Courier* asked bitterly. "Why his mission was to get money for the European and North American Railway!"[10] The New Brunswick legislature, also under the impression that the European and North American had been abandoned, refused to accept the Halifax and Quebec as a substitute. On April 5, 1851, it approved resolutions rejecting outright "the plan suggested in the correspondence between the Honourable Mr. Howe and the Right Honourable Earl Grey." Regretfully reporting this to Grey, Head wrote:

. . . my own opinion (irrespective of my Executive Council) decidedly is that the Legislature of New Brunswick would have acted wisely in accepting the general terms offered by Her Majesty's Government. I trust sincerely that the course of events may be such as not to expose us hereafter to the reproach of having impeded our own progress, and retarded the general prosperity of the whole of British North America.[11]

[8]P.R.O., C.O. 217/205, Hawes to Howe (draft), March 10, 1851.
[9]Lewis Papers, Head to Lewis, March 31, 1851. Grey's despatch on the Halifax and Quebec Railway was tabled in the New Brunswick assembly on April 1, 1851.
[10]Saint John *Courier*, March 29, 1851.
[11]P.R.O., C.O. 188/114, Head to Grey, April 6, 1851.

An opportunity remained for avoiding such reproach in the fact that Grey in his despatch announcing the new plan had suggested an intercolonial conference at Toronto to consider it. When this was in due course called by Elgin, Head persuaded his council to send Chandler as the New Brunswick delegate. He himself drafted Chandler's instructions in the council chamber, wording them very carefully in such a way as to leave scope for New Brunswick participation in the discussions without directly contravening the expressed wishes of the legislature.[12] The real change in the situation, however, was brought about by Joseph Howe who was to be Nova Scotia's representative and who joined Chandler at Dorchester *en route* to Canada. Howe explained to Chandler that New Brunswick opposition to his scheme was based on an error, that far from the European and North American having been abandoned, the Colonial Office letter of March 10 had included it in the British guarantee as "part of the plan" for building the Halifax and Quebec. In public addresses at every opportunity as he passed through New Brunswick and Maine, and when he made a side trip to Fredericton to visit Head, Howe repeated this explanation and was received with sudden acclaim.[13] Some may have simply stifled their remaining doubts, as did Head who later confessed: "I never could clearly make out where the pledge to advance money for the Portland line was to be found. Still it was no business of mine to know what might have passed with Mr. Howe."[14]

At Toronto further efforts were made to ensure a reversal of the New Brunswick decision of the past session. It was conceded by Nova Scotia and Canada that instead of New Brunswick being asked to build the whole portion of the main line passing through her territory—by far the longest section—the line should be built on the joint account of the three provinces each sharing equally. New Brunswick would thus be given a reasonable chance to do her part and at the same time have sufficient resources left over to build for herself, with the aid of the British guarantee, the branch to the American border.

[12]P.A.C., N.B. Executive Council Minutes, May 19, 1851. Two minutes, one appointing Chandler, the other giving him his instructions, are here, both drafted in Head's handwriting.
[13]P.A.C., Head Papers, Head to Elgin, May 26, 1851; Howe Papers, Howe to Grey, May 28, 1851. P.R.O., C.O. 217/206, Howe to Keating, July 20, 1851.
[14]P.A.C., Head Papers, Head to Chandler, December 16, 1851.

The prospects that this seemed to open up for the development of the province were enormous, and Chandler's report was received with enthusiasm by the New Brunswick executive council early in July.[15] Almost over night the whole atmosphere of provincial affairs became altered. Squabbles over the appointment of Carter and Wilmot and over the salaries of the judges which had seemed so important in the spring were almost forgotten, and talk of annexation ceased. Railways became the focus of all attention. With the help of Chandler, now at the height of his influence, Head seized this golden opportunity to carry out his long-contemplated scheme for breaking the back of the Opposition by offering the surveyor-generalship to R. D. Wilmot and bringing him and J. H. Gray into the council. The path of these new members in their parting from their former friends could be wonderfully smoothed by the argument, as Chandler put it: "that the great Railway question supersedes all minor questions."[16]

As part of the strategy for securing New Brunswick's co-operation with regard to the railway proposals, at a time when this had still seemed likely to be difficult, it had been agreed in Toronto that the Canadian legislature which was still in session should be asked to give its approval at once. In Nova Scotia, the legislature would first be dissolved and after an election on the issue, which Howe felt confident of winning, a special railway session would be called in the autumn. The pressure on New Brunswick to fall in line with the others would then become enormous.

The first threat to the success of this scheme occurred when the Nova Scotia electorate, its enthusiasm considerably dulled by the prospect of becoming responsible for building somewhat more than its own share of the line, returned Howe with a much smaller majority than he had hoped for. As the time for legislative action approached, fear of failure grew in the Government of Nova Scotia. It was shared by that of New Brunswick which had had the much greater initial handicap to overcome and could not be sure until the test was actually made how great the swing in opinion had been. Howe, Chandler, and Head corresponded with one another frequently, concerting their last-

[15]P.A.C., N.B. Executive Council Minutes, July 2, 1851.
[16]P.A.C., Howe Papers, Chandler to Howe, August 3, 1851.

minute efforts.[17] A suggestion by Howe that New Brunswick go first instead of waiting for the lead of Nova Scotia, was rejected by the New Brunswick council. Explaining this privately to Howe, Head wrote:

I confess I think they are right—after the adverse action of last session I should be sorry to bring the Railroad before the Legislature again, unless on a definite & final issue. Now the opinion of the Legislature of Nova Scotia is the most material element in giving this shape to the question.

I am sure that if that point were left open the opposition & the timid people here combined would be able to thwart any proposition made by the Government. . . . The enormous variety & conflicting character of local interests is so great in N.B. that there are always stragglers ready to attach themselves to any one in this matter.

It is most important to keep it clearly understood *that no definite line is decided on* through N.B. or will be so without full inquiry & consideration of the merits of the respective routes. By this many who would oppose their neighbours' line will support the general measure in the hope that the chance of events may give their own neighbourhood the benefit of it.[18]

Even when the Nova Scotia legislature met in November and after "temperate and dignified" discussion passed the railway bills by large majorities,[19] Head remained doubtful of similar action by New Brunswick. He notified Howe early in December:

My Council are just about to meet and I hope we may be able to get our Legislature together in the first week of January. . . . I will own to you that I am not very sanguine. The people at St. John are jealous of Halifax. . . . There is no enlarged view of the interests of New Brunswick as a part of British North America & there is no proper appreciation of the enormous gain to their Province involved in opening the whole mass of ungranted land and of timber now rotting on the ground.

My power of action is, as you know, limited by my position. I can only work through others but I assure you I feel the importance of the object & the difficulty of the game we are playing as much as anybody can do.[20]

At just this point the "game" took on an entirely new character. While Head was writing this letter to Howe, the latter was already reading "with regret and deep mortification" a despatch

[17]P.A.C., Howe Papers, Howe to Head, private, September 15; Head to Howe, private, September 20; Chandler to Howe, October 16; Chandler to Howe, November 29; Howe to Head, private, December 4; Head to Howe, private and confidential, December 9, 1851.

[18]P.A.C., Howe Papers, Head to Howe, private, September 20, 1851.

[19]P.R.O., C.O. 217/206, Harvey to Grey, November 13, 1851.

[20]P.A.C., Howe Papers, Head to Howe, private and confidential, December 9, 1851.

from Grey informing him that there had never been any intention on the part of Her Majesty's Government to include the European and North American Railway in the terms of the guarantee to the Halifax and Quebec. Finally, late in November, months after documents had begun to arrive containing Howe's interpretation of the agreement, the Colonial Office had awakened to what this was and had repudiated it.[21]

Head was of course much concerned to find this new "stumbling block" in the way of the railway linking the colonies and so important to their future, but he was not prepared to abandon it yet. "I fear legislation here will not be easy," he wrote at once in answer to a letter from Howe,[22] "but the matter requires consideration." To Chandler, he immediately forwarded Howe's letter and hastened to add:

My own opinion is unchanged. I believe that the way to get both lines is to get the money for the Q. and H. line from England. In fact I think it not at all improbable that if the H. and Q. line were guaranteed by the English Gov^t the money for the other might be got from capitalists on *terms nearly as favourable.* However this may be it is most important that no violent or sudden rejection be made on the part of N.B. Keep the door open for getting the money as long as you can at any rate. I fear that Howe & Sir J. Harvey will be annoyed.[23]

It was on this note too that Head opened the legislative session on January 8, 1852, with a Speech from the Throne parts of which read more like a speech from the hustings:

I feel convinced your interests are part and parcel of the interests of British North America. . . . In my opinion a Railroad uniting Canada, New Brunswick, and Nova Scotia, especially in connection with the United States, would produce an abundant return to this Province. I believe that your Revenue would increase very largely without imposing additional burthens on anyone—that millions of acres now untrodden would supply food for man, and that millions of tons of timber now standing worthless in your forests would find a profitable market.

To bolster Head in these strenuous efforts to avoid another rejection of the scheme by New Brunswick, three members of

[21]Harvey's speech opening the special session of the Nova Scotia legislature was what first attracted Colonial Office attention to Howe's "mistake"; P.R.O., C.O. 217/206, Harvey to Grey, November 13, 1851. Grey to Harvey, November 29, clarified the British view. Howe's reaction is to be found in Howe to Harvey, December 11, 1851, enclosed in Harvey to Grey, December 11, 1851.

[22]P.A.C., Howe Papers, Head to Howe, private, December 16, 1851.

[23]P.A.C., Head Papers, Head to Chandler, December 16, 1851.

the Canadian executive council, led by Hincks, went through
the "martyrdom" of a mid-January journey by sleigh from
Quebec to Fredericton.[24] They were sent by Elgin to "concert
measures under the eye of Sir E. Head who will no doubt exercise
a salutary influence over their discussions."[25] After having agreed
on what was in Head's opinion "the last possible scheme," they
proceeded on to Halifax taking Chandler with them. There,
following much bargaining with a disgruntled Nova Scotia
government, the ingenuity of the Canadians was successful in
working out one further compromise acceptable to all. By its
terms, the three governments proposed to support the St. John
River route from Halifax to Quebec rather than that along the
North Shore favoured by Major Robinson. In return for this concession which would satisfy Saint John and leave New Brunswick
with a much shorter line to the Maine border to build alone, New
Brunswick would assume responsibility for five-twelfths of the
joint project, leaving only one-quarter to be borne by Nova
Scotia and one-third by Canada.[26]

The concurrence of all three legislatures in this arrangement
was obtained with less difficulty than had been anticipated and
early in March Hincks sailed for England to begin final negotiations with the Colonial Office. Chandler followed as speedily
as possible but Howe who was supposed to accompany him kept
postponing his departure for one reason or another and eventually
decided not to go at all. Meanwhile, on February 20, the Russell
Government had been defeated and Grey's tenure of the Colonial
Office had come to a close. Sir John Pakington, his successor, was
not opposed to the guarantee but lacking Grey's keen interest
in it failed to urge it upon his colleagues in the way Grey would
certainly have done. The result was that the scheme gradually
lost momentum and before Head's arrival in England on leave
of absence toward the end of May, the cabinet had decided
against applying to parliament for aid to a railway passing so
near the American border and lacking the military advantages
expected if Major Robinson's route had been accepted.[27] The

[24]P.A.C., Head Papers, Head to Harvey, January 23, 1852.
[25]A. G. Doughty (ed.), *The Elgin-Grey Papers*, III, 988, Elgin to Grey,
January 16, 1852.
[26]P.R.O., C.O. 217/208, Harvey to Grey, February 5, 1852; *N.B. Assembly
Journals*, 1852, documents tabled on February 13, 1852.
[27]P.R.O., C.O. 188/118, Board of Trade to Colonial Office, May 17, 1852, and
minutes. Pakington's decision was announced in Pakington to Head, May 27,
1852.

original object of his mission being unobtainable, Chandler seized the opportunity while in England to contact English capitalists for help in financing the European and North American Railway. Hincks and later Howe began similar negotiations. In 1853, on the initiative of the English backers of railway schemes in all of the provinces, discussions on an intercolonial were briefly revived but had come to nothing before the Crimean War put a stop to them.

In the meantime, during the year or so in which railways had claimed the economic spotlight, progress had been made in that other great matter of intercolonial interest, reciprocity. Agitation in favour of reciprocity had reached its height in New Brunswick in 1850, especially in connection with the election campaign fought in the summer of that year. In fact, it had become so loud and insistent that it tended to hinder rather than help the negotiations being conducted in Washington by the British minister on behalf of the North American provinces. A warning from Grey that "undue eagerness" on the part of New Brunswick was merely encouraging the United States to put forward "unreasonable demands,"[28] crossed *en route* a private letter to him from Head showing that the latter was already aware of the danger and was trying to cope with it: "I have no more difficult task than to check against the impatience of members of my Council who do not see that loud talking is injurious to negotiations in Washington. The substratum however of the agitation here is the supposed discontent in Canada—by herself New Brunswick cd. not hope to produce much effect."[29]

The main problem from the time that the negotiations had begun late in 1849 had been to find some means of arousing the interest of American opinion. Retaliatory action of one sort or another had been suggested from time to time. In Canada, a favourite proposal was to close the St. Lawrence seaway to American shipping. New Brunswick, in a similar vein, wished to see the establishment of an exclusive British North American coasting trade. Both provinces toyed with the idea of imposing differential duties on imports from the United States. This latter suggestion met of course with the special opposition of Grey, although even he was prepared to admit that colonial demands would have to

[28]P.R.O., C.O. 188/112, Head to Grey, May 20, 1850, minute by Grey.
[29]P.R.O., C.O. 188/113, Head to Grey, private, June 14, 1850.

be satisfied eventually in some way. Head too had exerted what influence he could against retaliation. "I do not think the English Govt. would readily [consent?] to establish differential duties here in their naked form," he wrote to Hincks on one occasion when the latter was in Washington on a reciprocity mission. "Moreover, I have some doubts as to the result of holding out any threats of this kind too openly. 'Jonathan' is very touchy on the subject of threats and the conviction on his part that the step may be taken is a powerful motive."[30]

Instead of any such openly retaliatory action, Head's thoughts had turned more and more to the matter of the fisheries. It was the prospect of provinces other than Canada, "more particularly those which enjoy any exclusive rights with regard to the cod fisheries," being included in the reciprocity negotiations which had attracted the notice of the American secretary of state back in 1849. Why not give him something more along this line to think about? With this in mind Head wrote to the colonial secretary as early as June, 1850:

It appears to me at the present moment important that the privileges granted to the American Fishermen in these waters should be defined somewhat accurately & that the instructions given to the officers commanding any of H.M. vessels here should be carried out in such a manner as to show the value of the rights of Fishing which England is possessed of on the coasts of British N. America. At the same time I feel that the subject is so important & so delicate as affecting the relative position of the two governments that I am unwilling to do more at present than call your Lordship's attention to it & recommend the officers employed off the shores of N. Brunswick to attend to those portions of the coast which are most likely to be encroached on.[31]

It was exactly the kind of action that Head suggested in this despatch that was to bring rapid results two years later. Britain was slow to recognize, however, that the fisheries constituted her one trump in an otherwise weak hand. Head's despatch was simply passed in a routine way by the Colonial Office to the Foreign Office and thence to the Advocate General's Office and soon these departments were deeply involved with one another in a discussion as to whether the line bounding the three-mile limit

30P.A.C., Head Papers, Head to Hincks, January 30, 1851.
31P.R.O., C.O. 188/113, Head to Grey, June 4, 1850. This letter enclosed a memorandum and map by Moses H. Perley of Saint John, an expert on New Brunswick's economy and the person who seems to have been initially responsible for arousing the interest of Head and others in this question.

within which British fishermen were acknowledged by the treaty of 1818 to have exclusive rights should be presumed to run from headland to headland across all bays or only across the smaller ones. The main question that Head had raised—whether within that limit, whatever it was, British fishermen should be given real protection against American encroachments—was discreetly shelved.[32]

By 1851, the fisheries were becoming important to New Brunswick for a new reason. The lifting of the depression in world trade and the progress of the economic transition that the province was undergoing were resulting in a revival of prosperity. Fishing, previously neglected, was on the eve of a particularly rapid advance. Fish exports were already beginning the steady rise that was to more than double their value between 1850 and 1854. The new significance of the fisheries in themselves, and also the part that they might play in bargaining for reciprocity with the United States, were both factors in leading the New Brunswick legislature to pass addresses to Her Majesty in the spring of 1851 praying that the shore fisheries be more adequately protected against the trespasses of American fishermen. The protection hitherto offered, the legislature explained, had been largely nominal. Two men-of-war from the Royal Navy's West Indies Squadron arrived after the early herring fishery had begun and left before the late line fishing ended. Their officers were unfamiliar with the waters and alarmed by the fogs. The ships were too large and unwieldy to move freely among the small harbours of the coast. What was wanted instead was a larger number of smaller vessels capable of enforcing the provisions of the treaty of 1818, and also of assisting in connection with local fishery and revenue regulations.[33]

The plan put forward in the addresses was an elaboration of the same subject to which Head had drawn the attention of the Colonial Office some months before, and he now wrote a separate and confidential despatch to Grey recommending strongly that it be given at least a year's trial.[34] He was convinced, he added, that the alternative to some such protection of colonial fishermen against illegal American competition would be a vigorous re-

[32]P.R.O., C.O. 188/113, Head to Grey, June 4, 1850, minutes; Foreign Office to Colonial Office, September 4, 1850.

[33]P.R.O., C.O. 188/114, Head to Grey, April 27, 1851, and enclosure.

[34]P.R.O., C.O. 188/114, Head to Grey, separate and confidential, April 27, 1851.

newal of demands that had been heard for some time for a provincial bounty on fish. The long and heated argument that had taken place between Grey and the New Brunswick legislature a few years before with respect to the hemp bounty might then, he feared, be repeated with increased bitterness over the much more important question of the fisheries. As additional re-insurance against such an eventuality, Head took occasion to set forth in this despatch his own opinion on the subject of bounties in general, an opinion rather different from that of Grey:

It has always appeared to me that the question of bounties within the Colony rested on a footing somewhat different from that of differential duties. I myself entertain the strongest opinions as to the impolicy, whether in the old country, or in the new one, of bounties of any kind, but the difficulty is that the Assembly and the people of this Province cannot be convinced that bounties paid from their own Revenue are a proper matter for interference on the part of the Home Govt. . . . But the question is not the expedience of the thing itself so much as the expediency of positively prohibiting their enactment by the Local Legislature and thus adding another to the many subjects of jealously which exist between the authorities in the Colony and H.M. Govt. in England.

While the British decision on this whole matter was still pending, an opportunity occurred for a further step to be taken by the colonies. At the Toronto conference in June, 1851, called to deal with Howe's Halifax and Quebec Railway scheme, Nova Scotia and New Brunswick raised the question of protecting the fisheries and a new plan was agreed upon by all three provinces. This differed from the one put forward by the New Brunswick legislature in that the delegates, recognizing that local as well as Imperial interests were involved, decided to recommend to their governments the employment of a number of small vessels at provincial expense to supplement whatever sort of protection continued to be offered by the Royal Navy.[35] Vice Admiral Seymour of the West Indies Squadron endorsed this plan and also the New Brunswick suggestions for the adoption of improved methods by the Royal Navy.[36] Grey was prepared to acquiesce and was about to submit the whole question for the decision of the cabinet when the latter was defeated in the House of Commons and on February 20, 1852, resigned.[37]

[35]P.A.C., N.B. Executive Council Minutes, July 2, 1851.
[36]P.R.O., C.O. 188/115, Admiralty to Colonial Office, August 26, 1851, enclosure; Vice Admiral Seymour to Secretary of Admiralty, August 5, 1851.
[37]Cf. P.R.O., C.O. 217/208, Harvey to Grey, February 19, 1852.

It was perhaps as well that Grey left office before a final decision on the protection of the fisheries was actually made. The subject was one that he approached with the greatest reluctance because while he recognized the need to conciliate colonial opinion he believed that the enforcement even of undoubted British rights in coastal waters "would not be calculated to protect the well-understood interests either of the Mother-country or of the Colonists." Wholesome competition in the fisheries as elsewhere was, in his opinion, better than "the old and narrow view of monopoly and commercial jealousy."[38] His successor, Sir John Pakington, was less doctrinaire. The new Government despatched a small flotilla of naval vessels in the spring with instructions to deal firmly with illegal American fishermen, and it agreed to leave the colonial governments free to take what steps they wished to encourage their own fisheries.[39] A new phase of the reciprocity negotiations was about to begin.

At this time, in the summer of 1852, when the political and economic affairs of the province were in a more flourishing state than in any period since his arrival, Head paid his first visit home to England. He had been away for four years but had been too preoccupied with political and railway matters to think of leave of absence. Otherwise he might have taken it the previous year in order to see the Great Exhibition. "I am very much afraid you people who live at Knightsbridge will not let the Crystal Palace stand till I see it," he had written to Lewis in the fall of 1851.[40] "However, it cannot be helped." A short time later Henry Taylor added his voice to that of Lewis who had for some time been urging Head's return home. "When will you come and see us all again—all the bald and grey-headed generation of us?" Taylor asked. "Does leave of absence never enter your imagination? Does Lady Head never mention it to you? If not, don't give my love to her."[41]

The visit when it finally came lasted from May until August. It was marred somewhat for Head by the sudden calling of a general election which kept Lewis very busy in what was to be

[38]Earl Grey, *The Colonial Policy of Lord John Russell's Administration*, I, 286–87.

[39]P.R.O., C.O. 217/208, Harvey to Grey, January 22, 1852, minutes; Bazalgette to Pakington, June 9, 1852.

[40]Lewis Papers, Head to Lewis, November 4, 1851.

[41]E. Dowden (ed.), *Correspondence of Henry Taylor*, Taylor to Head, November 16, 1851.

an unsuccessful attempt to secure re-election, and also by the thought of having to leave his only son, John, behind to enter Harrow, when the rest of the family returned to New Brunswick. John was then twelve years old and his education had been a matter of concern to Head for some time. "He is sharp but careless about Latin & Greek," Head had written to Lewis shortly before the boy's twelfth birthday. "I have taken him through the first book of the [illegible] & a good deal of Latin & I now find that my temper is not good enough for teaching him. The stimulus too of emulation becomes necessary. No one, except myself, has taught him."[42]

One effect of the renewal of contacts with old friends in England was that Head became for a while at least more conscious of his comparative isolation in New Brunswick where, although he was on easy terms of familiarity with Chandler and a number of others, he remained to some extent set apart by his position and by his different intellectual background and interests. Even anticipation of having to leave England again was painful and Head confessed to Lewis: "I have no hope of getting anything which would enable me to remain in England though I should prefer it on many accounts. One must follow out the line which is open & take one's chances."[43]

When the Heads returned to New Brunswick early in September they were accompanied by Sir Charles and Lady Lyell. The journey itself was "tolerably prosperous" being completed in thirteen days from Liverpool to Fredericton, including a day in Halifax—very good time, especially in view of a storm part of the way severe enough to incapacitate almost everyone except the "young American," Amabel, born in New Brunswick in 1850, who, according to her father, "Never suffered one hour on board ship but ran about plagueing everybody pretty much as she does on shore." At home again, Head wrote to Lewis: "It seems like a dream to have seen you all so lately."[44]

When in England, Head must have discussed at length with Lewis and others the work of the Oxford University Commission

[42]Lewis Papers, Head to Lewis, February 9, 1852. It is not surprising that John at first found school life unpleasant. Writing to Lewis January 24, 1853, Head commented: "My Boy Johnny has got rid of his cough & is, I hope, returning to Harrow but he does not yet take kindly to it. I hope this will change."
[43]Lewis Papers, Head to Lewis, February 9, 1852.
[44]Lewis Papers, Head to Lewis, September 5, 1852.

to which he had agreed to contribute a brief and whose *Report* was about to appear. One of his first actions on returning to New Brunswick was to take steps to bring about the appointment of a similar commission to investigate King's College, Fredericton.

From the beginning Head had taken a keen interest in trying to improve the educational facilities of the province, as was to be expected of a person of his intellectual attainments and experience of university teaching. He has been justly linked with an outstanding predecessor, Sir Howard Douglas, as one of two men deserving special mention for the parts they played in the history of New Brunswick's educational development.[45] An example of the detailed nature of his interest is found in a letter to the Rev. G. L. Street, January 11, 1850: "I attach great importance to the appointment of teachers to the Grammar Schools and I always fear the examinations may not be stringent enough. Mr. Cay must improve himself in Greek which is properly speaking essential."[46] This particular aspect of Head's concern with education is also made clear in a note from Chandler to Joseph Howe toward the end of 1851:

Sir Edmund Head when here the other day, suggested (what I believe has for some time been a favorite scheme of his) that Nova Scotia and New Brunswick should join in the establishment of a training school to be located at some convenient point at the head of the bay at Westmorland or Amherst and requested me to write to you on the subject. Pray turn the subject over in your mind, or call the attention of your able Superintendent of Education to the suggestion.[47]

As official visitor of King's College, Head had a special function in matters of higher education in the province, and he did not consider it to be merely nominal. Rather, he looked upon his relationship with the college council as being much the same as that with his "responsible" executive council. The college council's decision should normally be final, but if in any instance it should seem to him to contravene the charter or regulations of the college, his duty would be to withhold his sanction.[48] The lack of support shown by the college in connection with Robb's lectures on agriculture had aroused doubts in Head's mind as early as 1849 concerning its appreciation of the real

[45]J. H. Rose, A. P. Newton, and E. A. Benians (general eds.), *Cambridge History of the British Empire*, VI, 791.
[46]P.A.C., Head Papers, Head to the Rev. G. L. Street, January 11, 1850.
[47]P.A.C., Howe Papers, Chandler to Howe, October 23, 1851.
[48]P.A.C., Head Papers, Head to Dr. Jacob, April 11, 1849.

educational requirements of the province. By the fall of 1852, his private opinion must have been that expressed by Lyell in a letter written while he was staying with Head at Government House. The college, according to Lyell, was

. . . rendered useless and almost without scholars, owing to an old-fashioned Oxonian of Corpus Christi, Oxford, having been made head, and determining that lectures in Aristotle are all that the youth in a new colony ought to study, or other subjects on the strict plan which may get honours at Oxford. I trust that Sir Edmund Head may succeed in his exertions to get something taught which the pupils can afford to spend their time in learning. At present they must go to the United States.[49]

An official letter to the college council which Head, in his capacity as visitor, was probably engaged in writing during Lyell's visit, and which he ordered printed and widely distributed a few weeks later, was less outspoken, but it dealt vigorously and in detail with the same problem of "how far the institution meets the wants of the country in a manner commensurate with its legal position and legal endowments." He suggested that a committee be set up to pursue the matter further and offered to co-operate with it in every possible way.[50] Sending a copy of the letter to Lewis, he explained his motive for writing it:

. . . The Institution was entirely a mistake in a new country of this kind as you may suppose by what I have stated. My real end & object is what I say—to save the endowments if I can, for if popular agitation against their misapplication of public money begins in earnest it will be impossible to obtain any funds for superior education, whereas by popularizing the instruction in some degree & convincing the assembly that we wish to make it practically useful, I think it may be preserved & profitably applied.[51]

Head's letter to the college council provoked the discussion he had hoped for and resulted the next year in the appointment of a commission modelled on that for Oxford. Head ensured that its membership was of high calibre choosing, among others, to act upon it, J. W. Dawson, then superintendent of education in Nova Scotia and Egerton Ryerson of Canada. He himself attended its meetings and occasionally took part in its discussions. "He impressed me very much," Dawson remarked afterwards, "with

[49]Mrs. Henry Lyell, *Sir Charles Lyell,* II, 179, Lyell to Leonard Horner, September 12, 1852.
[50]P.R.O., C.O. 188/119, Head to Newcastle, April 9, 1853, contains a copy of this printed letter which is dated September 28, 1852.
[51]Lewis Papers, Head to Lewis, October 18, 1852. There were only 24 students in 1851.

his earnestness and zeal in educational matters, his extensive information and his advanced views on the subject. He was also well versed in natural science, especially in geology and mineralogy."[52]

What Head wanted for King's College was a departure from its policy of placing almost its entire emphasis on classical and literary subjects. His own special training and ability in these fields—he spent much time while in New Brunswick re-reading the Greek classics—prevented him, of course, from minimizing in any way their value. But he was strongly of the opinion that, particularly in a new country like New Brunswick, there should be a greater opportunity for study along practical lines, for example in the natural sciences, medicine, and law. He opposed, on the other hand, any religious test or instruction since this was a state-supported college, although he hastened to add that no inference should be drawn from this as to his views "with reference to the necessity of theological instruction as part of a thorough and complete education." Another matter to which Head drew attention was the small size of the constituency from which the college drew its students, and he put forward a suggestion that was to be repeated many times afterwards, that one institution of higher learning should be established to serve the whole of the Maritime Provinces. This might be organized along the lines of the University of London, examinations and degrees being received from a central body while instruction continued to be given in local institutions making use of existing buildings and endowments. Head's ideas, and his initiative in the matter of the commission of inquiry, were of real importance in the development of a more progressive policy with regard to higher education in New Brunswick.

The last years of Head's administration in New Brunswick, following his return from England in the fall of 1852, were years of comparative political tranquillity and economic prosperity. His own authority was now firmly established, and his prestige was at its highest point. "My political affairs are prosperous . . . ," he wrote to Lewis toward the end of 1852, "& my influence in the Govt. never was greater. It is quite as much now as is expedient in this kind of Colony." Again, a month or so later, he wrote:

[52]R. Dawson (ed.), *Fifty Years of Work in Canada*, pp. 86–87.

My position here at present is far easier than it has hitherto been. . . . The mixed system resistance on principle & concession when no principle was involved has borne its fruits & I have at this moment more real power, without the show of it, than I ever had. Nothing has done me so much good as the knowledge of law which I picked up before I came out. By means of this I can meet my council on equal terms in almost all matters & they are very shy of proposing to me anything of a doubtful character.[53]

In these circumstances, and with a middle-of-the-road sort of ministry, pledged to railway building and other practical measures, political controversy was kept at a minimum. All of this was very satisfactory so far as it went. "One of my great objects," Head wrote to Herman Merivale some time later, "has always been to keep down the abusive virulence and bitterness of feeling which has characterized parties in Nova Scotia and done so much mischief there."[54] From time to time, however, Head took occasion to remind new colonial secretaries and the general public of the province that many of the basic problems of Responsible Government still remained to be solved. In a Speech from the Throne closing the session of 1853, for example, and in a long despatch to the Duke of Newcastle drawing attention to it, he emphasized the continuing dangers arising from the absence of municipal institutions. Only one county had been incorporated under the terms of the permissive act of 1851 with the consequence that numerous local and private bills were still being passed by the legislature. These tended, in Head's opinion, to degrade that body and, indeed, its whole function of law making:

It will be a curious calculation what per-centage of persons out of our small population will in 1864 be affected directly or indirectly by laws of an exceptional character. Such acts do not easily admit of classification or codifying. The Law of the Land will be the exception & not the rule. . . . The generality which is one of the characteristics of law, as such, has disappeared.[55]

Again, in 1854, Head made a fresh survey of the whole financial set-up of the province, examining in great detail the departmental and other changes needed for the efficient administration of its rapidly growing revenues and expenditures. The heart of the problem remained the fact that the executive did not yet

[53]Lewis Papers, Head to Lewis, December 16, 1852; January 24, 1853.
[54]P.R.O., C.O. 188/120, Head to Merivale, private, November 19, 1853.
[55]P.R.O., C.O. 188/119, Head to Newcastle, May 6, 1853.

have the sole right of initiating money votes. Head commented, as he had so frequently done in the past:

A great deal has been said in these Colonies on the question of 'Responsible Government' but the one peculiar subject on which the Executive Government ought to be more especially responsible to the Representatives of the people—the relation of expenditure to income—is practically conducted so as to exclude all responsiblity. The preparation of the estimates and the due care that the aggregate of money votes introduced shall not exceed the probable income, are matters for which no public officer is answerable—I had almost said they are left to chance.[56]

It has sometimes been suggested, as a result of Head's great influence during these final years in New Brunswick, that he was fundamentally reactionary, grasping power for himself and opposed at bottom to colonial self-government. This was what that vigorous Opposition editor, G. E. Fenety, implied when he wrote after Head's departure: "As a strong-minded, self-willed man, His Excellency left the Province without a peer among Governors."[57] In fact, Head was not only strong-minded and self-willed: he was also clear-headed, and knew what was really involved in making Responsible Government function in practice. That this was his consistent objective may be illustrated by a particularly appropriate example taken from his last year in the province.[58]

An act of the session of 1854 provided for an important reorganization of the law courts. Public opinion and that of the Bar was strongly in favour of the change which had been carefully studied and recommended by a special law commission. The judges, however, and especially one or two most affected personally, were entirely hostile and looked to Head and the colonial secretary to intervene on their behalf and disallow the act. Head himself thought the act faulty in some parts but he rejected, rather rudely, the judges' appeal, insisting that the matter was one of completely *"internal concern,"*[59] and therefore within the complete competence of the legislature. The judges' argument that Head had refused in 1850 to accept the advice of the executive council in a similar matter of judicial change

[56]P.R.O., C.O. 188/121, Head to Newcastle, January 14, 1854.
[57]Fenety, *Political Notes*, I, 476.
[58]P.R.O., C.O. 188/121, Head to Newcastle, separate, May 20, 1854. The account that follows is based on this long and important despatch except where otherwise noted.
[59]P.A.C., Head Papers, Head to Judge Parker, private, April 26, 1854.

and that his refusal constituted a precedent which might now be followed, Head would not admit for a moment. The present change took the form of an act passed after careful consideration by both Houses of the legislature; the earlier proposals had merely consisted in the advice of the executive council on an executive matter and the council "had the remedy in their own hands when their advice was rejected: they might have resigned and appealed to public opinion." So far as the rights and interests of the judges were concerned, Head added:

I think the Judges generally will do me the credit of saying that in 1849 and subsequently I have done all I could to ward off from them the perpetual danger which has been threatening them in every successive Session. Almost the only serious difficulty which I have had in the Administration of this Government has arisen from these attacks. Hitherto I have succeeded in avoiding or staving off all injury to the emoluments or rights of the existing Judges; but I have done so at the constant and imminent risk of quarrels with my Executive Council and under the dread of provoking at any moment a most troublesome conflict between the authority of the Queen's Government in England and that of the House of Assembly here.

Had the positive and substantial injustice threatened in every one of these cases been confined to a partial change in the nature of the duties to be discharged by a Judge and the kind of law which he was to administer, I am not sure that I should have felt justified in incurring the risk.

On the more general subject of the way in which this matter of the judiciary impinged on the whole readjustment of constitutional relationships involved in the introduction of Responsible Government, Head wrote—and this was his final word on Responsible Government in New Brunswick:

No questions are more difficult than those involving the relation of the Judges to the Colonial Legislature under the present system of 'Responsible Government.' So long as justice is administered in Her Majesty's name the Advisers of the Crown are in a certain sense responsible for all measures affecting such administration. But the introduction of 'Responsible Government' in the Colonies is in fact a great constitutional revolution, and I apprehend that the share of such responsibility which falls on the Advisers of Her Majesty in England is under this system much less than it formerly was, whilst the share imposed on the Executive Council and the Colonial Ministers is proportionately increased. We cannot take the system by halves. To give to the Local Legislature professed freedom of action, and at the same time to interfere on matters affecting the Colony itself because that Legislature do not use their powers exactly as we should wish, is, it appears to me, to augment a great moral power of resistance for the express purpose of provoking its exercise against ourselves.

The largest single topic of interest in New Brunswick during Head's last years there was reciprocity. The results of the far more aggressive fisheries-protection policy put into effect in the summer of 1852 were soon evident. After a few vessels had been caught flagrantly violating the three-mile limit and had been seized, a great storm of protest arose in the United States. It was led by Daniel Webster, now secretary of state. Having formerly represented Massachussetts in Congress, Webster had a personal interest in the fisheries question and in a speaking campaign in connection with the forthcoming presidential election he loudly claimed that England was depriving American fishermen of their "just Treaty Rights."[60] This gave the British minister an excellent opportunity to point out exactly what these rights were and how they had been systematically exceeded by American fishermen for many years. As a result, he was not long in receiving a letter written by Webster on July 17, 1852, stating: "I have recommended to the President that we take up the whole subject of the Fisheries, and the Canadian Trade at once, as a matter of negotiation."[61]

This was the opening that Britain and the colonies had been waiting for and the Foreign Office requested the Colonial Office and the Board of Trade to draw up as soon as possible a joint statement which might be adopted by the cabinet as a basis for negotiations and transmitted to the minister in Washington. Pakington decided to consult the colonies in this connection, and on October 30, 1852, addressed a confidential despatch to the governors asking them for a full report on the wishes and interests of their several provinces.[62]

Head's method of fulfilling this request is a revealing example of the control he now exercised over his council especially in matters of this sort which were only partially local in their nature. He first wrote to Chandler:

Everything leads me to think that it may be very important to supply the English Govt. with full and complete information on the subject of the relations of these Provinces and [the] U.S. with as little delay as possible. The Election of the President points to the possibility of speedy negotiations

[60]P.R.O., F.O. 97/26, Foreign Office Memorandum: "Protection of British Fisheries in North America," March 8, 1853.

[61]P.R.O., C.O. 42/585, Admiralty to Colonial Office, August 17, 1852. Enclosure: Webster to Crampton, July 17, 1852.

[62]P.R.O., C.O. 42/585, Foreign Office to Colonial Office, October 13, 1852, minutes, and draft despatches.

being commenced and I wish to be prepared. I propose therefore to summon a Council next week for the purpose of obtaining a confidential report on the subject of the demands which might be advisable with reference to the interests of New Brunswick. . . . Would it suit you to be at Fredericton on Tuesday 23rd Nov., or thereabouts?[63]

When the council met, Head laid before them a memorandum asking for a detailed report on the concessions they would be prepared to offer to the United States and what they would expect in return, and for any other observations they might care to make. He concluded:

His Excellency the Lieutenant Governor need not point out to the Council the fact that the conduct of any negotiations must rest entirely with Her Majesty's Government and the result (if any) must be governed by principles affecting the whole Empire. . . . His object is to be prepared for affording information at any moment. He does not pledge himself beforehand to make his own opinion on the details coincide with that of his Executive Council but he is anxious to receive their advice in perfect candour and good faith.[64]

The advice which Head eventually received in a minute dated December 11, 1852, differed in one significant detail from the opinion expressed by the New Brunswick executive council at the time the province had first been included in the reciprocity negotiations in 1849. Now, as then, the council stated their willingness to surrender the exclusive fishing rights of the province in return for various American concessions. But, then, they had declared they "would not hesitate" to make such a surrender. Now there was a definite note of hesitation: the council were "clearly of opinion, that the prosperity of the Province, is not now altogether dependent upon receiving the concessions proposed to be granted in return. They conceive that the exclusive enjoyment of those Fisheries may become, under a proper system, a source of unbounded wealth to the present and future population of New Brunswick." Moreover, they stressed their conviction that "the Fisheries on the Coasts of New Brunswick are the natural rights and property of its people and should not be alienated, conceded, or affected without their consent."[65]

In most details Head concurred in the views of the council, although he did not share their new-found doubts at the desir-

[63]P.A.C., Head Papers, Head to Chandler, November 15, 1852.

[64]P.R.O., C.O. 188/117, Head to Pakington, confidential, December 4, 1852, enclosure.

[65]P.R.O., C.O. 188/117, Head to Pakington, December 16, 1852, enclosure.

ability of New Brunswick's being included with the rest of British North America in a reciprocity treaty at the cost of sacrificing her exclusive fishing rights. He forwarded the executive council minute along with his own detailed comments on it as New Brunswick's answer to the Colonial Office request for an expression of the provincial viewpoint.

In addition, and at the same time, Head wrote another long despatch, marked "separate and confidential," which dealt with the wider and more fundamental issues of British North American policy, issues that were affected by the question of reciprocity and that helped explain the attitude of the colonies to it.[66] This despatch, dated December 14, 1852, covered much the same ground as had his secret memorandum of 1851 on union and his other despatches sent to Grey, and it may well have been written primarily for the purpose of drawing the attention of the new colonial secretary to these topics. In general, his opinions do not seem to have altered significantly since those earlier documents were written. His stress was still on his belief that "it is practicable so to govern British North America as to make its population cling to the essence of British Institutions and the alliance of the British Crown; supposing even that the present legal tie which unites them to England were to be gradually weakened & at last dissolved." The objects of British policy in North America should be to maintain the legal connection as long as possible and particularly to prevent the annexation of the colonies to the United States. With these purposes in mind two principles should be adhered to. In the first place, there should be fostered in the colonies "such a sense of unity, common interest, and self-importance as will deprive them of any wish to become subordinate to the great Republican Confederacy on their borders." Secondly, by means of a reciprocity agreement, "the irritation & inconvenience caused by their holding the position of foreign states in relation to the people of the Union" should be minimized.

Writing with a confidence based on his thorough knowledge of the Maritimes, Head dwelt particularly on his belief in the importance of encouraging a closer association between these provinces and Canada, and he went on to give in some detail his views as to how this might be done:

[66]P.R.O., C.O. 188/117, Head to Pakington, separate and confidential, December 14, 1852.

Since I have been in New Brunswick I have watched with great anxiety
& much thought the aspect of public affairs and the phases of public
opinion in this Colony. I have done this during a time of great depression
& at a moment when disturbances in a neighbouring colony of superior
importance lent additional value to every movement of popular feeling. . . .

The cessation of differential duties in favour of the Colonies & the
abandonment of what is now called the 'Old Colonial System,' however
unavoidable & however beneficial . . . necessarily produced . . . a diminished sense of unity with the Mother Country. . . .

I know little of Canada . . . but it appears to me that the notion of
annexation to the United States has waned there, just in proportion as the
sense of their own progress & their own self-importance has increased. . . .

My desire would be to see the 'Lower Colonies' as they are called so
identified in feeling & interest with Canada, that one sense of self-importance & consequent independence with reference to the United States should
pervade the whole group of these Provinces protected as they are by the
British Crown & governed by British Institutions.

Among the things needed to create such an identity of feeling,
Head mentioned again a common currency and flag, and dealt
at some length with the question of a customs union and the
establishment of an exclusive British North American coasting
trade. All of these would have "the moral result of exhibiting
these colonies to the world in a consolidated form professing
commercial interests of the same kind & bound together by a
common allegiance & a common system. . . . above all their
physical connection by a rail-road would endow them with real
unity & substantial independence from the United States."

That Head made no overt mention of political union in this
despatch is of no significance.[67] Ostensibly he was writing on
reciprocity not union. The tone of his argument in favour of a
union of all of the British North American colonies is however
unmistakable:

It may be said that from local position & other circumstances, the feelings
of Canada, Nova Scotia, New Brunswick, & Prince Edward's Island are so
different as necessarily to impede the creation of any such common sentiment or such a reconcilement of interests apparently incompatible. I believe
on the other hand, that any such incompatibilty is much more apparent
than real & that the existence of any minor difficulties only makes it more
important to deal with the matter whilst the influence of the Queen's
Government is yet strong & whilst our relation to the United States is such
as to offer no obstacles practically insuperable.

[67]For a contrary interpretation in this respect see Whitelaw, *The Maritimes
and Canada*, p. 115, note 1.

The fate of this carefully written despatch was unfortunate. On the very day that it was sent, the Government to which Pakington belonged was defeated in the House of Commons, and when it arrived in the Colonial Office Pakington's successor, the Duke of Newcastle, was too busy to do more than read a Colonial Office synopsis of all the lengthy papers that had come in from the various colonies on reciprocity. Once again, as had happened in the case of Head's despatch of March 31, 1849, on the Halifax and Quebec Railway, an important exposition of his views on union and other fundamental problems in British North America was scarcely glanced at in the Colonial Office because of new circumstances that had suddenly arisen there.

As evidence of Head's thinking, however, this is one of the most important despatches he wrote from New Brunswick. It reveals an even surer understanding than before of the fundamental factors that were determining—and changing—the relationships of the colonies with the mother country and the United States and with each other. It was his last official statement on British North American union until after he left New Brunswick. He had no occasion to deal with the subject again because the problems that he had looked to union to help solve remained in abeyance during those years of economic and political serenity, and because the Halifax and Quebec Railway negotiations, although briefly renewed in 1853, were never near enough to success to make union seem an immediate possibility. A somewhat oblique reference in a letter written to Lewis at the end of 1853 would indicate, however, that his belief in the ultimate need for union did not wane until that time at least:

My views are very simple. I believe that Canada will never be annexed to the U.S. if we give her freedom enough, as we now do & foster her own sense of self importance. The Canadians are beginning to say 'We are too great a people to be tied on to any body's tail & we are not going to be slave catchers to the United States'.

This temper of mind is in my opinion the right one for us to encourage, especially if any sense of *united interest* in all the British Provinces can be created. Whether Canada belong nominally or not to England is comparatively immaterial. I don't believe it to be in the power of the U.S. to seize or crush Canada.[68]

Meanwhile, the reciprocity negotiations proceeded from 1852 on in an atmosphere of ever increasing hope of success. Head

[68]Lewis Papers, Head to Lewis, December 29, 1853.

continued to watch over New Brunswick interests and corresponded frequently in this connection not only with the
colonial secretary but also with Lord Elgin, the British minister
in Washington, Israel D. Andrews the energetic American consul
in Saint John, and many others. His own part during the last
stages of the negotiations was less important that it had been
earlier when the main lines of policy were being determined. His
special task was to keep New Brunswick's views clearly before
the negotiators while at the same time preventing colonial
opinion, made indifferent by prosperity, from turning against
an agreement altogether. Still believing that reciprocity was
essential for the continued political as well as economic welfare
of British North America, he was convinced that some apparent
sacrifice of particular New Brunswick interests, if necessary for
the sake of compromise, would be fully justified in the long run.
When the treaty was drafted and it became evident that several
of New Brunswick's principal demands had not been met and
her sacrifices would likely be heavy, Head wrote persuasively in
one of his last despatches of the many advantages that would
nevertheless result, and he added hortatively: "I cannot for one
moment suppose that the Provincial Legislature can be so blind
to their own interests as to hesitate to make the necessary
changes in our own tariff."[69] By this means, Head's influence
was perpetuated and had some weight in securing final ratification of the treaty by New Brunswick.

The interest that Head had shown from the beginning in a
large variety of local New Brunswick affairs continued throughout his administration. He still did a great deal of travelling about
each summer, frequently accompanied by Lady Head. Topics
as widely separated from one another as the encouragement of
agriculture, law reform, an exhibition at Saint John modelled on
the Great Exhibition of 1851 in Britain, and the delicate problems
arising out of the relationship in the colony between church and
state, all attracted his sympathetic and sometimes prolonged
attention.

The cold, but not unpleasant, winter weather remained a
constant source of amazement. "I must say however it agrees
with me very well," he wrote to Lewis during his last spring
in the province. "I have taken a cold shower bath & walked

before breakfast on the River every day since last November (with the exception of perhaps three or four)."[70] Riding as well was a regular form of recreation for Head and on one occasion he was thrown heavily when a dog rushed down a bank at his horse. "We were riding fast & the whole thing happened before I saw the dog."[71] Fortunately he escaped with only a broken rib and some severe bruises. Study, of course, remained a major interest, and in the year following his return from England, Head wrote a small book. "I have finished what would make a *small duodecimo* on 'Shall & Will' . . . ," he wrote in November, 1853. "It has no originality & is, I should think, very dull so that I doubt if it will be worth publishing."[72] It was first published in 1856 and then in a new edition and with two new chapters in 1858.

As the six years of his term in New Brunswick approached their end, Head's thoughts began to turn to the question of his next appointment. In December, 1852, in his farewell letter from the Colonial Office, Pakington had mentioned Jamaica among other possibilities,[73] and in the summer of 1853, the Duke of Newcastle made an offer of the governorship of British Guiana at a somewhat higher salary than Head was receiving in New Brunswick. After careful consideration Head decided against going to Guiana fearing the effect of the climate on Lady Head's health, "though I know that I must take my chance after shutting the door in the face of promotion of this kind."[74] Mentioning his decision in this matter to Lewis, Head added: "I should prefer even an Australian Govt. to a *W. Indian of any kind* though if Jamaica had been offered to me I should probably have taken it."[75]

The exact circumstances surrounding the final choice of Head to succeed Elgin as governor general of British North America, the most important post in the colonial service, are not known, but Elgin himself may well have had some share in it. At the end

[70]Lewis Papers, Head to Lewis, April 4, 1854.
[71]Lewis Papers, Head to Lewis, May 22, 1853.
[72]Lewis Papers, Head to Lewis, November, 1853. This was *"Shall"* and *"Will"; or, two Chapters on Future Auxiliary Verbs* (London: John Murray, 1856); and second edition, *To which are added, 1. An essay on certain affirmative and negative particles in the English language. 2. An essay on the provincial word "songle"* (London: John Murray, 1858).
[73]See Lewis Papers, Head to Lewis, November, 1853.
[74]P.A.C., Head Papers, Head to Merivale, private, August 22, 1853.
[75]Lewis Papers, Head to Lewis, November, 1853.

of August, 1853, shortly after Head had rejected the Guiana appointment, Elgin visited Fredericton to discuss reciprocity and other topics on his way to England; and it was only a few months following his arrival in London that rumours began to circulate in Canada that he would go to India and would be replaced in Canada by Head. Sir James Graham, now first lord of the admiralty, wrote to Head rather cryptically at about that same time, toward the end of 1853: "I doubt whether Lord Elgin will return to Canada; that post is widely different from Guiana."[76] Some considerable time was still to pass, however, before Head received, in June 1854, just immediately before the Duke of Newcastle left the Colonial Office, the offer of the governor-generalship.[77] On September 19 his new appointment was announced in the *Royal Gazette*.

[76]Cf. Lewis Papers, Head to Lewis, December 29, 1853. Head quotes this passage from a letter he had received from Graham, and adds: "Don't suppose for one moment that I entertain any visionary or extravagant expectation of going to Canada."

[77]Cf. Lewis, *Letters*, p. 282, Lewis to Head, July 6, 1854.

III

CANADA, 1854–1861

SIX

The Crimean War and Canadian Defence

ON December 19, 1854, Sir Edmund Walker Head was sworn in before Chief Justice Bowen at Quebec and became the first, and only, lieutenant governor of New Brunswick to assume office as "Her Majesty's Governor General of all Her Majesty's Provinces in North America and of the Island of Prince Edward," Captain General, Governor in Chief, and Vice Admiral in and over the same.[1] More than two months had elapsed since he had said his final farewells in Saint John late in September and had sailed with his family and suite for Boston on his way to Canada. "It was in some measure painful to me to leave New Brunswick," Head confessed to Lewis. "The addresses presented at St. John and Fredericton were of the most flattering & cordial character. It was difficult to answer them—especially one from the members of my Council who spoke I believe sincerely though far too strongly."[2]

At Boston, Head met his successor as lieutenant governor of New Brunswick, J. H. T. Maners Sutton. In view of their future differences of opinion on the subject of confederation, it is interesting to note that the personal relations of these two men started off, at least so far as Head was concerned, on a footing of friendship and esteem. "He will *get on capitally,*" Head wrote to Lewis shortly after their meeting. "His Church principles are quite safe—as much so as could be desired."[3] A few weeks later he added: "I have heard from Manners Sutton. He likes Frederic-

---

[1]P.R.O., C.O. 42/595, G. Grey to Head, September 21, and October 7, 1854. The commissions and instructions pertaining to these various offices, together with their heavy official seals, weighed exactly 896 ounces. Mr. Rowland Hill of the G.P.O. was scandalized at having to send them for the sake of speed through the United States paying 6¼ *d.* an ounce, or a total of £33.6.8. (C.O. 42/596, G.P.O. to C.O., October 2, 1854).

[2]Lewis Papers, Head to Lewis, October 17, 1854.

[3]*Ibid.* Head and Manners Sutton had met and worked together before when the latter was under-secretary in the Home Office during most of Head's service as one of the chief Poor Law commissioners.

119

ton much & he is sure to succeed. I don't think a better man could have been chosen."[4]

It had been Head's intention to spend only a short time in the United States, waiting to hear from Elgin that the Reciprocity Bill had been passed and two controversial measures concerning the clergy reserves and seigneurial tenure had been dealt with and the Canadian legislature adjourned. Elgin could then leave with his work completed, and Head begin his new régime under favourable circumstances. As time passed, however, and the debates at Quebec showed no signs of ending, it became evident that the visit in the United States would have to be considerably prolonged—an outcome not altogether displeasing to Head with his keen interest in American politics and his growing circle of friends in Boston and New York. Moreover, it gave him an opportunity to see, as he put it, "what a live President looks like."[5] At the end of October he wrote to Lewis:

Lady Head & I have passed the last week in taking a run to Washington, leaving the children here. We returned yesterday greatly edified by having seen the 'City of magnificent distances' as it has been called. Crampton took us in most hospitably & our weather was delicious.

I paid my respects to the President who looked very ill having been suffering from ague—a disease which they say no tenant of the White House escapes. President Pierce is an ordinary looking man and, I should think, possesses very ordinary faculties though it is unfair to judge him from an interview which took place when he was *ill, arrayed in a dressing gown & slippers*. Marcy the Secretary of State is a cunning, slow speaking, and intensely tiresome person. He has some humour but it is so long in coming out that the point of a story evaporates before one can catch it. He told one story about himself & General Scott in Sir Francis Head's time when Marcy was Governor of the State of New York, which curiously illustrated the difficulty in dealing with the U.S. Govt. It came out incidentally in the narrative that Genl. Scott & Marcy got the U.S. Marshall who was with them not to execute the warrant which he held against Van Rensselaer who had just violated the neutrality laws by invading Canada! . . .

The U.S. Govt. & its supporters are really most anxious for the defeat of the French & English in the Crimea—our success is gall & wormwood to them. I could clearly see this by the way the President talked—how 'he could not understand the way we got to Balaklava etc etc' unfolding his map. I did not give him much comfort but said (what turns out to be the case) that it could only be accounted for by the complete command of the surrounding country given us by the battle of Alma.[6]

[4]Lewis Papers, Head to Lewis, October 29, 1854.
[5]Lewis Papers, Head to Lewis, October 17, 1854.
[6]Lewis Papers, Head to Lewis, October 29, 1854.

It was not until November 10, when the work of the Canadian legislature seemed on the point of completion, that the Heads eventually reached Quebec City. The approach down the river from Montreal on the steamer *John Munn,* and the landing ceremonies in the early morning, must have been reminiscent of the arrival at Saint John almost seven years before. On this occasion, however, the legislature had not actually adjourned, and the debates continued on all manner of topics day after day, the Heads having meanwhile to remain as Lord Elgin's guests in their future home, Spencer Wood. Over a month passed in this fashion, until finally, as the holiday season came near, the remaining legislation was hurriedly put through and on December 18 the long-expected adjournment took place. The following day Head assumed office, and on December 22 Lord Elgin stepped into a canoe and was ferried from ice-floe to ice-floe across the St. Lawrence on his way through the United States home to England.

It has been too readily taken for granted that Lord Elgin's departure marked the sudden eclipse of the office of governor general, and that his successors played little if any part in Canadian history, unless through some failure to understand their constitutional limitations they managed to embroil themselves in a controversy. Such sudden change is rare in history. Elgin's own truer appreciation of the continuing importance of the office is made clear in a remarkably far-sighted despatch dated on the last day before he gave it up to Head:

. . . the maintenance of the position and due influence of the Governor is one of the most critical problems that have to be solved in the adaptation of Parliamentary Government to the Colonial system, and it is difficult to overestimate the importance which attaches to its satisfactory solution. As the Imperial Government and Parliament gradually withdraw from Legislative interference, and from the exercise of patronage in Colonial affairs, the Office of Governor tends to become, in the most emphatic sense of the term, the link which connects the Mother Country and the Colony, and his influence the means by which harmony of action between the local and Imperial Authorities is to be preserved. It is . . . by the frank acceptance of the conditions of the Parliamentary System that this influence can be most surely extended and confirmed. Placed by his position above strife of parties, holding office by a tenure less precarious than the Ministers who surround him—having no political interest to serve but that of the community whose affairs he is appointed to administer, his opinion cannot fail, when all cause for suspicion or jealousy is removed, to have great weight in the Colonial Councils—while he is at liberty to constitute himself in a special manner the patron of those larger and higher interests—such interests for example as those of education and of moral and material progress in all its branches, which unlike the contests of party unite instead of dividing the members of the body politic. The mention of such influences as an appreciable force in the administration of public affairs may provoke a sneer on the part of persons who have no faith in any appeal which is not addressed to the lowest motives of human conduct, but those who have juster views of our common nature & who have seen the influences that are purely moral, wielded with judgment, will not be disposed to deny them a high degree of efficacy.[7]

The fact is that although the role of the governor general had changed, and was continuing to change, it had not become unimportant. Indeed, in Head's time, while the British North American colonies were in the early stages of their advance along the narrow and untrodden path toward full equality within a united empire, something considerably more than being a "patron of those larger and higher interests" was still required. The governor needed to have "great weight in the Colonial Councils" as well. It was of not little significance that a man of Head's deep and sensitive knowledge of British North American affairs, and of the real duties and responsibilities of a governor of a self-governing colony, held office in Canada after Lord Elgin.

Although technically his commission as governor general extended his authority to all parts of British North America, Head, like his predecessors, confined himself in practice to the administration of the united province of Canada. In general, the problems he faced there were not unlike those with which he had become familiar in New Brunswick. They stemmed from the need to watch carefully over, and from time to time guide, the course of events following the recognition of Responsible Government and the break-up of the old mercantile system of empire. In its details, however, the Canadian situation was very different from the New Brunswick. Administrative reforms which had engaged so much of Head's attention in New Brunswick formed no part of his political problem in Canada, nor was he obliged to supervise minutely the work of his ministers. Except on a few occasions and with regard to a few matters, Head had little to do in Canada with immediate day-to-day administration of the government. He intervened personally only in certain defence questions and in major political crises, notably the one

7P.R.O., C.O. 42/595, Elgin to G. Grey, December 18, 1854.

arising out of the seat-of-government dispute in 1858. He felt a special responsibility as well in connection with some issues which involved Imperial interests, as for example the Grand Trunk Railway whose shareholders lived in England, and he kept himself informed with regard to these issues when they were being dealt with by his ministers. Otherwise, in accordance with the principle of Responsible Government, he left the task of government to his thoroughly competent and experienced Canadian executive councils led by their own prime ministers.

Under these circumstances, it was not in the main as an administrator that Head made his contribution in Canada, but in two other respects. He acted, as Elgin had foreseen would be necessary, as an interpreter between the colonial and Imperial governments, smoothing the path for their changing relationship with each other; in his period the fields of this change were, in particular, defence and tariffs. He acted also—and this was the result of the special quality of Head's own mind and experience— as a designer of long-range policy. It was a period in British North American affairs when a governor general, well prepared for intensive thinking along these lines, could play a uniquely valuable part. In the Maritimes, the effective functioning of Responsible Government in small separate provinces had still to be assured. In Canada, sectional differences between French and English, and the difficulty in particular of choosing a permanent seat of government agreeable to both, were evidence of approaching political deadlock. Farther west, the Hudson's Bay Company was finding its authority challenged, and the annexation of its territories to Canada, or even possibly to the United States, was being widely talked of. Head's responsibility being primarily for Canada, his efforts in these years were directed quite largely toward getting to know the special character of the sectional issue there and dealing with its various manifestations as they occurred. From time to time, however, in considering long-range policy for Canada, especially in the period from 1856 to 1858, he was obliged to turn his thoughts as well back to the eastern provinces with which he was already thoroughly familiar and westward to the Hudson's Bay lands which, by a strange chance, he would later govern. His search for the basic principles underlying British problems in North America had already begun in New Brunswick. In Canada, where his horizons were wider and his prestige greater, his mature views were of profound importance in moulding the future of that colony and of the Empire as a whole.

Head's most immediate tasks in the spring of 1855 were very largely concerned with military affairs, and these were to continue to occupy much of his attention for the next two years. There were a variety of reasons why such matters, hitherto almost entirely remote from his experience, should fall to his lot more than was normally to be expected by the holder of his commissions from the Colonial Office, the War Office, and the Admiralty. In 1855 and until the spring of 1856, Britain was engaged in her only large military adventure of the mid-nineteenth century, the Crimean War, and in 1857 the Indian Mutiny occurred. Both had their repercussions on the defence policy of the Empire which in any case was already undergoing a major revision as part of the same Imperial transformation that was bringing in colonial self-government and ending mercantilism.

As early as 1851, Grey had set forth the military aspect of the change:

Canada (in common with the other British provinces in North America) now possesses . . . the advantage of self-government in all that relates to her internal affairs. It appears to Her Majesty's Government that this advantage ought to carry with it corresponding responsibilities, and that the time is now come when the people of Canada must be called upon to take upon themselves a larger share than they have hitherto done, of expenses which are incurred on this account, and for their advantage. Of these expenses, by far the heaviest charge which falls upon this country is that incurred for the military protection of the province. . . . [It] is far from being the view of Her Majesty's Government that the general military power of the empire is not to be used in the protection of this part of Her Majesty's dominions. But . . . it is the conviction of Her Majesty's Government, that it is only due to the people of this country that they should now be relieved from a large proportion of the charge which has hitherto been imposed upon them for the protection of a Colony now well able to do much toward protecting itself.[8]

The Duke of Newcastle had begun to implement this policy in 1853 by reducing the number of Imperial troops stationed in Canada. He had continued to withdraw troops, more rapidly, after Britain entered the Crimean War on March 27, 1854, and by the time of Head's arrival at the end of the year, a large pro-

---

[8]Grey to Elgin, March 14, 1851, extracts quoted in C. P. Stacey, *Canada and the British Army, 1846–1871*, pp. 79–80.

portion of them had gone. But their replacement by an effective Canadian militia was still in its embryonic stage, and simultaneously a serious crisis in relations with an unfriendly American government was boiling up.

Hostility rather than friendship was the normal attitude of the United States toward Britain during much of the nineteenth century, and the aggressive spirit of "manifest destiny" characterized her relations with her neighbours on the North American continent. All of this was personally familiar to Head as a result of his recent visit in the United States and his con-versations with the president and the secretary of state and many other Americans. What he saw and heard led him to conclude: "Their policy is . . . always to smooth down difficulties in private communications with foreign ministers & then, if popularity requires it, to burst out in an entirely different sense with some bombastic assertion of American rights. . . . They may commit some desperate act in the hope of receiving popularity by an Anti-British cry."[9]

An excellent opportunity for such a cry was being provided in the first months of Head's administration by the foolhardy attempts of British agents to enlist residents of the United States for service in the Crimea. Under the terms of a foreign enlistment act passed in Britain in December, 1854, a recruiting depot had been set up in Halifax and Sir Gaspard Le Marchant, now the only soldier among the governors in British North America, had been given authority to look for men in any direction he thought fit.[10] The intention was to try to get recruits from the United States where a severe depression was causing unemployment, and at the same time to evade that country's neutrality legislation which made official recruiting there illegal. Le Marchant, in turn, entrusted Joseph Howe with a secret mission to the United States to supervise recruiting, and to arrange transportation to the British colonies for those intending to enlist. Within a short time Howe had obtained the support of a number of influential persons, including Mr. Crampton, the British minister in Washington. Soon he was ready to despatch recruits.

Head had, of course, been kept informed in a general way of what was being done but his first direct involvement came with

[9]Lewis Papers, Head to Lewis, October 29, 1854.
[10]18 Vict., c. 2 and P.R.O., C.O. 42/600, Herbert to Le Marchant, confidential, February 15, 1855.

a telegram on April 4, 1855, from Howe asking if five hundred men could be received and cared for in Canada. With his usual caution in handling what he knew to be an extremely delicate matter, and fearful of Howe's well-known tendency in the opposite direction, Head replied shortly: "No Authority," and then wired to Le Marchant and Crampton (in cypher) for further information. Le Marchant confirmed that Howe had "an understanding" with him but Crampton said no action was necessary in Canada. The subsequent appearance after office hours at Spencer Wood of an individual who claimed to be a British recruiting agent in New York but could produce no credentials, and the receipt of more telegrams from Howe all sent openly through American companies, convinced Head that a most dangerous situation was developing. Lieutenant General Rowan, the commander of the troops in Canada, with whom Head was keeping in close touch, was of the same opinion. Both were further alarmed by a telegram to Rowan from Howe stating among other things: "Mr. Crampton co-operating." Head explained his concern subsequently to the colonial secretary:

The use of Mr. Crampton's name in an open telegraph message, on such a matter as this, satisfied me that it would not be prudent to commit myself in any way by written communications to Mr. Howe. Indeed from my previous knowledge of that gentleman when I was in New Brunswick, I doubted whether discretion or caution in the use of official documents & messages was quite so characteristic of him, as energy and resolution in carrying through what he had undertaken.[11]

It was necessary on the other hand not to impede any good work that Howe might be doing, and Head sent his private secretary, Viscount Bury, to Niagara, where Howe had last been heard from, with instructions to receive recruits if this seemed desirable but not even to confer with Howe except on Canadian soil. Bury's trip was fruitless as Howe had already departed. A short time later, however, Crampton himself visited Head in Quebec, went on to Halifax, and then returned to Quebec, with the aim of arranging a more carefully co-ordinated effort.[12] But the damage had already been done. The efforts of Howe and Crampton and their various recruiting agents had not been kept sufficiently secret. A public outcry arose in the United States and eventually the government took the position that "Great Britain, in attempting by the agency of her military and civil

[11]P.R.O., C.O. 42/598, Head to Russell, military and confidential, May 2, 1855.
[12]P.R.O., C.O. 42/598, Head to Russell, military, May 23, 1855.

authorities in the British North American Provinces, and her diplomatic and consular functionaries in the United States, to raise troops here, committed an act of usurpation against the sovereign rights of the United States."[13] In May, 1856, Crampton's recall was demanded.

The War Office had at some stages of the recruiting effort been inclined to think Head not active enough.[14] Howe undoubtedly felt this, which probably accounts for his remark years later when he heard that Head had been named governor of the Hudson's Bay Company: "Old Head will chill it to death or I am much mistaken."[15] On the other hand, Head himself, immediately after conferring with Crampton at Quebec in the spring of 1855, wrote: "I saw no reason to doubt the propriety of the course which I had pursued with reference to Mr. Howe."[16] A year later, at the time of Crampton's recall, he was more definite still, and also more explicit in a letter to Lewis:

I think the aspect of affairs in the U.S. very ugly. . . . As I have often said to you before I never congratulated myself on anything more than on my caution in the Recruiting business. Had a bitter feeling been created on the Canadian frontier it might ere this have turned the scale. I fear very much now all that is happening at home in the U.S. is so discreditable that the Govt will run any risk to turn men's attention to foreign affairs. The Sumner business shows a pleasant condition of things & the Civil War (for it is nothing less) in Kansas is equal to it.[17]

Fear of annoying the United States was wise in any case in the generation of her war against Mexico and of Commodore Perry's "negotiations" with Japan, and there seems little doubt, in retrospect, that Head's caution was justifiable. So too were his equally careful preparations for the defence of Canada should that need arise.

[13]J. A. Chisholm (ed.), *Speeches and Public Letters of Joseph Howe*, II, 310, note.

[14]P.R.O., W.O. 1/568, Head to G. Grey, military and confidential, February 23, 1855, minutes.

[15]P.A.C., Howe Papers, Howe to Watkin, December 24, 1863.

[16]P.R.O., C.O. 42/598, Head to Russell, military, May 23, 1855.

[17]Lewis Papers, Head to Lewis, June 9, 1856. Lord John Russell, who became colonial secretary for a few months at the height of the crisis, was in full agreement with Head's views, writing to him privately at the beginning of June, 1855: "I am very thankful to you for your judicious proceedings, both in respect to recruiting for the Foreign Legion & in regard to the formation of a Canadian Regt. . . . I am delighted to find Canada in such good hands. You will always find me ready to assist you if you shd. ever want it." P.R.O., P.R.O. 30/22/117, Russell to Head, June 1, 1855.

Canadian defence in the 1850's was still largely an Imperial concern, and Head's direct and personal responsibility was therefore great. It was made more difficult for him to fulfil by his own lack of any military training and especially by a short-sighted decision on the part of the War Office that one of the first cuts in the Imperial establishment in Canada should be the elimination of the governor general's military staff. Since Lord Durham's time the governor general had been allowed a military secretary and two aides-de-camp, paid by the British government. Orders had been given, however, that on Lord Elgin's retirement all of these offices should be discontinued. When notified of this at the time of his appointment Head made a mild protest: "To myself personally, from my previous habits and position such a change is wholly immaterial. My only fear would be lest the position of the Queen's Representative might on public occasions contrast disadvantageously with that of a Lieut. General with his Staff commanding Her Majesty's troops in the some colony."[18] Later, when Head had had an opportunity to talk with Elgin at Quebec, he discovered that the governor general had also had an aide-de-camp paid by the province, and he was able to solve the problem in a reasonably satisfactory way, so far as social duties were concerned, by obtaining permission for another to be seconded, with an allowance as an extra aide-de-camp, from one of the regiments remaining in the colony.[19]

The absence of a military secretary continued, however, to be a most serious handicap at a time when military correspondence was unusually voluminous owing to the Crimean War, the tense international situation, and the various problems connected with the transfer of responsibility in matters of defence from the Imperial to the local government. Only in 1856, after numerous appeals from Head, supported by the Colonial Office and by Lewis—the one known occasion on which Head asked Lewis to use his influence on his behalf—and only after the receipt of numerous military despatches written in Head's own "execrable" hand, did the obstinate War Office agree to provide a secretary. And by then, the worst need was over.[20]

[18]P.R.O., W.O. 1/568, Head to G. Grey, military and separate, August 7, 1854. See also, same to same, July 29, 1854, and minutes.

[19]P.R.O., C.O. 42/595, Head to G. Grey, military and separate, November 25, 1854.

[20]P.R.O., C.O. 42/607, W.O. to C.O., April 14, June 30, August 9, August 30, 1856, and minutes and draft replies by the C.O. This series of documents presents

At the time when Head's responsibility began, arrangements for the assumption by Canada of a larger share of her own defence were just on the point of advancing beyond the discussion stage. Newcastle's scheme for the accelerated withdrawal of troops from British North America, which he had worked out in conjunction with Elgin and Hincks in London shortly after the Crimean War began, had been based on strict adherence to Grey's principles of 1851: that is, part, but only part, of the defence burden hitherto borne entirely by Britain would be transferred to Canada. Since this would be a permanent and not simply a wartime adjustment, Newcastle decided quite logically —and also, of course, with an eye to the Canadian reaction—that part of the lands that had been held by the Imperial government for ordnance purposes should be transferred simultaneously. He proposed that, in Canada, only lands at Montreal, Quebec, and Kingston—places of first-class strategic importance where Imperial garrisons would remain—should continue in Imperial possession. Some others, important in case of war but not in the first rank, should be surrendered on the understanding that the provincial government retain them for defence. The rest, comprising by far the largest class, should be handed over unconditionally but with the hope that Canada would decide to use the proceeds from their sale for organizing a more effective militia.[21]

This scheme was before the Canadian government when Head arrived, and in February, 1855, a special commission which had been appointed to study it reported in favour of acceptance. The commission proposed as well that the old "sedentary" militia, based on universal service and one annual muster, be supplemented by volunteer or active companies. These would have arms and uniforms and be expected to undergo ten consecutive days' training a year for which they would receive full pay. On May 19, a militia act framed along these lines was given the royal assent by Head. When it came into effect on July 1, an

only the final stage of the whole long haggle. See also Lewis Papers, Head to Lewis, November 14, 1855: " . . . I am overwhelmed with military correspondence. . . . Nor does the diminution of the number of the Queen's troops in the Colony make the correspondence less in proportion. On the contrary there is more trouble & correspondence connected with disposing properly an insufficient number. . . . I have proof of this on my table at the present moment in the shape of several letters respecting the transfer of two companies to one place and 20 or 50 men to another."

[21]P.R.O., W.O. 1/568, minute by Duke of Newcastle, August 7, 1854; G. Grey to Elgin, confidential and military, September 8, 1854.

able soldier, Colonel de Rottenburg, was appointed adjutant general of militia. While he was beginning to organize the new force, several members of the executive council went to London to negotiate the final terms for the surrender of the ordnance lands and to purchase arms.[22]

By this time, the danger from the United States seemed to be approaching its peak and every effort was made to speed preparations against possible attack. This was hindered somewhat, so far as the Militia Act was concerned, by certain political difficulties. "There was when it was passed a strong party in the Legislature opposed to the expense it would cause, and it is necessary to act cautiously so as not to alarm this party unnecessarily or give them good ground for an outcry." Special care had to be taken in the issuing of commissions to avoid giving the militia a political tinge. "On the whole I have succeeded in this," Head reported the next spring, "by consulting individual members of the Council, and members of the Assembly as to their own localities and taking care to blend all parties as much as possible. The Act is becoming popular. The volunteers or active portion come forward readily, and gradually I have no doubt we shall make it work well."[23]

In the meantime, however, when the critical winter of 1855–56 began, the militia was still incompletely organized and it had had virtually no training. Nor had it arms. Those ordered in England had failed to arrive before the St. Lawrence was frozen over. A secret and confidential memorandum dated March 1, 1856, "On the defensible condition of Western Canada," written in Head's own hand and copied at the Colonial Office for the War Office, the Queen, and the cabinet, revealed an appalling situation and one that was *"irremediable* at the moment."[24] At Toronto, to which the seat of government had

[22]Stacey, *Canada and the British Army,* pp. 92 ff.

[23]P.R.O., C.O. 42/603, Head memorandum, "On the defensible condition of Western Canada," March 1, 1856. That Head's caution regarding the commissions was well advised is shown in the following comment made at this time by a member of the executive council about its leader, Sir Allan MacNab: "I observe that the newspapers state that a Canadian battalion is to be raised. . . . I suppose Sir Allan will provide all the compact root and branch with commissions. . . . I think Sir Allan's judgment would dictate all that is reasonable and fair enough but he has such an infernal lot of hangers on to provide for." P.A.C., Macdonald Papers, vol. 260, John Ross to Macdonald, August 23, 1855.

[24]P.R.O., C.O. 42/603, Head memorandum, "On the defensible condition of Western Canada." There were small and inadequate Imperial garrisons at Quebec, Montreal, and Kingston.

been transferred from Quebec in the autumn of 1855, and indeed in the whole region west of Kingston, there was little means of defence.

As regards Military force 700 or 800 men including the two companies of Rifles and the Pensioners could probably be got together with four or six field pieces, and this is pretty nearly all that could be done until the navigation is open. . . . The total absence of Military stores available for our purpose even at *Kingston* would make it difficult to attempt more in the way of regular organization at present.

Every expedient was being adopted to remedy this weakness. Six hundred stand of percussion muskets had been moved up "quietly" by sleigh from Montreal to Toronto.

Before this transfer took place there was not a spare musket, I believe, west of Kingston. The last rifles in store at Kingston were given out a short time since at my request to a volunteer corps formed at Brockville, of these, however, being I think 50 in number, *one half were flint.* [Among other stores, originally intended as Indian presents, were] 46 Chief's rifles with loading rods etc and some percussion caps. I have ventured to ask the Commissariat officer . . . to place them, such as they are, at the disposal of the Adjutant General of Militia. . . . *A very large proportion* of the musquets [*sic*] in store at Montreal, Quebec, and Kingston, are old flint musquets.

The Cavalry Swords are of an old pattern, and *have no belts.* . . .

In the mean time during the current winter if an attack should come I must do the best that can be done with the means at my command. I feel sure of the readiness of the people of Upper Canada to repel aggressors from the United States. How far they could do so successfully with their present means and imperfect organization is very doubtful.

In fact however the mass of the people here do not believe in the probability of war at the present moment and scarcely contemplate such an event.

However small this probability may be the total absence of means to meet it is not a pleasant state of things.

A few days after he wrote this gloomy memorandum, Head received on March 5, 1856, a despatch which showed that the Imperial government was also greatly concerned about the lack of arms in Canada. It stated that a shipment including 5000 muskets was on its way to Halifax and would be sent overland through New Brunswick to Canada. Head immediately took steps to prepare to receive it, and wrote to Manners Sutton giving him the names of lumbermen who would probably have teams that could be hired and that would already be in the woods near the road. For the sake of security he suggested to everyone that the code name "Railroad Iron" be used for the supplies. The futility of the whole scheme, however, was clearly evident to him: the snow might well melt closing the road before the supplies could get through, and in any case they could not possibly arrive more than a little while before navigation re-opened in the St. Lawrence. "I should not myself have advised it but it is done."[25]

It was in this same week, when he was most conscious of the "*irremediable*" nature of Canada's military weakness, that Head received an earnest and persuasive visitor who had a fantastic story to tell. This was a certain Alexander Manning St. George, an Englishman, who called himself a half-brother of Henry Manning, and told of a meeting at Thomas's Hotel, Washington, where a plot for the military annexation of Canada to the United States had been worked out in detail. It had been attended by Americans and a number of well-known Canadians. "The Attorney General (McDonald) heard the story and as every name was recited he recognized it." In view of the filibustering currently engaged in in other directions by believers in the "manifest destiny" of the United States—William Walker had just established himself as generalissimo of a puppet government in Nicaragua—St. George's story however alarmist could not be disregarded. Head informed Merivale in a private and confidential letter:

What I hear from other quarters makes me believe the truth to be this. . . . I think Seward and some of the northern members of the Senate, who, for their own purposes, have taken the warlike tone, have to justify this tone in the Free States. They could do this best by committing the President to a scheme which would increase the power of the Free States in the Senate by 4 votes. Such is said to be the proposed division of Western Canada. The inducements held out to the President may be conjectured to be as follows—
1. The facility of appropriating Western Canada before the navigation opens.
They reckon of course on the sympathy of the population as reported by their friends here. These reports are, I am convinced, utterly delusive. . . .
2. The Free-soil war party hold out to the President the glory he would earn by securing the Lakes to the United States. As to Lower Canada—they would leave that to be dealt with afterwards.
Now against any scheme of this kind taking effect there is, it appears

[25]P.A.C., G 14/43, Head to Manners Sutton, confidential, March 5, 1856. See also, G 19/21, Head to Major General Home, confidential, March 5, 1856.

to me, the strong argument that Pierce *dare* not take measures for annexing 4 *free* states to the Union, without having actually secured for his Southern friends a corresponding accession of strength. This could not be done simultaneously: and in fact it could never be done at all; because when war was declared there would, with our naval superiority, be an end of dreams respecting Cuba etc etc. . . .

If Pierce therefore gave way to Seward & his friends he would have to renounce all reliance on the South without really gaining the North, who, as well he knows, hate him.

For these reasons mainly I do not believe in the imminent danger of War; but I do believe that a scheme such as I have described has been agitated at Washington.[26]

Although Head at no time thought war likely, it remained a disquieting possibility as late as the summer of 1856 because of the electioneering tactics being pursued by American politicians driven almost to desperation in this last presidential year but one before the steadily widening gulf between North and South reached its inevitable culmination in war. Risking international even to avoid civil war was no excuse for them of course. With an understandable lack of sympathy Head wrote to Lewis in June:

That men should be such fools as to play their tricks and stake all on such trumpery grounds is perfectly incredible if one did not see it. . . . If we have a war I suppose we shall have to stand the first blow. There is nothing as yet to hinder my being taken prisoner any day for as things now stand the Yankees would have command of the Lakes.

If I am carried off to Boston or New York I will apprise you of the change in my address but I think we should have a fight for it first.[27]

In fact, however, Britain's skilful and firm diplomacy and Head's caution in Canada were successful in staving off whatever official or unofficial aggression might have taken place during this critical year. The British attitude, influenced no doubt by Head's account of Canada's defencelessness, had remained most conciliatory toward the United States even when Crampton's recall had finally been demanded in May. On March 30, however, the Treaty of Paris had ended the Crimean War, and it was not many months before Palmerston was able to despatch five regiments

[26]P.R.O., C.O. 42/603, Head to Merivale, private and confidential, March 8, 1856. In 1861, when there was again danger of American invasion, Head was to hear this same story brought up to date by a man now calling himself George Manning. This time he was not impressed. See P.R.O., C.O. 537/96, F.O. to C.O., secret, June 20, 1861, and enclosures; same to same, secret, July 1, 1861, and enclosures; L. B. Shippee, *Canadian-American Relations, 1849–1874*, pp. 121–22.

[27]Lewis Papers, Head to Lewis, June 15, 1856.

to British North America, partly as a show of force, partly to dispose of troops no longer needed elsewhere.[28] The danger which, in so far as it had existed at all, had been mainly due to Canada's weakness and the American election, was over by the fall.

The sending of reinforcements to British North America at this time was welcomed by Head but strongly criticized by Lord Elgin from his place in the House of Lords—an interesting difference of opinion between two men whose views on the relationship between mother country and colony were essentially the same. Head had been asked privately by Henry Labouchere, now colonial secretary, what effect the presence of considerable numbers of Imperial troops might have on Canada's own defence measures, especially on recruiting for the militia. Having first consulted with Colonel de Rottenburg, the adjutant general of militia, Head replied in a private letter written in his own hand.[29] After Elgin's attack on the Government, this letter was placed in the Colonial Office files and copies were prepared for the War Office, the cabinet, and the Queen. Head's views, supported by Colonel de Rottenburg, were as follows:

> I think the presence of an increased military force, if it be stationed at Quebec, Montreal & Kingston, will not interfere with the spirit or energy of the militia now in course of being organized.
> In Lower Canada it is principally in the cities that the volunteer corps will be formed. They consist in great part of gentlemen or respectable tradesmen; and I do not think their readiness will be diminished by the presence of the military force.
> In Upper Canada, where our main reliance is on the yeomen and gentleman farmers in the country the case might be different; but if Kingston is the last considerable post westward occupied by the Queen's troops in time of peace, I do not apprehend any change in the present temper of the Country. . . .
> Upon the whole however I advise that the *main reliance in all Canada west of Kingston be professedly on the Militia*. The regular force in the strong military positions below will give confidence and stimulate rather than deter the military advance of Upper Canada.

Elgin's argument in the House of Lords, on the other hand, was that by sending troops Britain was resuming a large share of the burden of Canadian defence and discouraging Canada's own efforts. He was opposed to what he considered a reactionary

[28]P.R.O., C.O. 42/604, Labouchere to Head, May 2, 1856.
[29]P.R.O., C.O. 42/604, Head to Labouchere, private, May 15, 1856. For Elgin's views see Stacey, *Canada and the British Army*, pp. 99–101.

departure from the policy laid down by Grey in 1851 "because he thought that it would be unjust towards the mother country, and also because, although it might be a boon to the colonies, in the first instance, it would be a boon followed by a speedy reaction, and would put an argument in the hands of those who were disposed to denounce our colonies as burdens."

The fact is that Elgin's views and Head's, in spite of superficial differences, remained very close in principle. Both accepted the stand taken by Grey in 1851, that Canada having obtained Responsible Government should assume greater responsibility for her own defence. But both, Elgin no less than Head, recognized the continuing responsibility as well of the mother country especially if war threatened—war brought near quite probably as a result of Imperial rather than colonial causes. It was in applying principle to practice that they differed because their estimation of the current American danger was not the same.

Geographic location and personal experience have an influence on even the most objective thinkers. Elgin in London could regard a blustering "Jonathan" with a degree of equanimity that Head could not quite achieve in exposed and isolated Toronto. And when Elgin thought of the United States, he remembered the Reciprocity festivities and the friendly salute of guns wishing him farewell when he had sailed from New York just over a year before. He was convinced that there had never been a time "when the substantial interests which bind the two countries together were so manifold and so important, and when the differences between them were so trifling and peurile." Head's impressions were more recent. He had watched the anti-British sentiment, always latent across the border, being fed in recent months by controversies over recruiting and other matters, and he had seen it flare up dangerously in a bitter election campaign. While he agreed with Elgin in discounting "the imminent danger of War," he thought "the aspect of affairs in the U.S. very ugly"; and he was more immediately conscious than anyone in England could be of the fact that the very weakness of Canada was in itself a serious temptation to a Government prepared to "run any risk to turn men's attention to foreign affairs."

Labouchere, in announcing that troops were being sent, made it clear that the Government shared with both Head and Elgin an understanding of the principles involved. He stated explicitly that this action must not be taken as evidence of Britain's willingness to shoulder once again a larger part of the burden of Canadian defence. Grey himself had always contemplated the retention of certain posts garrisoned by Imperial forces. The size of the garrisons might be increased or decreased from time to time as the need arose without changing general policy. Her Majesty's Government, Labouchere asserted, "desire to place their main dependence on the well-proved loyalty and courage of Her Majesty's Canadian subjects to repel any hostile aggression should the occasion ever unfortunately occur, although in that event Her Majesty's Government would not fail to give to the Province the full support of the whole power of the British Empire."[30] Even verbally, this was almost an exact repetition of what Grey had said five years before.

The "ifs" of history are imponderable, and it is not easy to judge, even in retrospect, what might have happened had Head rejected the reinforcements proffered on these terms. A border incident or something more serious might have occurred; proof that this was a real possibility was to be given within the next ten years in the San Juan filibuster of 1859 and the Fenian Raids. As to the effect of the reinforcements on the militia programme: it is true that the funds provided for the militia were to be greatly reduced when the act came up for renewal in 1859, but this can be adequately explained by the apparent lessening in Anglo-American tension and by the need for strict economy in view of the commercial depression that had cut deeply into government revenue. The vote for the militia was to be raised again in 1860 when these conditions had once more changed.

In military matters, Head's responsibilities as governor general impinged upon those of the commander of the regular British forces in North America. The possibilities of a conflict of jurisdiction, of misunderstanding between the military and the civilian viewpoints, or even of petty jealousy between the two leading figures in provincial society, were almost endless in this relationship. Head's numerous letters among the Eyre Papers in the Public Record Office afford an unusual opportunity to assess his skill in handling a delicate situation of this sort—and they show too his sustained and detailed interest in Canadian defence problems, and particularly in the militia.

Lieutenant General Sir William Eyre was one of several officers who served as commander of the troops during Head's term in

[30]P.R.O., C.O. 42/604, Labouchere to Head, May 2, 1856.

Canada. He arrived in the summer of 1856 with the reinforcements from the Crimea, and Head immediately took steps to place their association on a close personal basis. The Eyres were invited for a visit to Toronto and a mutual interest in "talk on metaphysical subjects" was discovered; an unusually frequent and frank private correspondence was immediately inaugurated; Lady Eyre's painting was praised and encouraged—at what cost to Head's integrity as an art critic cannot now be judged. Genuine friendship and mutual esteem seem to have followed what may at first have been policy on Head's part, and the result was very close and effective co-operation. Irritating difficulties regarding the transfer of the ordnance lands and frequent squabbles between regular and militia officers were only some of the many disputes that were dealt with smoothly by channelling them to the top for amicable solution by the two men.[31]

A special project in which Head and Eyre were both greatly interested had its origin in the outbreak of the Indian Mutiny in May, 1857. When Head was in England later that summer, it was suggested to him that Canada assist in the emergency by raising a regiment to serve as a regular part of the British Army. He wrote to Eyre who was administering the government during his absence:

I was quietly refreshing myself in Cornwall when I got a letter from Mr. Labouchere saying that serious thoughts were again entertained of raising a regiment in B.N. America; and desiring me to see Lord Panmure and the D. of Cambridge on the subject. Much to my disgust I came up yesterday (from Bodmin in 12 hours). I have not yet seen Lord Panmure, but I have just come from the Horse Guards where I have talked the matter over with the Duke of Cambridge & General Yorke.

It is evident that H.R.H. is *very anxious* the thing should be done: General Yorke, I can see, on the other hand does not like encroaching too much on the patronage of the Horse Guards and would give nothing to the Colonists but the subalterns' commissions. The Duke proposes to write to you confidentially & ask you to consult de Rottenburg & prepare a scheme. This scheme, if it is ready, I am to see when I pass through London in October. It will not of course be made public or communicated to the Canadian Government until approved and settled here.[32]

[31]P.R.O., P.R.O. 30/46, Eyre Papers, *passim*. See especially Box 18, Head to Eyre, private, October 31, 1856. Head's letters to Eyre, even when he had a copy made first for the file, were always sent to Eyre in his own handwriting, no doubt with a view to establishing an atmosphere of intimate personal understanding—albeit at considerable sacrifice of legibility.

[32]P.R.O., P.R.O. 30/46/18, Head to Eyre, confidential, August 22, 1857.

Further interviews and much correspondence while in England and after his return to Canada resulted eventually in Head's being able to lay a satisfactory proposal before his executive council. Its approval given, Head and Eyre worked closely together for many months to solve the numerous problems connected with choosing the officers for, recruiting, equipping, training, and finally sending overseas, the 100th Royal Canadian Regiment of Foot, the first regiment raised in a colony for general service.[83]

In dealing with defence, as with any other problem, Head's thoughts turned instinctively from practice to the consideration of fundamental principles. It is probable that no one saw, or explained, more clearly than Head the military implications of the new idea of empire that he was helping to work out in North America—the idea of an empire that would come to consist of a mother country associated in a sort of federal way, possibly by intangible bonds, with adult and self-governing colonies. This had been the idea of Grey and Elgin as well but both had ceased to be directly concerned with the North American scene before the full effect of the military changes came to be felt. Too often those who succeeded them in the determination of Imperial policy seemed to be tinged with "Little Englandism." Head revealed his anxiety regarding this tendency in an unusually frank letter to Eyre, written in December, 1856, in connection with the detailed arrangements that were being made, not without controversy, for the transfer of the ordnance lands:

To speak with perfect candour I think the English Government have not acted with a clear and consistent policy with regard to this colony. Perhaps you will say that Canada is not singular in this respect: but the facts appear to me to be thus—

Mr. Gladstone and his colleagues seem to have adopted a theory that all that England had to do was to keep Canada in good humour for the short remainder of her *wedded* life so to speak—that they could give it up when they pleased and how they pleased, and that its abandonment was only a question of time. This sort of feeling coincided perfectly with the advance in self government in the Colony itself and the colonial authorities acted upon it so as to clench the bargain with regard to the Ordnance Lands. . . .

[83]P.A.C., G 14/43, Head to Panmure, private, August 23, 1857; P.R.O., C.O. 42/612, W.O. to C.O., October 17, 1857; C.O. 42/613, Head to Labouchere, January 13, 1858; P.R.O. 30/46/18, Head to Eyre, private, December 12, 1857, March 20, 1858, May 10, 1858.

Now it is not my business to criticize this policy or to do anything beyond carrying it out. As the chief of the colonial Government I represent the interests of Canada, and must act specially with that in view *when those interests are not adverse to the policy or the instructions of the Queen's Government.*

There is no such opposition between the *avowed* policy of the English government and the wishes of the Executive Council here. I may have my own opinion as to the consistency of the course taken in the cessation of the Ordnance Lands, unconditional and sweeping as it is, with the 'solidarité' of defensive interests between England and Canada.

I may doubt whether it would be easy to give up Canada if we wished it—whether we could do so without dishonour in time of war, as the Duke of Wellington observed: or get any minister bold enough to propose it in time of peace. But whatever these doubts may amount to, my duty is to carry out the principles avowed and adopted, and work out the problem as it lies before me.[34]

In spite of his professions in this document, Head was by no means content to sit back and merely "carry out the principles avowed and adopted" by the British Government when they seemed to threaten the " 'solidarité' of defensive interests between England and Canada." In frequent despatches he hammered home to the Colonial Office his own viewpoint as to the correct principles on which Imperial military relationships should be based.

He always stressed first the responsibility of the colony, which seemed to him to follow almost axiomatically from the achievement of Responsible Government:

In pursuance of the principles of Colonial rule now adopted by England, Canada practically exercises a control over her own affairs. Her experience in Parliamentary and Municipal government is gradually and surely building up her institutions, and forming the political habits of her people, without destroying the tie which binds her to Great Britain, and without impairing her loyalty to the British throne.

But so long as violence and wrong exist in the world, no community, though making its own laws, and substantially governing its own people, can be said to assume the character of a political whole, without possessing some organized means of self-protection. . . . For such a community to rely upon a distant mother country for aid in . . . local emergencies (as distinguished from regular war, or continuous hostilities amounting to war) is to confess its own helplessness, and to assume a position inconsistent with the proud and just maintenance of its own rights.[35]

[34]P.A.C., G 19/21, Head to Eyre, private and confidential, December 22, 1856. This is a file copy with corrections made by Head. The original, entirely in Head's hand, is among the Eyre Papers (P.R.O. 30/46/18).
[35]P.R.O., C.O. 42/613, Head to Labouchere, February 8, 1858.

On the other hand, Head was, if anything, still more insistent on the continuing responsibilities of Great Britain in the matter of colonial defence: "I hold in the strongest manner, that as the control of the foreign relations of the Colony still rests with the Mother-Country, so the obligation on the latter to carry the former through difficulties which these relations create or regulate, is unquestionable."[36]

Head's subtle mind was aware, however, that the emphasis had really to be placed on the *joint* responsibility of both mother country and colony, rather than on simple insistance that the latter should now bear a share, but a share only, of the burden borne hitherto entirely by the former. Grey, Elgin, and New-castle had agreed that Imperial forces should be kept only at a few posts of strategic importance—Quebec, Montreal, and Kings-ton—and that, aside from these, the main reliance should be on the militia organized by Canada. Head accepted this arrange-ment as a matter of practical convenience, but he saw its dangers, and was careful to reject the implication that it meant any real differentiation of defence responsibilities. He stressed, for ex-ample, that:

The interests of Great Britain and of Canada . . . coincide in the main-tenance of a proper Militia force. It ought to be the aim of both to foster and encourage in the Colony such Military arrangements as may meet its ordinary wants, and may, if a foreign war should unfortunately arise, in-crease the efficiency of the Imperial Forces, and lighten the labours of sus-taining an extraordinary crisis. . . .

It may be said that in this theory the line which separates the duty of the Mother Country and that of the colony is vague and undefined. It would be singular if it were otherwise; for the present relation of Great Britain to her freely governed Colonies is, I believe, new and unprecedented in the history of the world, and political duties and relations can only be rendered definite by experience and practice.[37]

Head was conscious of how delicate were the practical adjust-ments required under such circumstances, when the border line

[36]*Ibid.* Head argued this subject vigorously with the authorities in England during his visit there in 1857. See P.R.O., P.R.O. 30/46/18, Head to Eyre, private, July 28, 1857: "I have had a long interview with Lord Panmure & after much discussion in which I stood up stoutly for the principles of Colonial defence by England, I think I got him to give up the demand for the old muskets & for the practice ammunition for the Field batteries. I have had the whole of the same ground to go over again with Sir Charles Wood at the Admiralty as to the general principle involved in expecting a colony to defend itself. I suppose I shall have it a third time with Sir John Burgoyne whom I shall see tomorrow."
[37]P.R.O., C.O. 42/613, Head to Labouchere, February 8, 1858.

between Canadian and British responsibilities was vague and was in fact undergoing a continuous transition. And since this transition was in the direction of the assumption by Canada of larger responsibilities, he was particularly concerned to avoid even the appearance that it was being forced upon her arbitrarily. He was always careful to insist on the need for consulting his executive council before committing Canada to any military policy, and on several occasions when the insensitive War Office made awkward proposals, he argued against them firmly. To take only one example: in 1858 the War Office suggested that Canada pay the expenses necessary in connection with renting officers' quarters in Montreal, pointing out that this was being done in Australia. Although the amount involved was small, less than £2000, the Colonial Office, more imbued with Head's opinions, doubted the wisdom of asking Canada to pay it. To make sure, one way or the other, it decided to ask for Head's advice first.[38] In response he made it clear that in the colony the understanding was that the defences in Montreal and other centres where Imperial garrisons were retained were the responsibility of the mother country. The present request would reflect on Britain's willingness to observe this arrangement. Nor was the comparison with Australia valid. Australia had no exposed frontier liable to be overrun at any moment, probably as a result of a quarrel arising from Imperial causes and where no direct colonial interest was concerned.[39]

In his theorizing on Imperial defence, Head did not confine himself to considering the joint responsibility of the mother country and the colony solely in connection with the defence of the latter. He was quick to realize that a wider vision was necessary, that if the mother country were to continue aiding the colonies in their defence, it was only just that they in turn, as they grew in wealth and population, should assume increased responsibility not only for their own defence but for that of the Empire as a whole. The decision to recruit the 100th Royal Canadian Regiment was the occasion for Head noticing this aspect, and he pointed out that the extension of the principle involved in this step might well have a revolutionary effect:

Great Britain is, as it were, placed in the centre of a circle: every man who emigrates to Canada or Australia has hitherto ceased to be available for any

[38]P.R.O., C.O. 42/616, W.O. to C.O., April 27, 1858, and minutes.
[39]P.R.O., C.O. 42/614, Head to Stanley, confidential, June 7, 1858.

142 *Sir Edmund Head*

military purpose, other than the defence of the single and distant point on the circumference which he may have adopted as his new home.

But if a regiment for general service can be, from time to time, drawn from one [of] these outlying points, it will be so much gained: the population, not of Great Britain & Ireland, but of the whole Empire may contribute in some degree to the military strength of the whole. . . .

The increase of the larger Colonies may thus tend to augment the active military force of England, and the inhabitants of each may be available for something more than the passive protection of its own soil. In this case, the British Army would grow with the growth, and strengthen with the strength of her Provinces as well as with her own, and would be so constituted as to represent them & combine in itself elements contributed by each.[40]

Head thus carried over into the military field his conception of the new form of Imperial integration which allowed for, and in fact was based on, the principle of political decentralization. His forecast of the way in which the military forces of the Empire would eventually be organized was inaccurate in detail. He could not visualize the extent of the military decentralization that would take place in the next hundred years. But he did understand, more clearly than most, that it was necessary to look ahead to a new order in which there would be a free flow of power, including military power, amongst the various governments of the Empire so that the progress of each would go to swell the strength of the whole.

[40]P.R.O., C.O. 42/613, Head to Stanley, May 1, 1858.

SEVEN

"The Future Prospects of British North America"

WHILE military affairs were in some respects the most urgent, and were the most demanding on Head's time, during his early years in Canada, other difficulties began to emerge that required more and more of his attention. The form that these difficulties would take had been by no means evident in the weeks spent with his predecessor at Spencer Wood in November and December, 1854. Elgin had laboured hard and with considerable success to solve the particular problems of his own administration before departing. He could congratulate himself especially on the introduction of a workable system of Responsible Government in which both French and English had learned to participate. With the ratification of the reciprocity treaty, he had laid the foundations for a period of economic prosperity and had ended the threat of annexation. In the last troubled and long-drawn-out session of the legislature, the closing of which he and Head had looked forward to so impatiently, he had enjoyed his final triumph, the settlement of the ancient and bitter controversies centring around the clergy reserves and seigneurial tenure. Calmer waters had seemed to lie ahead at the time of the new governor general's inauguration. It was only gradually, in the next year or so, that Head became aware that the apparent calm was in reality a brief period of transition from one phase to another of certain basic Canadian problems. The old sectionalism, for example, far from disappearing was about to be revived in bitter disagreement over the choice of a permanent seat of government. Other issues that concerned the Maritimes and the Hudson's Bay Territories as well as Canada were approaching a climax. By the autumn of 1856, when a visit from an old friend, Robert Lowe, helped to bring all of these topics into sharper focus, Head was beginning to perceive the special lines along which his main contributions to Canadian development would be made.

Meanwhile in 1855, apart from the military dangers, all seemed most auspicious in Canada. During a comparatively tranquil session of the legislature in the winter and early spring, and in the course of the numerous social functions that accompanied it, Head had an opportunity to get to know at his leisure the men with whom he would have to deal in the years to come. Bluff old Sir Allan MacNab, partially crippled with gout, had been brought to the fore as prime minister in a Liberal-Conservative coalition after the election of the previous year when there had been a general shifting of the political kaleidoscope as a result of the passing of former disputes and of the politicians associated with them. Just after the New Year, a slight further reconstruction of the executive council had substituted E. P. Taché for A. N. Morin as leader of its French Canadian section. More important was the acceptance at the same time of his first ministerial office by G. E. Cartier, soon to be recognized as one of the greatest spokesmen of French Canada. Supplying the real driving force in the coalition was the forty-year-old attorney general west, John A. Macdonald, already acquiring a friendship for Head that he was to enjoy with no subsequent governor to the same extent.[1] Vigorous in opposition were the great editor of the Toronto *Globe*, George Brown, and his following which included J. S. Macdonald, William Macdougall, and an increasing number of western Liberals. These were associated sometimes, in an uneasy relationship, with a small Rouge group from Lower Canada. Able, idealistic, and aggressive individuals, these Liberals would shortly constitute a serious menace to the Government's continuance in office, but they suffered from the weakness common to Opposition parties in Canada that they could offer no generally acceptable alternative to the Government's slow and circumspect progress down the centre of the political highway. Their cry of "Representation by Population" would win them support in Upper Canada, now beginning to outgrow its partner and changing rapidly therefore its attitude to the provision in the Act of Union that gave each equal representation in the legislature. But what the Liberals might gain in Upper Canada by such a slogan, they were bound to lose in Lower

[1]Joseph Pope, *Memoirs of Sir John Alexander Macdonald*, I, 133. See also Donald Creighton, *John A. Macdonald: The Young Politician*, pp. 216, 242.

Canada. By emphasizing sectional differences, Brown and his friends could not but hasten political deadlock and the dissolution of the union. Head, with the scholar's preference for moderation and the administrator's wish to avoid disruptive controversy, was certain in the long run to sympathize more with his middle-of-the-road coalition Government than with an Opposition of this character. "The triumvirate of the future—Head, Macdonald and Cartier"[2] would be the result in due course. In the session of 1855, however, there was little to indicate to contemporaries how deep these political and sectional divisions would become. There was no need for Head to consider being involved himself in the party disputes of Canada.

After the session ended, Head spent the summer of 1855 becoming familiar with Canada itself. Showing the same keen interest in travelling about and seeing new places that he had while in New Brunswick, he first took a trip up the Saguenay,[3] and then visited various parts of Lower Canada, before going on west as far as London, spending some weeks at Niagara Falls, and finally entering Toronto, to which in the meantime the seat of government had been transferred, on November 2.

Letters to Lewis portray vividly his reaction to what he saw.[4] For example, in one dated from Hamilton on October 20, he wrote:

I write this whilst waiting for breakfast at Sir Allan McNab's—Sir Allan himself being laid up with gout. I have just been going through a round of receptions or public greetings in some of the principal places of Western Canada. Lady Head has been with me whilst the children & governess are left at the Clifton House—a large inn at Niagara Falls. Our House at Toronto is not quite ready.

When I was in Canada in 1850 I don't think there were 20 miles of railway open. Now besides the Grand Trunk (which is to run from Quebec to Toronto and which is complete from Quebec to Montreal) they have the Great Western which traverses the whole peninsula between the great Lakes—a length of 200 miles. We went on the 18th from Niagara to 'London'—dined with people at London & returned yesterday visiting two

[2]Creighton, *Macdonald*, p. 217.
[3]About this "trip to the Saguenay with Sir Edmund and Lady Head," John Ross wrote to Macdonald, September 17, 1855: "The contact with His Excellency will do you good and as you have a great game to play before very long this excursion may have in some measure facilitated that which must come." P.A.C., Macdonald Papers, vol. 260.
[4]For the two letters quoted, see Lewis Papers, Head to Lewis, October 20, 1855 and November 14, 1855.

or three flourishing places in the way. The growth of wheat this year is enormous & the price about 8/ to 10/ (Currency) a bushel whilst 5/ a bushel is acknowledged to be a paying price. The Consequence is that everything is prosperous & in good humour. I have been received everywhere as if the Queen herself had come—and both in this district and on the shores of Lake Ontario—at Kingston, Cobourg, and Hamilton where I had the same thing to go through, the feeling about the war & Sebastopol is quite curious. The enthusiasm in favour of England seems strong in proportion to the disfavour of the Yankees toward the allies.

You would have been much amused with the scenes one has to go through. The making speeches in answer to addresses &c after dinner or luncheon becomes a little tiresome because one has to say exactly the same thing over & over again.

The condition of the Country & the growth of the towns is perfectly *astounding*. The country looks settled & cultivated with good farm houses & buildings of every kind. The uncleared land in this tract is diminishing rapidly—unsold land there is none. London has already 12000 or 14000 inhabitants with substantial brick streets getting up in all directions and shops filled with smart goods. In short much as I had heard of the prosperity of Western Canada I have been surprised at the visible evidence of it. The contrast with the sort of sleepy look which prevades Lower Canada is most remarkable. There everything seems to have been asleep through the French Revolution (Laws & all) and now the state of society among the 'habitants' is a sort of reflection of what it was in France in the time of the Regency. I am perfectly satisfied with my tour so far as my personal position is concerned.

A few weeks later, Head continued his account in another letter to Lewis:

Here we are at Toronto with the workmen in the house and very little power of seeing anybody yet. We went to London in Western Canada & elsewhere & finally made a public entry into Toronto. Nothing could be better than my reception has been. The whole population turned out & they say no Govr Genl was better received. I got into one scrape with the Lower Canadian papers by some incautious words in a speech at Hamilton, but I have set that right again with all but those who are determined to be opposed to everything English. They are a small minority & powerless.

I like what I see of the people here. My boy is here & goes to the grammar school or Upper Canada College as they call it, where the instruction seems tolerable. I am sure that he cannot do less than he did at Harrow.

The speech at Hamilton with its repercussions was the first warning, which for the time being Head failed to take seriously enough, of the dangerous undercurrent of sectional feeling in Canada. Carried away by his impression of the rapid growth in population and wealth of the western regions, he had attributed this at Hamilton to several factors including "the superiority of race from which most of you have sprung," a remark which brought the expected cheers and obviously in its setting and circumstances had no intention of implying any invidious comparison. It was a careless remark to make in Canada, however, and was eagerly seized upon by Rouge newspapers and interpreted as meaning that Head had fallen under the baneful influence of Sir Allan MacNab and other alleged opponents of French rights in Canada. A brief flurry, sufficient nevertheless to attract the attention of the Colonial Office, partially subsided when Head made an explanatory statement on the occasion of his Toronto welcome.[5] But considerable damage had been done and his words were to be recalled and magnified and distorted more than once as sectional bitterness increased.[6] The depth of prejudice that existed in Canada was not at first easy for Head to appreciate with his cosmopolitan outlook, and his upbringing which had given him an unusual familiarity with other languages and countries, particularly France.

Head also failed in the beginning to see the seat-of-government question in its proper light. Following the burning of the parliament buildings in Montreal during the Rebellion Losses riots of 1849, and after considering various possibilities, including the "old plan of adopting Byetown [sic] as the seat of Government,"[7] it had been decided to alternate every four years between the old provincial capitals of Quebec and Toronto. At the time of the transfer to Toronto in 1855, Head was inclined to think that in spite of its obvious disadvantages, a movable capital had much to commend it in Canada. "It has certain benefits which are not the less real because they do not catch the eye so readily as its evils."[8] One, for example, was that during the four years of sessions at Quebec, Upper Canadian members had learned something of the nature of that part of the province and had been freed of some of their prejudices "by living in good fellowship and brotherhood with their French brethren."[9] Similar benefits would no doubt accrue to French members while they lived in Toronto.

[5]P.R.O., C.O. 42/599, Labouchere to Head, confidential, November 30, 1855; Head to Labouchere, confidential, December 22, 1855.

[6]Cf. Sir Joseph Pope, *Correspondence of Sir John Macdonald*, Macdonald to Rose, June 29, 1883.

[7]A. G. Doughty (ed.), *The Elgin-Grey Papers*, II, 470.

[8]P.R.O., C.O. 42/598, Head to Molesworth, August 7, 1855.

[9]P.R.O., C.O. 42/599, Head to Labouchere, December 23, 1855, enclosure.

What Head did not take sufficiently into account in this early stage of his thinking on the subject was that quite apart from the expense and inconvenience arising from the transfer of the capital every four years, the very fact that it was not fixed in one place tended to give the whole arrangement the appearance of being temporary and to keep alive sectional jealousies and suspicions. Toronto feared, on into the spring of 1855, that influence at Quebec might prevent the government from actually leaving, and Quebec was afraid it might never return. Other localities kept hoping that something might after all still occur to give them a chance to become the permanent seat of government. Anxiety and bitterness were bound to grow throughout Canada, city rivalling city and section section, until some one place was chosen, expensive buildings were erected, and the government established there so firmly that no question could be entertained of moving it again.

Head was brought to a truer appreciation of this whole problem by the first serious ministerial crisis of his régime in Canada, which began on the evening of May 10, 1856. The House had been in continuous session for thirty-two hours, and finally a vote was taken on a want-of-confidence amendment challenging the ministry's policy regarding the seat of government. The amendment was defeated 70 to 47, but 6 more Upper Canadian members had voted against the Government than for it. John A. Macdonald and two of his colleagues from Upper Canada took this "defeat" of their section of the party as an excuse for resigning from the ministry. Their purpose, which they had had in mind for some time,[10] was to force their leader, Sir Allan MacNab, out of office and open the way for the more liberal element among the Upper Canadians to come forward under Macdonald.

The problem that faced Head under these circumstances was not an easy one. Quite apart from the ruthlessness of the stratagem employed against MacNab, it had involved the principle that the Government required majority support from both Upper and Lower Canada and not merely from the two combined—the so-called "double majority" principle—and this, lacking any constitutional foundation, could not be officially condoned by Her Majesty's Representative. On the other hand, viewed realistically,

[10]See note 2 above. Also, P.R.O., C.O. 42/604, Head to Labouchere, private and confidential, May 26, 1856.

the resignation of the three ministers was something that Head could not in any case prevent, and if it led to the result they hoped for, it might have the beneficial effect of making the Upper Canadian section of the ministry stronger and more popular. Head disapproved their method, but recognized their aim to be sound, and resolved to further it in so far as he could without himself departing from the path of strict rectitude.

The course he took, therefore, was first to urge the three ministers to reconsider their decision, pointing out that the grounds they had given for it were not constitutionally valid. When they remained adamant, he made his own position clear in a written memorandum to MacNab:

His Excellency desires it to be understood by the whole Council that he considers the mere fact of an adverse vote in one section of the Province, whether Upper or Lower, as no constitutional reason for resigning Office. What His Excellency looks to, is the confidence or want of confidence in a ministry of the Legislative Assembly as a whole representing the people of the United Province of Canada.

At the same time, he stated that in his opinion it would be impossible to replace Macdonald and his friends without a complete reconstruction of the Government. Nor could he consent to a dissolution to test the confidence of the country in "the remaining portion of the Government, or in any modification of it to be made on the spur of the moment." He thus definitely forestalled any possible attempt of MacNab to cling futilely to office.[11]

The final outcome was the retirement of MacNab and the formation of the Taché-Macdonald Government which was able to complete the session. Although the crisis had had its unpleasant features, it had produced certain results which Head was inclined to look upon with satisfaction. Summing up immediately afterwards in a letter to Lewis, Head wrote:

. . . I have had to steer very carefully in order to avoid interrupting all the ordinary business by a dissolution—a movement under such circumstances of a very mischievous character.

On the whole I have escaped with less personal abuse than could be expected. . . . The peculiarity of the matter was that although the Gov^t had a fair majority on the whole, yet there was a majority of Upper Canada members against them. Three members of the Council made this a *pretext* for resigning—Baldwin having formerly done the same thing under different circumstances.

The real object of these Gentlemen was to get rid of Sir Allan McNab

11P.R.O., C.O. 42/604, Head to Labouchere, May 26, 1856, enclosure A.

who though laid up in bed for two months consecutively would not relieve them by resigning voluntarily. If I had turned him out by any action of my own he would have got up a quarrel between me & the whole Conservative party. I sat still. These three gentlemen resigned—and I acted in such a manner as to make their resignation a break up of the Government—whilst I protested strongly against the absurdity in *one* legislature of requiring *two* majorities. In fact it is ignoring the Union. This obnoxious dictum has now been repudiated by the Gov^t as remodelled & rejected by the House, though it is avowed & rightly that it would not do to impose measures *continuously* & *systematically* on Upper or Lower Canada by the voice of a majority of the other half. You may judge how the difficulty of my position has been complicated by this Quasi-federal question which I am bound to treat as theoretically absurd, though I know full well that in practice it must be looked to. However at the present moment I have a Gov^t consisting of eight of the old Council with two new ones who will be able to finish the session. They only got a majority of five the other day but they have done what I wanted in staying in notwithstanding a sectional majority against them. How far this is consistent with the former conduct of some of them it is for them to think: my business is to adhere to the sound principle of a majority of the House as *one* House—not *two*— and to get the business done.[12]

The impression left on Head's mind by the events of this crisis was twofold. In the first place, he was convinced by it that the time had come for settling permanently the seat-of-government question. His earlier belief that there were advantages in alternating between Quebec and Toronto was overwhelmed by proof of the greater disadvantages involved, and he informed the new premier immediately that he thought the Government would be wise "to take a decided course on the seat of Govt question, either by selecting a place themselves, or voting the money for the Crown to expend where it pleased."[13] Some time later, explaining his reasons for this new view to Labouchere, Head wrote:

To keep it open is to maintain in full flow a constant source of local bitterness and sectional animosity which by a little management can always be turned against the government of the day. . . . If the Province of Canada is to remain one, it is essential that its Seat of Government should be fixed and recognized by all."[14]

Secondly, the prominence given to the "double majority"

[12]Lewis Papers, Head to Lewis, June 9, 1856. See also Creighton, *Macdonald*, pp. 230 ff.
[13]P.R.O., C.O. 42/604, Head to Labouchere, private and confidential, May 26, 1856.
[14]P.R.O., C.O. 42/609, Head to Labouchere, March 28, 1857.

principle, and the indisputable fact that party lines were beginning to assume a sectional character, made it clear to Head how much more deep-seated than he had realized was the division between Upper and Lower Canada. It was this division that had caused the crisis just past, and it would lead to others still more serious in the future unless some remedy were found. For the moment, the best remedy seemed to lie in the support of a moderate government of "conservative progress" such as the one that had emerged under the leadership of Taché and Macdonald.[15] In a final confidential summing-up, Head wrote to Labouchere:

Should the Session terminate smoothly, I hope that the constituency of Upper Canada . . . will support a middle party consisting neither of ultra liberals nor of 'Tories', and that the majority of the Lower Canadian members will rally round a Council formed on these principles. At any rate our present course opens the fairest chance of a tranquil administration of the Govt. of Canada.[16]

It was only a few months after this ministerial crisis, and at the time when the dangers of American aggression were just beginning to lessen with the arrival of veteran British regiments from the Crimea, that Head received a very interesting visitor at Toronto and had conversations with him that were to lead to far-reaching results. This was Robert Lowe, later Viscount Sherbrooke, who was then vice-president of the Board of Trade in the Palmerston Government. Lowe had passed through Toronto first in mid-August, 1856, on a combined business and pleasure tour of the United States and Canada in company with Captain Douglas Galton, the British government's leading railway expert. Head had been away at the time, but wrote to Lowe later at New York and persuaded him to return for a brief visit. In

[15]P.R.O., C.O. 42/604, Head to Labouchere, private and confidential, May 26, 1856.

[16]P.R.O., C.O. 42/604, Head to Labouchere, separate and confidential, May 31, 1856. Lewis's comment on this crisis is worth noting: "I was much interested in reading your official and private letters about your ministerial crisis which were sent around to the Cabinet. You were doubtless right in remaining passive, and throwing the responsibility upon the ministers and the Assembly. It seems to me that half the mistakes which people make in politics arise from doing too much. . . . The imperfect fusion of the provinces and the necessity for a double majority is an evil. . . . To a certain extent we have it at home. We are often told that an Irish measure was carried against a majority of the Irish members . . . a measure affecting the manufacturers against a majority of the manufacturing members, and so on." Lewis, *Letters*, pp. 313–14.

Toronto, the two old Oxford friends enjoyed lengthy discussions on a wide variety of subjects, ranging all the way from the sagas of Iceland, in which both were keenly interested, to matters of an immediate and practical nature such as the advantages of choosing Ottawa as the permanent capital of Canada—the whole interspersed with a wealth of classical allusion that greatly impressed Galton.[17]

Lowe was a very clever and unusual man and his mental outlook tended to complement that of Head, as did also his very different background of knowledge and experience with regard to British North America. An albino, with a delicate physique, weak eyesight, and a quick temper, Lowe had been accustomed all his life to overcoming obstacles apparently insurmountable. His clear, alert mind was always ready to take up a new problem, and he had the courage to push through to a conclusion, no matter how visionary it might seem. Head's outlook was sufficiently similar for him to be able to respect that of Lowe, but it contained a greater admixture of caution and less fire. Head was quite as willing to explore a new idea as was Lowe, but he was inclined to do so with scholarly thoroughness rather than intuitive brilliance. And when it came to North American problems, Lowe, whose colonial experience was confined to Australia, was familiar only with some of their more general aspects, except in the case of a few specific matters that were of chief concern to the British Government at the moment. Even in these, however, his knowledge was bound to be superficial when compared with Head's background of study and long administrative experience.

In these circumstances, it is not surprising that it was Lowe who put forward the very comprehensive—and impractical—proposal that was to give these conversations some significance in the history of Canada. He suggested "that the Government of Canada should construct, at the cost of the province, a line of railway (which the Imperial Government seems very anxious to have opened) from Quebec to Halifax, and that as compensation for this outlay, Rupert's Land should be annexed to Canada."[18] What Lowe had in mind was a joint solution for the two problems that he knew were of greatest current interest to the

---

[17]A. Patchett Martin, *The Right Hon. Robert Lowe, Viscount Sherbrooke*, II, 131–34; D. G. G. Kerr, "Edmund Head, Robert Lowe, and Confederation," *Canadian Historical Review*, XX (1939), 409–20.

[18]H.B. Co., A 7/2, Simpson to Shepherd, confidential, November 15, 1856.

Imperial Government so far as British North America was concerned: the defence of Canada and the government of the Hudson's Bay Territories.

The problem of defence was bound to cast its shadow over any discussion of North American affairs in 1856, and the difficulty experienced in sending arms overland through New Brunswick the previous winter had proved once again the vital necessity for military purposes of all-year-round communication by means of a railway through British territory between Canada and the seaboard. This was a matter with which Head, in particular, had long been concerned, and he and Lowe were in perfect agreement as to its significance.

The Hudson's Bay Company problem on the other hand was one that had not hitherto attracted Head's special attention. By its charter of 1670, the company owned and governed all lands drained by waters flowing into Hudson's Bay. These were commonly known as Rupert's Land and included the only settlement to be established in the period of company rule, that at the Red River. In 1821, the company had received in addition, by licence, the right to the exclusive trade and government—but not the title to the land—in what came to be known as the North West Territory, the region between the chartered territory and the Rocky Mountains. This licence, granted originally for twenty-one years, had been renewed in 1838 for another twenty-one. Further rights of the Hudson's Bay Company at various periods on the Pacific coast need not be considered here.

In the 1850's, the westward advance of settlement across the continent was placing a triple pressure upon the Hudson's Bay Company. In the first place, the expansion of American population in the middle west brought the threat of encroachment by individuals, or possibly an eventual attack by the government, on the company's comparatively empty lands north of an imaginary and not yet fully explored boundary line. Secondly, the growth of the Red River Settlement itself, and its increasing contact with the outside world, made it more restive under company rule; however admirably the company had managed an almost uninhabited wilderness, it could not be expected to govern satisfactorily areas populated by nineteenth-century North Americans. And finally, there was Canada, approaching the end of its own ungranted lands and stirred by the example of the United States to turn its eyes westward to the great prairies

owned by the Hudson's Bay Company. It was not very difficult
in the 1850's to see that under these circumstances the days of
government by the company, in parts at least of its vast
territories, were numbered: what was puzzling was to find a
satisfactory alternative to its rule.

It had been with this in mind that Lowe had suggested the
annexation of Rupert's Land to Canada. By this means a government could be provided that would meet the wishes of the inhabitants of the Red River Settlement, while at the same time
Canadian agitation for expansion westward could be satisfied
and American threats frustrated. Lowe happened, moreover, to
know that the issue he had raised was of some immediate
importance. Before leaving England, he had heard that old
"Bear" Ellice of the Hudson's Bay Company had approached
Labouchere on the subject of the renewal of the North West
Territory licence, due to expire in 1859. In the course of a preliminary exchange of views, the alternative had been mentioned
of annexing all of the territories to Canada so that they would
not fall into American hands when the grip of the company
began to weaken. Lowe himself, and so far as he knew, the
majority of the cabinet, were anxious for this possibility to be
seriously explored.[19]

Head's reaction when Lowe proposed that Canada build the
Halifax and Quebec Railway and receive Rupert's Land as compensation was one of considerable scepticism. Such a scheme
would be a long step toward the solution of defence and Hudson's Bay problems. It would no doubt be welcomed by Britain
because it would throw the whole responsibility on Canada. But
would the Canadian government be willing or able to accept this
responsibility, even though it carried with it the glory of a very
large accession of territory? Head feared the answer would have
to be in the negative. The annexation of Rupert's Land, far from
offering compensation for the money to be spent on the railway,
might itself impose too great a burden on Canada for her government to bear. According to the Hudson's Bay Company solicitor,
John Rose, to whom Head mentioned these conversations a few
weeks later, "he thought it woud add to the importance and
future prosperity of Canada to obtain this large accession of
territory, but that the difficulty which presented itself to his
mind was how, in its present condition, they were to provide for

[19]H.B. Co., A 7/2, Simpson to Shepherd, confidential, September 27, 1856.

the Government of so extensive and remote a territory difficult of access from every side."[20]

Nevertheless, although he could not accept Lowe's plan as immediately feasible, Head had found it a most stimulating topic for discussion with a man of Lowe's calibre. This was true also of the other issues that they went over together such as sectionalism and a seat of government in Canada, and the problems of Responsible Government in the Maritime Provinces. Moreover, he had learned from Lowe that far-reaching decisions on some at least of these were on the point of being made in Britain. A few days after Lowe's departure, therefore, he wrote privately and confidentially to Labouchere as follows:

Mr. Robert Lowe has been here, and I have had much pleasure in seeing him even for so short a time as he was enabled to spare us. During that time short as it was, conversations with him have suggested to me the propriety of my communicating with you confidentially on one or two subjects of great importance to the future prospects of British North America.

These subjects are the position and prospects of the 'Lower Colonies' as they are called—that is to say, New Brunswick, Nova Scotia, and P. E. Island—and the relation of the Hudson's Bay Territory to the other British possessions on this continent as well as the Crown of England.

Both of these—more especially the former—have long occupied my thoughts—but I hope you will understand two things distinctly.

First. Mr. Lowe did not advise or suggest that I should address you on the subject. I alone am responsible for taking this liberty.

Secondly. I have no wish to thrust on you or the Queen's Government advice which is not asked for or desired. Nor do I profess to have any scheme 'ready cut and dried' to meet the difficulties belonging to either subject. If it is your wish that I should do my best to form a definite opinion on one or other of these matters, I will readily give my attention to them, and embody in a confidential memorandum of some kind the result of such consideration. . . .

If it shall be H.M.'s pleasure that I remain in Canada another year I could easily after next Session (if all is peaceful and quiet) visit England. Indeed at all events I should probably ask leave to do so on my own account as it will be five years since I was at home.

Should you wish me to inform myself on the subjects referred to in this letter, and to make up my opinion (valeat quantum) upon them, I will readily do so, and communicate the results of my consideration either by word of mouth or on paper as circumstances may permit, and the Government desire that I should do so.[21]

[20]H.B. Co., A 7/2, Simpson to Shepherd, confidential, November 15, 1856.
[21]P.A.C., G 206, Head to Labouchere, private and confidential, September 3, 1856.

It was this offer, made by Head as a result of his conversations with Lowe, which, on being immediately accepted at the Colonial Office, led to his writing during the following winter two most important memoranda, one on Maritime union, the other on the Hudson's Bay Territories. These, and a third recommending Ottawa as the capital of Canada, which he prepared in the spring, are among his most important achievements in long-range planning for British North America.

EIGHT

Advice on Basic Problems

H EAD spent much time during the winter months of 1856–57 in Toronto studying the basic British North American problems he had discussed with Lowe. So far as the Hudson's Bay question was concerned, he pored over Blue Books and other documents and maps, forwarded at his request from the Colonial Office; and he kept in close touch as well, by private letters and conversations and through official and public channels, with important new developments that were currently taking place.[1] These developments must be considered somewhat fully because they mark the beginning of the long negotiations for the transfer of the Hudson's Bay Territories to Canada which Head as governor of the company was to bring to the verge of completion just before his death some twelve years later.

The possibility of the Territories being transferred to Canada had already been mentioned in official circles before Lowe's visit to Canada, as Head had learned from Lowe himself. This had been in the summer of 1856 when Ellice had put out his preliminary feelers with regard to the renewal of the licence for exclusive trade in the North West. The company's position when this matter was raised was a delicate one. Sir George Simpson, the governor of Rupert's Land, writing from Lachine on the very day that Lowe had sailed from England, had asked Governor Shepherd, "whether it might not be advisable to make a merit of necessity," and surrender not only the licence but the charter as well. The latter involved the company in increasingly heavy responsibilities while the exclusive trading rights were in practice almost nullified by the activities of American adventurers and their half-breed allies. Indeed these rights were in a sense a

---

[1]P.A.C., G 206, Head to Labouchere, private and confidential, September 3, 1856; Lewis, *Letters*, Lewis to Head, November 5, 1856: "I send you a list of works upon the Hudson's Bay Company, copied from the catalogue of the Colonial Office. You will probably be able to select from it what you want."

drawback because in *laissez-faire* England they subjected the company to odium as a monopolist. Why not surrender the charter, Simpson concluded, "on receiving compensation on some such basis as was allowed to the East India Company"?[2] London officials preferred the less drastic course of applying for a renewal of the licence and asking for military support from Britain for the preservation of law and order, but Simpson adhered to his view that the "loss of the Charter could not materially add to the difficulties of our present position."[3]

Unofficial discussions which continued through September and October by means of private letters and conversations between Labouchere and Ellice made clear the official attitude that each side would eventually adopt. The company, Ellice pointed out, had governed the Territories with great skill and success for the past thirty years since its amalgamation with the old North West Company. It was willing to continue to do so if it received reasonable support. Otherwise, it would be prepared to dispose of its rights for "a million of money." Reminding Labouchere of the disorders of the old days of unrestrained rivalry between the Hudson's Bay and Montreal traders, Ellice warned against letting the company be prematurely destroyed in the meantime.

Before you lay the train, or permit Sir E. Head to lay the train, which may set fire to this instrument that has worked so well, both for the governors and the governed, be very sure that you see your way clear to some better substitute. . . . I would advise the greatest caution in writing to Head. . . . He should be told that the Government had no indisposition to the Provincial Government acquiring the rights and interests of the Hudson's Bay Company, on the condition that arrangements should be made for an equally satisfactory state of Government in the territory, and that they should bear the expence of it. But that if the responsibility was still to be thrown on this country of maintaining peace and order there, they might still be obliged, even with all the objections they entertained to the principle of monopoly, to consent to the renewal of the License of exclusive trade as the least evil before them. . . . In the meantime you desired the opinion of the Canadian Council, not with respect to the abolition of the monopoly alone, but with respect to some practicable scheme of Government for the Hudson's Bay Territory.[4]

This was sound advice and it went to the root of the problem not only as it appeared to the company but as it appeared also to

[2]H.B. Co., A 7/2, Simpson to Shepherd, confidential, October 2, 1856.
[3]H.B. Co., A 7/2, Shepherd to Simpson, private, September 1, 1856; Simpson to Shepherd, confidential, September 27, 1856.
[4]H.B. Co., A 7/2, Ellice to Labouchere, September 30, 1856.

responsible members of the British and Canadian Governments. Each party had its own interests to serve, but all three would gladly have found some "better substitute" for the company's rule—and all three realized how difficult it was to do so. Labouchere made it clear in his answer to Ellice that he, for one, understood the hazards of making any change: "You cannot suppose that I have any wish wantonly to stir these embarrassing questions—on the other hand sometimes difficulties are avoided by looking forward betimes." He went on to suggest that some portions of the Territories adjacent to Canada might be found fit for settlement and might be transferred to that colony by equitable arrangement. "I have merely written to Head to say that I want to be kept informed of any thing that takes place on this question, & that I also will myself look into it."[5]

A degree of mutual understanding between the company and the Colonial Office having thus been achieved, formal negotiations began in November, 1856, when a deputation from the company consisting of the governor and two of the leading directors waited on Labouchere at the Colonial Office. They were received in a friendly spirit, but Labouchere pointed out that as theirs was the only remaining trade monopoly, parliament and the country generally would expect a full inquiry before the licence was renewed. He proposed, therefore, to bring forward at an early date in the coming session a motion to appoint a select committee of investigation. Before it, both Canada and the Hudson's Bay Company might be represented by witnesses, and the resulting evidence could be used by the Government as the basis for its final decision.[6]

When, shortly afterwards, Labouchere notified the Canadian Government of these intentions,[7] that Government became suddenly more conscious of the awkwardness of its position. Popular agitation in Canada, provoked to a considerable extent for political or private reasons, had created in the public mind an impression of the company and its territories that was not wholly true. It was thought that the Hudson's Bay Territories were of inestimable value and offered boundless possibilities for settlement and trade, and perhaps even for mining. And the whole

---

[5]P.A.C., Ellice Papers, Labouchere to Ellice, October 5, 1856.
[6]H.B. Co., A 7/2, Shepherd to Simpson, private and confidential, November 21, 1856.
[7]P.R.O., C.O. 42/605, Labouchere to Head, December 4, 1856.

southern portion as far as the Pacific, some believed, belonged by right to Canada and had done so ever since the days of the French and the Montreal traders and explorers.[8] It had been wrongfully usurped by a monopolistic and tyrannous company which had used this large section of the continent for its own purposes for all of these years with no consideration for the interests of the Empire as a whole or for the wretched inhabitants of the one populated district, the Red River Settlement. So widespread were views such as these that no Canadian Government could hope to survive if it showed any unwillingness to take over the Hudson's Bay Territories, whatever fears its more responsible members might have that these rich but vast and distant lands would prove difficult and expensive to exploit and govern. In these rather embarrassing circumstances, the expressions of joy with which the Canadian executive council greeted Labouchere's announcement of an inquiry have a hollow ring, and their answer contained in a minute dated January 17, 1857, is understandably vague despite the large number of emphatic words used: "The general feeling here is strongly that the Western Boundary of Canada extends to the Pacific Ocean. . . . Situated as Canada is, she necessarily has an immediate interest in every portion of British North America, and the question of the jurisdiction and Title claimed by the Hudson's Bay Company is to her of paramount importance."[9]

Meanwhile, ever since Lowe's visit in the late summer of 1856, Head had been carefully studying the whole background of Hudson's Bay affairs. At that time he had professed to have "no *formed* opinions" on the subject, except that he could not agree with those who insisted that Canada had "an inherent right" to share in the future spoils of the Hudson's Bay Company. "We do not, as I have told them, now govern properly the territory belonging to Canada." Head was inclined to think that instead the formation of separate colonies would be necessary.

I have an impression but it is a very vague one that if ever this territory is taken in hand by the English Government the extreme western portion of it will have to be settled and ruled from Vancouver's Island which is accessible to our Navy and open to the important commerce of the Pacific. Even then, I conceive that between the western limit of Canada and the

[8]A. S. Morton, *A History of the Canadian West to 1870–71,* p. 829.
[9]P.R.O., C.O. 42/609, Head to Labouchere, January 17, 1857, enclosure.

Government of Vancouver's Island there would have to be some district under a Governor or Lieut. Governor of its own.[10]

The reason for Head's belief that separate colonies would be necessary and for his doubts about the feasibility of annexation to Canada was that he could not at that time see how Canada could govern "so extensive and remote a territory difficult of access from every side."[11] More careful consideration, after a thorough examination of all available information, changed Head's first impressions only to the extent that he was able to visualize an eventual solution for this problem of government. Accordingly, his final conclusions, sent to Labouchere on March 2, 1857, took the form of a confidential memorandum containing "Heads of a bill for the Formation of a separate province out of the Hudson's Bay Territory to be ultimately annexed to Canada."[12]

In this outline "bill" and in "notes" opposite each article, Head suggested the creation of a "separate province" to be removed from the company's jurisdiction and to extend from the Rocky Mountains to the Canadian frontier—wherever that might be (possibly in the vicinity of Lake Nipigon)—and from the north branch of the Saskatchewan to the American border. It would, therefore, "include all the tract west of Lake Superior likely to be settled or occupied from Canada." The region west of the Rockies "according to my view would be best dealt with from Vancouver's Island as the seat of Government." The new central province might be called either Saskatchewan or Manitoba. " 'Manitoba' is the most easily pronounced and spelt—but may be thought *ill-omened* as I believe it means 'Evil Spirit.' " The capital would, of course, be at the Red River Settlement. Ultimately, following an address to the Queen from both Houses of the Canadian parliament stating Canada's readiness to establish a fair and adequate system of government in the new province, the whole, or from time to time parts of it, might be annexed to Canada.

[10]P.A.C., G 206, Head to Labouchere, private and confidential, September 3, 1856.
[11]H.B. Co., A 7/2, Simpson to Shepherd, confidential, November 15, 1856. As late as January, 1857, Head was reported to see "difficulties and objections" in the way of annexation. See H.B. Co., A 7/2, Simpson to Shepherd, private, January 6, 1857.
[12]P.A.C., G 180B, Confidential Memorandum, March 2, 1857.

The Canadians clearly could not complain if they got the territory so soon as they asked for it and professed their readiness to receive it and govern it. To thrust it upon them at once would be imprudent. If it were offered clamour might oblige the Government here to take the responsibility and do the best they could. Justice however would not be done to the territory by this premature occupation.

For the meantime, in order to provide an easy transition to ultimate annexation, Head proposed a most ingenious form of government for the territory, one which if it had been adopted might have prevented the damaging events of 1869. He suggested that the new province be governed under a commission issued to the governor general of Canada, but that there also be a lieutenant governor appointed by the Crown and resident at the Red River. The lieutenant governor would conduct his correspondence with the Colonial Office through the governor general and would be assisted by a small council composed of one member named by the Hudson's Bay Company, one-half of the others appointed by the governor general on the advice of his Canadian ministers, and the rest elected by the freeholders living within thirty miles of the Red River. The rights of the company and of the inhabitants, and "the revisionary interest" held by Canada, would thus all be safeguarded. The Canadian members of the territorial council "would be supposed always to keep an eye on the future union with Canada . . . [and they] would afterwards be well acquainted with all the particulars of the territory when it was annexed. By changing these men occasionally—supposing the intermediate state to last ten years— eight or ten persons at least might be so qualified to discuss the interests of Saskatchewan from personal knowledge of its affairs." At the same time, the Canadian parliament might at its leisure begin "to legislate by anticipation," creating the necessary legal and administrative machinery for the future government of the province—provided always that such legislation should take effect only when the whole or a part was annexed.

To meet the already existing danger of American encroachment, Head had two suggestions to make. One was that the lieutenant governor should be given immediate power to organize a militia. "This would be one of the first things to be done— unless (*which at first would be far better*) a regiment of irregular mounted rifles in the Queen's service were set on foot. Land might be part of the consideration for their military services. Men would emigrate thither on these terms and they would be paid only when called out for drill or service—say three months in a year." In the second place, ordinary settlement by British subjects should also be encouraged as rapidly as possible in order to help forestall the Americans. With this object in mind Head felt it might be unwise to wait until Canada was ready to absorb the whole territory and he had therefore included in his scheme a provision which would make possible the annexation of it in portions if deemed desirable at the time. This would "allow certain portions along the frontier to be settled first—indeed tracts of (say) 25 miles square ought as soon as possible to be set out and surveyed along the whole frontier line to be sold very low or given to *British subjects* willing to settle on them."

Head touched but lightly, in concluding his memorandum, on what arrangement might be made with the Hudson's Bay Company for giving up its rights. That would depend on the report of the select committee and on the negotiations that would follow it in London. What he foresaw as a possibility was that the company would abandon its right of property in the whole soil of the region and its exclusive trading privileges. It might retain a reasonable amount of land, particularly around its posts, and could, of course, continue to trade like anyone else. The question of compensation, Head did not mention at all, that being for the moment beyond his purview.

The second memorandum that Head was engaged in writing during the winter of 1856–57 was on the subject of British North American union. In preparing it, he entered into correspondence with the lieutenant governors of the other provinces,[13] and there is evidence to suggest that he discussed the broad implications of all the various British North American problems with which it was concerned with a number of the leading public men of Canada.[14] His memorandum was based primarily, however, on his own background of study and thought going back to the time of his first arrival in New Brunswick. His most important statements on union in that earlier period had been made in his memorandum to Lord Grey in 1851 and his despatch to Sir John

[13]E.g., P.R.O., C.O. 188/131, Sutton to Lytton, private and confidential, October 2, 1858.
[14]E.g., H.B. Co., A 7/2, Simpson to Shepherd, November 15, 1856, and January 9, 1857.

Pakington in 1852. At that time, he had stressed the need for a federal union of all the British North American colonies. Individually, they seemed very small to stand alone when their economic and political ties with the mother country were being loosened, and when the hegemony of the United States throughout the whole North American continent was rapidly becoming more manifest. Some of the colonies indeed seemed hardly large enough for the effective functioning of parliamentary or Responsible Government.[15]

Even while in New Brunswick, however, Head had begun to realize that Canada's position might be exceptional, that Canadians had begun to feel a sense of "their own progress and their own self-importance"[16] and were ready to say: " 'We are too great a people to be tied on to any body's tail.' "[17] When he travelled through Canada again in 1855 as its new governor general, one of the things that impressed him most was its tremendous growth in population and prosperity since his first visit five years before. And its loyalty to Britain, then engaged in the Crimean War, seemed most striking. "One might almost suppose the sympathy of the Canadian people with the cause of England to be more eagerly shown on account of the adverse feeling which is said to prevail in the United States."[18]

In these circumstances, and in his new Canadian environment, Head's interest in union had remained temporarily in abeyance. When the matter was drawn to his attention, as in a paper by a Mr. James Anderson which was referred to him at the beginning of 1856, he wrote quite non-committally to Labouchere:

There are few persons to whose minds this scheme has not presented itself in some shape or other. I have myself reflected on it a great deal, and I cannot say that the difficulties surrounding it have diminished in proportion to the consideration which I have given it.

If it is your wish, Sir, I am prepared to discuss the various schemes of this character, but I scarcely think that without the expression of such a wish on your part, I should be justified in appending a full and elaborate commentary to Mr. Anderson's paper. Many of the points involved in such

[15]See above, chap. v.
[16]P.R.O., C.O. 188/117, Head to Pakington, separate and confidential, December 14, 1852.
[17]Lewis Papers, Head to Lewis, December 29, 1853.
[18]P.A.C., G 204, Head to Molesworth, October 22, 1855.

a question could only be satisfactorily discussed in personal communication between parties well acquainted with the facts.[19]

Perhaps in this last sentence there is some hint of a reviving interest on Head's part in the question of confederation, and this is given colour by the fact that Head is known to have intended to ask for leave of absence to visit England in the summer of 1856.[20] He may have had in mind "personal communication" with Labouchere at that time.[21] Certainly when the state of Anglo-American relations made it impossible for him to leave his post in Canada that year, Head seized eagerly the opportunity for "personal communication" with another member of the British Government, Robert Lowe. There is no evidence beyond the fact that Lowe proposed the annexation of the Hudson's Bay Territories to Canada, and associated this with the building of the Halifax and Quebec Railway, to show how their conversation happened to turn to the subject of confederation, or what they said to each other about it.

It may be that Lowe's proposal naturally suggested a confederation of British North America that would eventually include the Hudson's Bay Territories as well as Canada and the Maritimes. Or possibly Head's mind had begun to toy with this idea again because of his concern with the defence problem which had been most urgent during the previous year and was still critical. The military danger had clearly emphasized once more the fact that the route through the Maritimes constituted a vital link between Canada and the mother country. An obvious weakness in this link was lack of the railway which Lowe was anxious to have built. Head's subtle mind may have perceived another weakness even more dangerous and more difficult to remedy: the possible break-down of Responsible Government in New Brunswick, and troubles there that might lead to that province ceasing to be a link of empire altogether, and being annexed instead to the United States.

Head had continued to correspond with Manners Sutton and probably with other friends in New Brunswick. The public press

[19]P.R.O., C.O. 42/603, Head to Labouchere, January 26, 1856.
[20]P.A.C., G 221A, Head to Labouchere, separate and confidential, March 23, 1857.
[21]This phrase seems to stand out and to have some such significance as this. It puzzled Merivale at the time, but possibly only because he read "explanation" for "communication." (See minutes on the despatch.)

alone, however, would have been sufficient to inform him that controversy of a serious nature had arisen there after the coming into effect of a prohibition law at the beginning of 1856. Indeed, the disorders and clamour of the early months of the year, and the obstinacy of the Government, which continued to try to enforce the measure, had been such as to lead Manners Sutton to dissolve the assembly contrary to the advice of his executive council, and in the election which followed in July, to conduct what amounted to a "governor's campaign" against his former ministers. He had been temporarily successful in this, but it must have seemed to Head in August that the difficulties that he himself had experienced in connection with the functioning of Responsible Government in New Brunswick, far from dying out, were becoming more critical. For many years he had been fearful that New Brunswick might be too small to stand alone in the new self-governing Empire that was emerging. Might not the situation in which Manners Sutton found himself, of more open involvement in New Brunswick politics than even Head had found necessary, be indicative of an approaching collapse? In which event, might New Brunswick not turn, as had been threatened in 1849, to the solution of annexation? How could Canada be defended if this link with the mother country, imperfect as it was without the railway, should be completely broken? Was it possible, however, that this disaster which might result in the loss of all of the colonies, could be averted by bringing New Brunswick into a larger British North American union of some sort before it was too late?

Questions such as these may well have been occupying a prominent place in Head's thoughts at the time of his conversations with Lowe. It is certain at any rate that he discussed thoroughly with Lowe, in this or in some other connection, the whole subject of confederation, because that, and in particular Maritime union, was one of the two topics "of great importance to the future prospects of British North America" which Head offered, as a result of Lowe's visit, to study and report on to the colonial secretary.

Head's views on confederation, by the fall of 1856, were different in one important respect from those that he had held earlier in New Brunswick. He made this clear in the letter that he wrote to Labouchere immediately after Lowe's departure:

I may say shortly that I do not now believe in the practicability of the federal or legislative Union of Canada with the three 'Lower Colonies'. I once thought differently but further knowledge and experience have changed my views. I believe however that it would be possible with great advantage to all parties concerned, to unite under one Government, Nova Scotia, Prince Edward's Island, and New Brunswick. . . . Each of these Colonies, certainly two of the three, are very small for 'Responsible Government'. The field of ambition to able men is very limited. It is difficult to find materials for forming any administration, and impossible to supply men fit for the Government on the one hand, and the Opposition on the other. Public opinion has a narrow range and is worth very little in itself. Its average quality is in the inverse ratio of the number of the population. New Brunswick which of course I know best, seems to make little progress. Hemmed in between Canada and Nova Scotia it will, I fear, get into a semi-torpid condition. The Union of the three Colonies would remedy or alleviate many of these evils and it would, I conceive, add much to the weight and prestige of England on the North American continent.[22]

The significant difference between this and earlier expressions by Head of his opinions on confederation was that he did not now believe in the "practicability" of union between Canada and the Maritimes. It is not certain that he had ceased altogether to believe in the desirability of such a union, but he was inclined to think that under the existing circumstances the objectives he had in mind might be achieved satisfactorily, and much more easily, in the smaller scheme which he now advocated.

As he went on to study the subject more thoroughly during the winter, and obtained the views of the Maritime lieutenant governors and others, this impression was confirmed. Indeed it was strengthened to the point of making him definitely opposed on practical grounds to the wider union. In the memorandum which he prepared for Labouchere and delivered to him personally when in England the following summer,[23]

[22]P.A.C., G 206, Head to Labouchere, private and confidential, September 3, 1856.

[23]See Alice B. Stewart, "Sir Edmund Head's Memorandum of 1857 on Maritime Union: A Lost Confederation Document," *Canadian Historical Review*, XXVI (1945), 406–19. Miss Stewart tells the chequered history of this memorandum and prints an almost complete copy of it which she discovered in the Canadian Archives. What is clearly the copy sent privately to Merivale early in 1860 has now been discovered in the Public Record Office (C.O. 537/137). It is signed by Head, and inscribed on the back in Pennefather's handwriting: "Written in 1857." The last lines, missing in Miss Stewart's copy, are: " . . . memorandum except that of suggesting what appears to me the readiest remedy for the sort

Head explained fully his reasons for this change from the stand that he had taken earlier in New Brunswick:

More experience in Colonial Government, and especially a knowledge of Canada more accurate than I then possessed have led me to a different conclusion. . . . With regard to a federal government of any kind with functions limited to particular subjects, the interests common to all the colonies are too few, and the knowledge of one another's wants existing in each is too scanty to give such a government the matter for constant or beneficial action. Such a body would have little which it could do properly, and having little to do would very probably make subjects for itself out of grievances against England. It would be powerless for good but effective for mischief. I think this view of the case is greatly strengthened by the obvious fact that the rapid growth of Canada is *westward*; that is to say, precisely in the direction which must from day to day present and develop fewer points of interest common to Canada and the Lower Colonies.

This fact, I repeat, was not apparent at all, or, at any rate, was not known to me at the time of my believing in the expediency of uniting all the British North American Colonies. It is a fact which appears decisive against any scheme of the kind including Canada as now constituted. I need not say that the separation of the St. Lawrence from the Lakes is an alternative not to be thought of for a moment.

The arguments against British North American federation did not apply to a union of the three Maritimes provinces by themselves: "I confess I think that the common interests of these three colonies, so far as I understand them, and the common character of their pursuits and position are such as to favour a Legislative Union of these three only. The size of one Province embracing these three would not be enormous, and the form would be compact."

Although he strongly favoured Maritime union, and was opposed to any scheme "including Canada as now constituted," Head was far from taking the point of view of Manners Sutton that these were two mutually exclusive alternatives. Further on in this same memorandum of 1857, he remarked of Maritime

---

of stagnant state of petty misgovernment likely to overspread New Brunswick and Prince Edward Island. Of Nova Scotia, as I have said, I know little practically." Minutes on a separate sheet of paper show that the memorandum was sent by Merivale, now transferred to the India Office, to Fortescue, the parliamentary under-secretary for the colonies, on February 17, 1860. The latter's comment was: "This is a very able & interesting paper. Sir E. Head's opinions of Parliamentary Government for small communities are very much those of Lord Grey, expressed in his book on Parliamentary Reform." Newcastle added: "I have read this with great interest."

union: "All would see their interest in its adoption. Even those who look to a more extensive union of the North American colonies might conceive it to be a stepping stone towards that end." A year later, therefore, when it began to appear that Canada might not long remain constituted as she was, that a "separation of the St. Lawrence from the Lakes" might be the result of bitter sectional controversy, Head had no difficulty in switching from one alternative to the other and deciding that it might not be possible for the larger union to wait upon the completion of the smaller. His opinions, founded on a few basic principles and not attached to any one plan of action, were always much more flexible than those of Manners Sutton or of Mulgrave in Nova Scotia.

The principles underlying Head's belief in union, as he outlined them in this memorandum of 1857, were in fact the same as those that he had stressed in his earlier writings, though now he applied them to Maritime, not British North American union. He began by arguing the importance of preserving the connection between the mother country and her North American colonies:

There are many statesmen who doubt the advantage derived by England from the possession of British North America. . . . I dissent entirely from the opinions entertained by the persons in question.

I believe that the greatness of England rests quite as much on her moral supremacy as on her material superiority: anything which wounds the one impairs the other also. The honour of a nation is not a mere empty name, or phantom. It is not in itself material force but it is the stimulus which sets in action the material force. It is the motive which may cause thousands to turn out, and arm themselves in a cause the real merits of which they know nothing. . . . National honour, therefore, is a source of national power quite as real as material wealth or a standing army; for without national honour a people will soon be deprived of both.

The British Colonies in North America could not be abandoned by England under pressure of difficulties without loss of honour as a nation. . . . But except under difficulties of a very embarrassing nature is it likely that any British Minister would be got to take the responsibility of proposing to abandon the North American Colonies?

Moreover, it was necessary to consider "that the balance of power among nations will not hereafter be discussed with reference to European interests alone." The United States must be taken into account. Loss of the British North American colonies would not "be a mere question of foregoing so much strength on our own side, or of losing a point of vantage ground against a formidable enemy. If they are taken from us in their present condition they must be added to that of the enemy. They would be subtracted from one sum to swell the amount of the other."

Head's conviction that it was therefore both necessary and desirable to retain the colonies was the great fundamental principle on which he based his belief in their union. And it was not enough for the mother country simply to give up thoughts of abandoning them. Positive measures had to be taken as well to prevent their loss. The two essential points in this regard, points which he had stressed many times in the past, were:

1. The success of Parliamentary self government on English principles.
2. The gradual growth of the colonies with a sense of self importance sufficient to keep them from adhesion to the American Union.

That union would tend to create a greater "sense of self importance" was evident; that it would also contribute to the "success of Parliamentary self government" was something Head had long argued:

My own experience in New Brunswick, and the experience of all intelligent men with whom I have discussed the subject, seem to me to support the doctrine that Parliamentary Government on the English system in order to work successfully requires to be applied on a certain scale. . . . According to my view then, when the Colonies were governed from England '*divide et impera*' was a sound maxim. When they govern themselves by the machinery of a parliament and a responsible ministry, size is a necessary condition of success.

Citing facts and figures regarding the Maritimes, Head reasoned that each of these colonies, even Nova Scotia, was too small to ensure such success, or that "sense of self importance" necessary to keep them from drifting into the arms of the United States. Canada, on the other hand, seemed, for the time being at least, to be in a more satisfactory state. "I will assume that at the present moment she is loyal to England and tolerably well satisfied with her own form of Government. This may not always be so, but at the present time I think both propositions may be affirmed with truth." For these reasons, a Maritime union seemed highly desirable,[24] a larger union to include Canada unnecessary. Essentially, it is only in this conclusion, based on his estimate of

[24]In the final pages of the memorandum, Head suggested what steps might be taken to lay a scheme for legislative union before the three Maritime legislatures and what some of the principal features of their new united government might be.

the situation existing "at the present time," that Head's views in this memorandum of 1857 differ from those he had held earlier, and would return to the next year when the Canadian scene changed so drastically.

The third major topic that was engaging Head's attention in the winter of 1856–57, and on which he also wrote a memorandum for the Colonial Office, concerned the choice of a permanent seat of government for Canada. The previous spring, after the ministerial crisis brought on by this issue, he had reached the conclusion that some one place must be speedily fixed upon in order to avoid the continuance of disruptive controversy. A similar view had been taken by the assembly, and in the latter part of its 1856 session it had passed a resolution favouring Quebec. An appropriation for buildings there which it had made as well was, however, struck out of the supply bill in the legislative council so that no final decision had been made by the time of prorogation.[25] A few months later, when Lowe was in Toronto, the matter that "involved the most discussion" in his conversations with Head was, according to one account, this seat-of-government question. After taking all factors into consideration, both Head and Lowe agreed that Ottawa offered the best site.[26]

It was obvious however that the choice of any one place would be a most difficult undertaking because of the rival ambitions of all of the others. As early as May, 1856, when the Taché-Macdonald Government had taken office, Head had suggested to the new premier the possibility of reference to the Crown as a means of getting around this problem.[27] In March, 1857, this course was adopted and both Houses of the legislature passed addresses praying "that Your Majesty will be graciously pleased to exercise Your Royal Prerogative, and select some place for the permanent seat of Government in Canada." The assembly resolved also that an appropriation not exceeding £225,000 should be made for

[25]James A. Gibson, "Sir Edmund Head's Memorandum on the Choice of Ottawa as the Seat of Government of Canada," *Canadian Historical Review*, XVI (1935), 411–17. The text of this memorandum is also here.

[26]A. Patchett Martin, *The Right Hon. Robert Lowe, Viscount Sherbrooke*, I, 133–34.

[27]P.R.O., C.O. 42/604, Head to Labouchere, private and confidential, May 26, 1856.

providing buildings "at such place as Her Majesty may see fit to select."

In his public despatch forwarding these addresses, Head gave in considerable detail his reasons for strongly recommending that their prayer be granted. He concluded, however:

It would evidently be improper to convey to the Queen's Advisers in England any opinion or advice in this matter on the part of the Executive Council here. The whole reference is . . . of an exceptional character, and if it were to be finally decided on the advice of persons any of whom are responsible to the Parliament of Canada, the great object of removing it beyond the cross action of local politics and sectional jealousies would be altogether frustrated.[28]

There was no such impropriety, of course, in Head expressing his own personal opinions, and either on his own initiative or at the private request of the British Government, he wrote a confidential memorandum "containing reasons for fixing the seat of Government for Canada at Ottawa." This memorandum is undated but is known to have reached the Colonial Office before the end of July, 1857.[29]

Head's arguments in favour of Ottawa were clear and unequivocating:

Ottawa is the only place which will be accepted by the majority of Upper and Lower Canada as a fair compromise. With the exception of Ottawa, every one of the cities proposed is an object of jealousy to each of the others. . . . The second vote of every place (save perhaps Toronto) would be given for Ottawa. The question, it must be remembered, is essentially one of compromise. Unless some insuperable bar exist to its selection, it is expedient to take that place which will be most readily acquiesced in by the majority.

The main objections to Ottawa were its "wild position" and its small size, and these were by no means "insuperable." The former was a constantly diminishing fault as settlement progressed: the latter was probably no fault at all—"neither legislation nor the action of Executive Government gain much by the casual presence of strangers, each of which usually takes the opportunity afforded by the transaction of his own business, to press on the Ministry the 'jobs' which affect himself or the district to which he belongs."

On the positive side, the advantages of Ottawa were real and

[28]P.R.O., C.O. 42/609, Head to Labouchere, March 28, 1857.
[29]P.R.O., C.O. 42/610, Separate Minute by A. Blackwood, July 24, 1857.

important. Its distance from the American frontier was advantageous in two ways. It rendered Ottawa more secure from raid or attack than some of its rivals; and secondly: "Canada is long and narrow; in fact, all frontier. The rapid extension of settlement up the Ottawa, and on each side of it, would give breadth and substance to the country." Moreover—and this was a point that was growing in importance in Head's mind as the conflict between Upper and Lower Canada became more open— Ottawa formed part of a central region which he thought might be encouraged to develop between the two sections of Canada in order to prevent deadlock, threatened as a result of their political equality:

Ultimately, indeed in a short time, the question will arise 'which is to predominate, Upper or Lower Canada?' Upper Canada is conscious of its increasing strength, and of the fact that it pays the larger share of the taxes. The cry for increased representation to the most populous and richest portion will soon be heard, or rather it is already raised. The only solution of the difficulty will be the chance that the district of Montreal, and the English population about it and in the townships, may be got to side with Upper Canada, and thus turn the scale in favour of that section, which, for reasons beyond our control, must in the end prevail. All real conflict would then be useless, and Quebec must succumb. It is most important therefore that the middle district should be made to feel its importance, and should connect its interests with Upper Canada. This object will be greatly promoted by the choice of Ottawa, linked to Montreal by its trade, and literally in Upper Canada but close on the border of the other section of the Province.

This last argument in favour of Ottawa, and mention also of the Ottawa Valley route to the west, important in case "the Red River settlement and the Saskatchewan country are finally to be annexed to Canada," link this memorandum with the two others that Head was preparing at the same time. The cross reference to the Hudson's Bay memorandum is obvious. More subtle, but of great significance, is the connection between Head's belief that the bolstering up of a central region between Upper and Lower Canada would solve the conflict between them, and his belief, as expressed in the memorandum on Maritime union, that the Canadian political situation could be assumed to be satisfactory, although it "may not always be so." Head was clearly still of the opinion as late as the spring of 1857 that the seat-of-government question was on the point of being solved, and that its successful solution would assist directly, and indirectly as well, in reducing and finally ending the opposition of one section to the other within the Canadian union. And so long as this appeared to be the case, he saw no advantage in trying to include Canada in a British North American confederation.

From the first it had been the intention that Head would not only draw up memoranda on these important topics concerning the British provinces, but would go to England himself in the summer of 1857 for personal discussions with Labouchere. Before he went, it would be necessary for him to turn over the administration of the government to the commander of the troops, his friend Sir William Eyre. Head's preparations for this were most thorough, ranging from an invitation to Lady Eyre to visit Government House and get a preliminary view of its domestic arrangements,[30] to a confidential memorandum for Sir William's guidance on the constitutional position of the governor general.[31] This latter document, unlike the memoranda for Labouchere, was of a highly personal nature, explaining simply and concisely Head's own theory and practice of government. It was probably never seen, or intended to be seen, by anyone except Pennefather, who copied it, and Eyre, to whom it was sent and amongst whose private papers it has remained. It is all the more interesting, therefore, as revealing in an intimate and authentic form the basis for Head's decisions in the several political crises that occurred during his term in Canada. Moreover, it shows clearly the actual stage that the Canadian government had reached at this period in its gradual transition toward complete freedom of executive action.

Head dealt with two matters in particular: with "the practise in Canada in case of defeat of a ministry"; and with the ordinary day-to-day routine of relations between the governor and his ministers.

The first of these was a subject on which Head had already acquired some practical experience, and when the seat-of-government and double-shuffle crisis occurred the next year, his views were to be tested in a public controversy as bitter as any in Canadian history. The fact was, however, he explained to

[30]P.R.O., P.R.O. 30/46/18, Head to Eyre, private, March 25, 1857.
[31]P.R.O., P.R.O. 30/46/14, Memorandum, n.d. This is inscribed on the back: "Confidential Memo^m from the Governor General Sir Edmund Head." Internal evidence leaves no doubt as to the approximate date and the purpose of the memorandum.

Eyre, that the course to be taken on the defeat of a ministry was something about which "there is not, and, from the nature of the case, never can be any well established rule. . . . [I]f a slight change will set up the ministry again there is no obstacle to making such change. Whether it is judicious to do so or otherwise, must be decided by the Governor, who, I conceive, ought on such occasions to keep, as much as he can, in his own hands the discretion of the total or partial disruption of the ministry." After illustrating what he meant with a brief synopsis of his proceedings the previous year during the crisis which had resulted in MacNab's elimination, Head concluded as he had begun: "I repeat then that I cannot conceive any rule or principle in this matter applicable to all cases. What is wise in each instance must depend on the relative importance of the seceding members, their position with reference to the Legislature, and the ground of their resignation."

Turning to more routine matters, Head outlined the composition of the executive council and explained certain facts about it; for instance, that its leader need not hold any particular office—"at present he is the Speaker of the Legislative Council." He continued:

The Council are supposed to meet on the requisition either of the Governor, or at the request of any one or more of themselves conveyed by the Clerk. They then discuss *in committee*, the Governor not being present, the various measures or questions with which they have to deal. Practically during the Session, they sit nearly every day; at other times two or three times a week.

When the measures or questions have been discussed in committee of Council, the result of such discussion is embodied in a memorandum. Such memoranda when copied out fair by the clerk, filed and tied together are countersigned by the President of the Committees of Council. They are in this shape laid before the Governor. My practice usually is when there is no press of business out of the Parliamentary Session to approve the minutes and affix my initials to them *in the Council room* at the table with the members (four being a quorum). During the session however and if there is nothing in such minutes which seems doubtful, or if they appear mere matters of course, I often initial them without going into Council. On the other hand, if any doubt of the propriety of any one minute suggests itself to my mind either from the memorandum itself, or from the papers on which it is founded and which are placed in the box with it, then I go into Council and discuss the matter fully, or sometimes I send it back for reconsideration by speaking to some one of the members of the Council on the subject. As a matter of course I constantly call the attention of Council to particular petitions or particular subjects either by a special memorandum signed by myself or by a mere general reference of the papers to them. This is, in effect, calling for their advice on this particular matter.

The memoranda which when approved by me become minutes of Council are laid before me with a printed heading to the effect that each is submitted as the recommendation of the Executive Council. When approved they become the authority on which all executive departments act in cases requiring special direction.

Care is taken especially that extraordinary payments of money, not authorized by Act or Vote, should be so sanctioned. The advice of the Council is generally thus given in all applications for the remission of capital punishment. In these latter instances a report is laid before the Committee of Council by the Attorney General after obtaining the Judge's remarks on the case.

In money matters the Inspector General of finance (the finance minister) generally reports to Council. In land matters the Chief Commissioner of Crown Lands. In public works the Chief Commissioner of Public Works. These departmental reports are the foundation on which the advice of the Government as a whole is given to the Governor.

Ordinary appointments in each department are usually submitted on the responsibility of the head of the department—not of the whole Council— and are initialled by me. Many of these pass through the Provincial Secretary's office with a memorandum of the Attorney General or other head of a department as the basis on which they are laid before me.

Leaving Eyre with these detailed instructions on administering the government of Canada, Head sailed from Quebec on June 20, 1857, aboard the S.S. *North American,* for his first visit home since 1852. "We had . . . a fair passage—not remarkably speedy but not uncomfortable in any way." Arriving at Liverpool on Friday, July 3, the Heads went on to London immediately, and on the following day Head had his first interview with Labouchere at the Colonial Office.

The next week a round of business and social activity began that was to last for the rest of the summer. "We were invited to the Queen's ball on Thursday when Her Majesty & Prince Albert both spoke to me very graciously on the subject of Canada."[32] Head was in excellent health and spirits throughout this period— "in great feather, and very amusing," as one friend noted in his diary after a London dinner party.[33] Honoured and entertained

[32]P.R.O., P.R.O. 30/46/18, Head to Eyre, private, July 13, 1857. See also, London *Times,* July 3, 1857, ff.

[33]G. S. Hillard (ed.), *George Ticknor,* II, 365. Ticknor also said of Head (p. 363): "He is looking very well, and says he is better than he has been for many years." Ticknor was at many of the same functions as the Heads, and the information in the remainder of this paragraph is taken from the full record he sent home to his wife.

as governor general and by personal friends, he enjoyed fully
the strenuous round of social engagements in London and in
country homes throughout England: breakfast at Milman's,
dinner at the Lyells', a concert at Lord Lansdowne's, days at
"Ellerbeck" with the Cardwells and at Harpton with the Lewis's
—meeting at these and many other places Macaulay, who did
"pretty much all the talk," George Ticknor, de Tocqueville, Lord
Glenelg, Nassau Senior, Herman Merivale, Sir Henry Holland,
Lord Monteagle, and in general, most of the political and literary
figures of the day. "Sir Edmund is in great force: Lady Head is
charming, as she always is," was the comment of a fellow guest
at the Cardwells'.

Frequently, of course, business intruded even on social
occasions. "At dinner at Lord Granville's Lord Palmerston talked
a good deal on the subject of the Canadian militia & the proposed
Railroad. The chief difficulty will be—how are Nova Scotia &
New Brunswick to pay their share of the interest?"[34] In addition
to such chance encounters with the prime minister and other
leading politicians, Head conferred on numerous occasions with
officials at the Colonial Office, the War Office, the Horse Guards,
and other government departments. The most important topics
discussed were the three on which he had written his memoranda.[35]

On the seat-of-government question, Head's advice in favour
of Ottawa, which was supported by other information that had
been collected by the Colonial Office, was accepted. It is possible
that a sketch painted by Lady Head early in the summer, after
a luncheon party near the place where the parliament buildings
were later erected, may have been shown to the Queen, and the
natural beauty of the site as well as the more practical arguments
put forward by Head may have had some influence in determining her decision.[36] Although almost certainly known to Head
before he left England, the official announcement of the Queen's
choice of Ottawa was delayed on his advice so as not to reach

[34]P.R.O., P.R.O. 30/46/18, Head to Eyre, private, September 1, 1857.

[35]One personal matter of some interest was that he let Merivale know that
he would not object to being transferred to the Ionian Islands where Sir John
Young was in serious difficulty, as his predecessor had been, because of the
determined effort of the inhabitants to secure their annexation to Greece. Nothing
came of this although the subject would be raised again a year later, this time
by Merivale. See below, pp. 214–15 (Lewis Papers, Head to Lewis, February 12,
1859).

[36]R. W. Scott, *The Choice of the Capital*, p. 30.

Canada until early in the New Year in order that it might not become a subject of controversy during the general election that was to take place in December.[37]

Head's memorandum on a legislative union of the "Lower Colonies" was discussed by him at the Colonial Office in conjunction with another proposal for a wider federal union of all of British North America, made at the same time by the new premier of Nova Scotia, J. W. Johnstone. Johnstone and his colleague, A. G. Archibald, and John A. Macdonald and John Rose of Canada, were in London when Head was there in July, on a further, and futile, attempt to secure support for the building of an intercolonial railway.[38] The Nova Scotians were authorized as well to discuss the union of British North America, and Johnstone sent a note to Head on this matter to try to enlist his support. The separate despatch to Labouchere which Head wrote as a result, from the Athenaeum Club on July 29, is expressed in formal terms, and being a public despatch it quite naturally makes no reference to the memorandum he had himself been preparing privately on the subject in recent months. Nor, for the same reason, does it give any indication of whether he had yet discussed this memorandum with Labouchere, although from the fact that he had already seen the latter, probably a number of times, it would seem strange if there had not been at least some preliminary exchange of views.[39]

The despatch of July 29 differs slightly, but significantly, in tone from the memorandum Head had written a short time before in Canada:

> . . . I am induced to solicit the attention of Her Majesty's advisers to the matter [union of British North America], simply because I am impressed with its importance and because I have the honour of holding Her Majesty's commission as Governor General of Canada, New Brunswick, Nova Scotia, and Prince Edward Island. . . . It appears to me at any rate very important to direct attention to the question.
>
> It may be that an Union of all the four Colonies, including Canada, would be impracticable or would not be received with favour by all. It may be, on the other hand, that a Legislative union of the three 'Lower Colonies' i.e. Nova Scotia, New Brunswick, and Prince Edward Island,

[37]P.R.O., C.O. 42/610, Head to Blackwood, private, November 21, 1857.

[38]See W. M. Whitelaw, *The Maritimes and Canada*, pp. 116–21. See also P.R.O., C.O. 42/612, John A. Macdonald to Labouchere, August 14, 1857.

[39]This differs somewhat from the conclusion drawn by Alice R. Stewart, *Canadian Historical Review*, XXVI (1945), 411.

would be more practicable in itself, and would be desired by those Colonies. Such a step would not in any way prejudice the future consideration of a more extensive union either with Canada or Newfoundland if this measure appeared to Her Majesty's advisers to be expedient, and if it met the wishes of the Colonists themselves.

As I have said my only object at present is to solicit the attention of the Government to the importance of the subject, and to its bearing on the future strength, prosperity, and good government of these possessions.[40]

Head's preference, it is clear, was still for Maritime union only, but in the interval since writing his memorandum his opposition to the larger scheme seems to have weakened considerably. Whereas in the memorandum he had merely referred in passing to the fact that Maritime union might be looked upon by some as a preliminary step to federation with Canada, he appears in this despatch to be on the point of adopting such a view himself. Certainly he was quite prepared to recommend the subject of federation to the consideration of the British Government, and the only doubts he expressed with regard to it were on the grounds that it might not be practicable or might not be acceptable to all of the colonies. It may be of course that pending completion of his discussions with Colonial Office officials, Head was not ready to take a definite stand against confederation in a public despatch, a copy of which he may well have felt obliged to show to Johnstone. The very cautious language that he used, and his avoidance of mentioning his own views, tends to bear this out.

On the other hand, while this may be true, it seems probable that Head would not have written in quite the tone that he did, had not his opinions altered, slightly at least, since his arrival in England. This may have happened as a result of a number of factors: the arguments put forward by the Nova Scotian delegation and the evidence of an interest in confederation on the part of that province, the renewal of negotiations regarding an intercolonial railway, the work of the Hudson's Bay committee whose report was to be published two days later, or possibly the tenor of conversations he had already had at the Colonial Office. In any case, whatever Head's exact opinions were at this time, it is known that by the end of his discussions with Labouchere an understanding had been reached that on Head's return to Canada the whole subject of some form of British North American union

[40]P.A.C., G 180B, Head to Labouchere, separate, July 29, 1857.

should be given his close attention. Herman Merivale informed one of Labouchere's successors a year later:

Mr. Labouchere particularly requested him to take it in hand, when he (Sir E. H.) was last in England: though whether any official instructions are on record on the subject, I am not certain. Mr. Labouchere's view was, not that it was a thing to be urged from this side, but that we ought to be prepared for its proposal & rather encourage it than otherwise.[41]

Of greater public interest in England in the summer of 1857 than any other matter that concerned British North America was the fate of the Hudson's Bay Territories then being examined by the select committee of the House of Commons that Labouchere had asked for and of which he was the chairman. The membership of the committee was impressive: Lord John Russell, Lord Stanley, who was to be the next colonial secretary, Pakington, an earlier one, Gladstone, Roebuck, Robert Lowe, Edward Ellice Jr., and Goderich. Much time was spent studying evidence, and witnesses were heard representing the company, the inhabitants of the territory, and the Canadian Government. Head had no official contact with the committee but he was in London for some weeks while it was completing its work. Being governor general of Canada and on terms of personal friendship with a number of the committee members, he may well have been consulted privately by others in addition to the chairman who had already received his memorandum on the subject. Whether this was so or not, the main recommendations of the majority in their report of July 31 were very similar to those Head had made to Labouchere in March.

Thus: the committee advised that the connection between Vancouver Island and the company be terminated and that steps be taken to extend the jurisdiction of that colony over adjacent mainland regions west of the Rockies which were fit for settlement. Other areas in the North West Territory and Rupert's Land not fit for settlement should remain under the control of the company and with respect to these its licence for exclusive trade should be renewed.

So far as settlement east of the Rockies was concerned, Canada's principal witness, Chief Justice Draper, had made a suggestion before the committee which was clearly reminiscent of the scheme outlined in Head's memorandum. Draper had asked that Canada be granted "a free right to explore and survey, in

[41]P.R.O., C.O. 42/614, Head to Lytton, August 16, 1858, minute by Merivale.

order to ascertain the capabilities of the country, as well as the right to open communications and to place settlers along the roads"; and that as settlement proceeded and townships were established these portions of the territory should be annexed to Canada.[42] While the committee was still completing its work, Labouchere had found out by writing to the company that it would be willing to cede lands really desired by Canada for settlement, relying on the British Government to secure just compensation to the shareholders and traders.[43] Accordingly the committee reported in this connection, in words that Head must have read with approval:

... Your Committee consider that it is essential to meet the just and reasonable wishes of Canada to be enabled to annex to her territory such portions of the land in the neighbourhood as may be available to her for the purposes of settlement, with which lands she is willing to open and maintain communications, and for which she will provide the means of local administration. Your Committee apprehend that the districts on the Red River and the Saskatchewan are among those likely to be desired for early occupation. It is of great importance that the peace and good order of those districts should be effectually secured. Your Committee trust that there will be no difficulty in effecting arrangements as between Her Majesty's Government and the Hudson's Bay Company by which these districts may be ceded to Canada on equitable principles, and within the districts thus annexed to her the authority of the Hudson's Bay Company would of course entirely cease.

The committee recognized that, if Canada was not willing at an early date to annex the Red River settlement at least, some other provision would have to be made for removing it from the company's jurisdiction and providing it with a government of its own. It did not consider, however, as Head had done, the details of any such interim arrangement. This, and many other matters as well, would have to be worked out in negotiations still to be conducted by the Colonial Office, the company, and Canada. To what extent Head may have talked over with Labouchere, before leaving England, the course that these negotiations should take, is not known.

On Wednesday, August 26, 1857, the Heads and a number of other guests of the Edward Cardwells at nearby "Ellerbeck" were visiting the Manchester Exhibition when Head was handed

[42]Morton, *A History of the Canadian West*, p. 830.
[43]H.B. Co., A 7/2, C.O. to H.B. Co., July 15, 1857; and reply, July 18, 1857.

a letter by special messenger from London. His comment after he glanced through it was: "That is too bad; it is the second time Labouchere has summoned me back to London, since I have been on this excursion." However, five minutes later, following hurried consultations with Lady Head and arranging to meet her at Tewkesbury on the Saturday, he set off for "Ellerbeck" and thence to London, to be sworn in as a member of Her Majesty's Privy Council.[44]

The honour thus conferred on Head coincided with what was in many ways the high-water mark of his success and popularity as a colonial governor. It was a well-deserved recognition of his achievements in New Brunswick, and of his able guidance of Canadian affairs through several years which had been most critical so far as defence against possible American attack had been concerned. In particular, it signified the high regard of Her Majesty and of Her Majesty's Government for the advice that Head had recently given orally, and in his written memoranda, on the various British North American problems that he had been studying since Lowe's visit to Toronto a year earlier.

[44]Hillard (ed.), *George Ticknor*, II, 398; P.R.O., P.R.O. 30/46/18, Head to Eyre, private, September 1, 1857.

NINE

The Crisis of 1858

O N November 3, 1857, the Heads arrived back at Quebec aboard the S.S. *Indian* after a stormy passage from Liverpool. "We left England all green, and found icicles a yard long on the cliffs of Bellisle."[1] By an unfortunate coincidence it was not the weather alone that was inclement in Canada in the fall of 1857. Political clouds too were gathering as a general election approached in an atmosphere made tense by sectional jealousies, and they were darkened by the spreading across into Canada of a financial depression that had commenced in the United States in the late summer. Head was at the beginning of a stormy year of political crisis which would be in marked contrast to the pleasant summer just finished in England.

At first the extent of the danger was not evident, and in fact the Canadian political scene appeared relatively calm. "The state of politics is I think *very promising*," Head wrote privately to the Colonial Office shortly after his return to Canada.[2] "The Hudson's Bay agitation is dying out. The Lower Canadians care but little for it." All that appeared to be happening was "a tranquil sort of ministerial crisis," brought on by the long-standing desire of Colonel Taché to retire from political life, which he now did in order to permit a reconstruction of the Government before the election. G. E. Cartier took his place as the leader of the Lower Canadian section of the council and the first of a long series of Macdonald–Cartier ministries came into existence on November 26.

---

[1] G. S. Hillard (ed.), *George Ticknor*, II, 406, Head to Ticknor, November 21, 1857. The cold weather may have been responsible for the fact that Lady Head caught influenza during the last stages of the journey and passed it on to Head when they got back to Toronto. "I rarely suffer from cold & I am not therefore very patient or submissive under the present infliction, especially as serious ministerial arrangements require constant attention" (P.R.O., P.R.O. 30/46/18, Head to Eyre, private, November 10, 1857).

[2] P.R.O., C.O. 42/610, Head to Blackwood, private, November 21, 1857.

Among other changes made at the same time to bolster the new Government, two were most important. The former speaker, L. V. Sicotte, was appointed commissioner of crown lands, and John Rose became solicitor general. Sicotte was known to be slightly Rouge, and, in Head's opinion, his accession "to the ranks of a Government mainly consisting of liberal Conservatives has a direct tendency to hamper the organization of the ultra-liberal party."[3] Rose, Montreal's leading commercial lawyer, and solicitor of the Hudson's Bay Company, the Grand Trunk Railway, and a host of lesser concerns, would be a tower of strength in the Government, a potentially dangerous critic out of it, in the coming period of financial stress and when Hudson's Bay and Grand Trunk matters would be prominent subjects of controversy. Head anticipated "a strong administration" as a result of what was virtually a reconstruction of the Lower Canadian section—a reconstruction comparable with that successfully undertaken the year before in the Upper Canadian section when Macdonald had supplanted MacNab.

In commenting confidentially to the colonial secretary regarding these changes, Head drew attention to one feature of them that had a direct bearing on a point he had stressed in his seat-of-government memorandum written a few months before. Noting that more of the new ministers came from the vicinity of Montreal and fewer from Quebec than had been the case previously, Head argued: "All of this therefore tends in the direction of increasing the influence of Montreal and the central district, whilst it diminishes that of Quebec: a course of policy which, in my opinion, will ultimately afford us the only means of solving satisfactorily the question of the relative representation of Upper and Lower Canada."[4] His re-statement of this idea in such a definite way after his return from England shows clearly that, whatever the nature of his discussions with Labouchere regarding confederation, Head's own views had remained substantially unaltered. He did not yet think confederation necessary as a solution for Canadian sectionalism, but instead, still believed that this could be gradually overcome by the method of building up a central area between the two extremes of the province.

[3]P.R.O., C.O. 42/610, Head to Labouchere, separate and confidential, November 26, 1857. An attempt at the same time to win over A. A. Dorion failed. (J. C. Dent, *The Last Forty Years: Canada since the Union of 1841*, II, 357.)

[4]P.R.O., C.O. 42/610, Head to Labouchere, separate and confidential, November 26, 1857.

The easy optimism with which Head viewed the political scene in November cannot long have survived the election campaign of the next two months, and its bitter aftermath in the debates over controverted elections that occupied the opening weeks of the session of 1858. Violent accusations of corruption and chicanery were hurled at the Government. Nor did the latter's position improve when the House passed on to other business, much of which was concerned with such highly inflammatory matters as aid to the Grand Trunk or Government policy with regard to the Hudson's Bay Territories.

The latter topic was one on which the British Government had made definite proposals to the company and to Canada in January, 1858. These adhered fairly closely to the recommendations of the select committee, and included provision for the renewal of the licence for another twenty-one years with the reservation that Vancouver Island and subsequently any other region required for settlement—even in charter territory—should be withdrawn from the company's jurisdiction upon suitable compensation being given. In the meantime, the boundary between Canada and Rupert's Land should be determined by appeal to the Judicial Committee of the Privy Council. If Canada on her own wished to go further and contest the charter itself she would of course be free to do so.[5]

The company was prepared to accept this solution, and in fact was well satisfied with it.[6] In Canada, however, as was noted by a shrewd company official,

annexation of the Red River and Saskatchewan appears to be popular, but the condition of compensation to the Company is a stumbling block. . . . It is difficult to judge what position the cabinet may assume, as I know the various members entertain very different views. Some wish to have nothing to do with the Hudson's Bay and others who made political capital of it at their elections, feel bound to do something toward redeeming their pledges.[7]

In these rather delicate circumstances, the resolutions that were eventually introduced into the legislature by way of reply to the British proposals were of a vague and negative nature. They urged Canada's claims strongly but only in the most general

[5]P.R.O., C.O. 42/606, C.O. to H.B. Co., January 20, 1858; Labouchere to Head, January 22, 1858.
[6]H.B. Co., A 7/2, Shepherd to Simpson, private, February 26, 1858.
[7]H.B. Co., D 4/84a, Simpson to Berens, private, April 17, 1858.

terms, insisted that the responsibility for determining the validity of the charter and settling the boundary rested with Britain and not with Canada, and rejected any suggestion of paying compensation to the company for parts of its lands that might be annexed to Canada. So weak was the Government's position that it did not dare press for speedy action even on such unoffending resolutions as these.[8]

In fact, from the beginning of the session the Government had had to use every expedient to maintain itself in office. It had soon had to abandon all pretense of adhering to the "double majority" principle, and as midsummer approached and the necessity of bringing forward the more controversial issues became inescapable, only the most skilful manoeuvring on the part of Macdonald and his colleagues enabled them to keep the support of a majority even of the whole House. They lost this too, temporarily, on the evening of Wednesday, July 28, when a vote on the old, familiar, seat-of-government question was carried by the Opposition by a vote of 64 to 50.

That this question became the subject of controversy again in 1858, in spite of the reference to the Queen the previous session, was owing to the fact that George Brown and the other Opposition leaders had not scrupled to consider trying to "upset the decision" as soon as the choice of Ottawa had been made known.[9] Their opportunity occurred with this vote which was on an amendment expressing the opinion of the assembly that "the City of *Ottawa* ought not to be the permanent seat of Government of this Province"[10]—and they seized it with an enthusiastic lack of political discernment, to say nothing of their failure to respect the previous commitments of the assembly itself or the dignity of the Queen. They brought about the defeat of the Government, however, and although the latter was immediately sustained on a direct confidence motion by a majority almost as large as that which had previously been against it, Brown's *Globe* appeared the following morning of July 29 with the headline, "Ignominious Defeat of the Government," and a virulent article demanding that the ministers cease to cling insensately to office.

[8]P.R.O., C.O. 42/613, Head to Stanley, May 22, 1858.
[9]A. Mackenzie, *Life and Speeches of George Brown*, p. 193, Brown to Holton, January 29, 1858.
[10]*Canada, House of Assembly, Journals*, 1858, p. 931.

Macdonald had no need to wait for his opponents' advice. In fact, he realized much more clearly than they did the possibilities inherent in the situation that had now arisen. He saw that it afforded him an excellent opportunity to end an increasingly precarious tenure of office on a note of loyalty to the Queen, and at a time when the Opposition, although becoming more dangerous, was still too weak and disorganized to form a stable government itself. Already, therefore, early on July 29, he had presented himself, along with Cartier, at Government House and had submitted to Head the resignation of his Government. When the assembly convened in mid-morning, he was able to announce that this had been accepted.

The events of the following week are well known. A Brown–Dorion ministry was patched together, was immediately defeated in both Houses of the legislature, was refused a dissolution by Head, and therefore had to resign. It was replaced, after Head had first approached a leading independent, A. T. Galt, by a re-constituted Cartier–Macdonald ministry. In a tricky "double-shuffle" of government portfolios the ministry avoided the necessity of returning to their constituents for re-election—a final blow to their less fortunate and already badly outmanoeuvred opponents—and they were then able to conclude the session successfully.

At two points in these events, Head influenced the course of Canadian history in a more direct and immediate way than at any other time throughout his administration. The first was when he refused Brown a dissolution; the second when he brought Galt into prominence as the potential leader of a new government. In connection with both of these events, although particularly the first, Head's actions became at once the subject of bitter controversy, and they must be examined in some detail.

With regard to the question of a dissolution, Head's constitutional right to refuse Brown's request and his wisdom in doing so have both been challenged. The charge of unconstitutionality is much the less serious of the two. Herman Merivale, whose position as permanent under-secretary in the Colonial Office and whose experience as professor of political economy at Oxford give his opinion great weight, wrote unhesitatingly at the time: "By far the most important discretionary power now vested in a Governor, under responsible government, is that of dissolution. It is one in which from the the very nature of the case, he cannot be bound under all circumstances to take the advice of his ministers—the same rule, I apprehend, applying to him as to the Crown here."[11] Moreover, the rule of thumb which can always be applied in such cases is whether the sovereign or the sovereign's representative can or cannot succeed in replacing the ministers whose advice he rejects by others able to secure the confidence of the legislature and carry on the functions of government. By this criterion of success, Head's right to refuse Brown a dissolution was rendered valid by the event.

The question then remains: Regardless of constitutional correctness, was Head's decision wise in the existing circumstances and from the point of view of the ultimate best interests of Canada? This is a question for which of course no exact answer can be given even from the vantage point of the historian, but a study of Head's motives and of the results he achieved should make an approximate judgment possible.

Head's motives were fully explained by himself in various documents: in two memoranda presented to Brown and made public during the crisis, in a public despatch and again in a confidential one to the colonial secretary written immediately afterwards, and in private letters to Lewis.[12] These and *Globe* editorials imputing quite different motives, all analysed in the light of a knowledge of Head's general views and character, suffice to give a very clear picture of why he did not agree to a dissolution.

Head's first memorandum was written on Saturday, July 31— the day on which Brown agreed to form a government but before he was in a position to name its members. It was delivered to Brown by Head's secretary, along with a covering note, on Sunday evening. In it was repeated for the record what Head had already told Brown Saturday morning and what, in fact, he had said as early as Thursday when he had first asked Brown to take office. It stressed that Head would give *"no pledge or promise express or implied, with reference to dissolving parliament. When advice is tendered to His Excellency on this subject, he will make up his mind according to the circumstances then existing,*

[11]P.R.O., C.O. 42/614, Head to Lytton, August 9, 1858, minute by Merivale.
[12]P.R.O., C.O. 42/614, Head to Lytton, August 9, 1858, and the enclosed memoranda addressed to Brown dated July 31 and August 4; C.O. 42/615, Head to Lytton, confidential, October 22, 1858; Lewis Papers, Head to Lewis, August 9, 1858 and January 2, 1859. The following account is taken from these documents except where otherwise noted.

and the reasons then laid before him." The assembly might of course adjourn of its own accord until after the re-election of Brown and his colleagues whose seats would be vacated by their acceptance of office. Or prorogation until, say, November or December was a possibility if certain matters of immediate importance were first dealt with. However, "prorogation is the action of His Excellency and, in this particular case, such act would be performed without the advice of ministers who had already received the confidence of parliament." Head would nevertheless agree to prorogation; in fact, "His Excellency's own opinion would be in favour of proroguing."

Head later explained confidentially to the colonial secretary his reasons for writing this memorandum:

> It may no doubt be asked, what induced me to address a note of this kind to Mr. Brown? I was well aware of the impolicy on general grounds of prescribing conditions on the part of the Crown to an administration about to take office, but the circumstances were, as it appeared to me, very peculiar. . . .
> The memorandum, as originally written, contained nothing which had express reference to a dissolution of Parliament, but after it was drafted, I received from a source wholly unconnected with the late administration certain information which induced me to alter its form. I was told that Mr. Brown's friends were asserting positively that I had promised to dissolve Parliament if desired by him to do so. I know that in Canada and elsewhere there had sometimes occurred differences as to the fact of what had taken place in conversation between a Governor and those with whom he was in contact. I thought that in the present instance any such issue of fact with reference to a dissolution would be most injurious in itself, and I determined at once to prevent it arising by deliberately recapitulating in writing what I had already twice stated in words to Mr. Brown himself. . . . I had distinctly told him that I thought a dissolution would be a very serious evil, and that I would give no promise of any kind with reference to it. By repeating this determination in writing, I did not mean to imply any special mistrust of Mr. Brown's truthfulness, but the same conversation often conveys different impressions to the individuals who take part in it, and I did not choose to run the risk of having my own veracity as to what had really passed in such a conversation pitted against that of any other man.

Head's second memorandum was written on the following Wednesday, August 4. Brown's ministry, sworn in at noon on Monday, had been defeated in both Houses that same evening. On Tuesday, Brown had waited on Head to request a dissolution, and Head had asked him to give his reasons in writing. When these had been presented on Wednesday morning, Head prepared a reply in the form of this second memorandum which was handed to Brown in the afternoon and which led to his immediate resignation. It is a long and carefully worded document which answers directly and conclusively each of the arguments put forward by Brown and his colleagues, and then goes on to give other grounds as well for Head's feeling it necessary to take the opposite point of view. In particular, Head stressed the disadvantage of another election when one had taken place only a few months before and when the business of the session was still not completed. He concluded:

It would seem to be the duty of His Excellency to exhaust every possible alternative before subjecting the province for the second time in the same year to the cost, the inconvenience, and the demoralization of such a proceeding.

The Governor General is by no means satisfied that every alternative has been exhausted, or that it would be impossible for him to secure a ministry who would close the business of this session, and carry on the administration of the government during the recess with the confidence of a majority of the Legislative Assembly.

After full and mature deliberation on the arguments submitted to him by word of mouth, and in writing, and with respect for the opinion of his council, His Excellency declines to dissolve parliament at the present time.

In a public despatch that Head wrote a few days later, after Cartier and Macdonald had resumed office and won the approval of the legislature, he referred to one other argument, which "in itself would not have induced me to refuse to dissolve the House," but which, taken with all the rest, he had felt should be given some weight. This was that Brown was even weaker in the legislative council than he was in the assembly, having been defeated there on a confidence vote by 16 to 8 on the day that he took office. If he were, by chance, returned to power in the assembly as a result of a general election, "a collision of an obstinate kind between the two houses would have been inevitable." The legislative council was already partially elective in Canada and so was entitled to a serious hearing in affairs of government. There was no provision for its dissolution,[13] so that the difficulty Head foresaw, while a secondary one, could not be altogether neglected in practice however invalid any argument based on it might be from the point of view of constitutional theory.

[13]19 & 20 Vict., c. 140 (Canada).

Head's private account of this crisis, written to Lewis on August 9, adds little in the way of new information but portrays vividly his personal attitude and impressions:

I don't know whether I shall have time to write to you at length. In fact for the last 10 days I have been fairly in hot water having had 3 Governments in the course of that time!

My old Govt no. 1. resigned on a vote snapped in an amendment about the Seat of Govt—without any direct withdrawal of confidence on the part of the Assembly. I then sent for the Leader of the opposition—Brown— and the printed correspondence in the enclosed paper will tell the rest. The paper however is as you see on my side. On the other I have [illegible] abuse & probably shall go through a course of hanging & burning (in effigy) for some time to come.

Govt. no. 3. pretty much identical with no. 1 is now in again & likely to finish the session.

I have begged Merivale to send you some more papers when he has done with them as they may amuse you.

The fact was that Brown knew & I knew that he could not get a majority of the present House. I told him plainly I would not promise to dissolve for the reasons (among others) in my printed paper. He took office not-withstanding on the speculation that he could bully me into dissolving and he was mistaken. However the exercise of this discretion is a very serious thing. As things now look I have both Houses with me & most of the respectable classes. All Lower Canada is strongly in my favour—65 to 70 members of the Legislature left their names at Govt House the day after the documents were read. The Legislative Council (now pretty elective) have committed themselves thoroughly—voting thanks to me (as I believe) for what I have done.

In fact if I had dissolved & Brown had secured a majority in the Lower House, the Council was so compromised that a collision between the two would have been certain. Yesterday I went down to pass some bills: Brown's friends had intended I believe to get up a demonstration against me but they were told that it would be put down by the other party & I was cheered. But the 'dead-cats' &c are yet to come. I don't feel at all sure how the thing will be taken in the outlying districts. Old Ellice is in Canada but I have not yet seen him.

Head's reference to Ellice in this letter which is otherwise concerned entirely with the government crisis may not have been just by chance. Ellice's name had appeared a day or two before in a *Globe* editorial which formed part of the torrents of abuse that had begun to pour forth from the Opposition press as soon as Head's refusal of a dissolution was known, abuse which Head, as his letter to Lewis shows, was prepared to read with the equanimity to be expected of a former Poor Law commissioner. The *Globe*, under the title, "Sir E. Head's Closet Councillors," had claimed his subservience to Ellice and the Barings, and the British money interests generally. It had suggested with scathing sarcasm that he ought to do away with all pretence and frankly concede to the Barings the nomination of the inspector general, to the merchants of London, Manchester, and Glasgow, the two attorney generals, to the Hudson's Bay Company, the commissioner of crown lands, and then let Mr. Ellice indicate his preferences with regard to all the rest.[14]

The *Globe*, long expert in vituperation, quite naturally excelled itself during this crisis in which Brown himself played such a leading and unfortunate role. With great ingenuity and imagination, and stimulated by a supreme fury, it managed to express in masterly fashion its more than utter contempt for the "odious character of Sir Edmund Head's conduct during the Ministerial Crisis." The "petty special pleading" of his second memorandum was declared "worthy of the author of 'Shall and Will', or of John A. Macdonald, who is said to have been his constant adviser throughout the entire transaction." Head, one day, was pilloried as "a weak Governor" who time after time had "blundered so egregiously that few hesitated to deride his incapacity," and who now stood convicted of "obedience to backstairs dictation." On the very next day it was Head himself who was the dictator. He was compared with Lord Metcalfe—although "without the ability or courage of that unpopular Governor"—and the *Globe*'s readers were warned that his presumption to interpret, or indeed to determine, the law of the land, if submitted to, would result in him becoming "Dictator *de jure*, as he already claims to be *de facto*." Nor did the *Globe* neglect the obvious reminder of the misdeeds of Sir Francis Bond Head. "Sir Edmund really belongs to the Head family," it concluded.

The *Globe*'s charges, needless to say, throw little light on Head's real motives for refusing Brown a dissolution, and they do not have to be taken seriously when the passions from which they were engendered have themselves ceased to exist. There can be no doubt of Head's integrity or of his scrupulously correct behaviour towards Brown and his colleagues. The grounds which he gave to Brown publicly for rejecting his advice were quite sufficient in themselves to justify such a course. They appeared

[14]Toronto *Globe*, August 7, 1858. Each of these allusions was to a current matter of legislative controversy. Further quotations are from the *Globe* of this or the two preceding days.

so even to Sir E. B. Lytton, the colonial secretary, who was by no means favourably disposed toward Head at the time:

I think Not Dissolving may be defended very well—2 Dissolutions within *one year*—the 2ᵈ Dissolution at the request of a Govt in a decided minority in *both* Chambers—important business including some Estimates & the H.B. Compʸ question unsettled—all to be suspended—are strong reasons for the exercise of a prorogative which is undeniably constitutional. . . . This is really the sole question that affects Sir E. Head.[15]

Nevertheless, it is clear that in addition to these public, and entirely adequate, motives for opposing Brown's request, Head was personally unsympathetic towards him and his policies and had greater confidence in Macdonald and Cartier. These two men headed a moderate liberal-conservative government much like the one Head himself had formed and worked through in New Brunswick. They were practical politicians, avoiding disruptive issues as much as possible and carrying on a reasonably efficient and constructive administration. With all their compromises and expedients, Head preferred such a ministry to one led by a brilliant controversialist, however sincere and idealistic. Nor was Head convinced of Brown's sincerity or idealism. The issue on which Brown had succeeded in defeating the Macdonald–Cartier Government—the seat-of-government question—had for years had an unsettling effect on Canadian politics. To revive it after the Queen had given her decision at the request of the Canadian legislature seemed to Head hardly honest; certainly no high ideals or principles could be alleged. This and Brown's whole record of extremist agitation undoubtedly prejudiced Head against him. Recognizing his own prejudice, he was careful to treat Brown with the strictest constitutional rectitude, but his satisfaction with the return to office of his old advisers was unmistakable.

Even if Head's motives were good, the question still remains: Was his decision a wise one? Was his judgment proved sound by the course of subsequent events? A fair estimate on this point is difficult to make. O. D. Skelton, for example, has suggested that it was unfortunate that Brown was not given an opportunity at this stage to exercise his great constructive powers.[16] And it is certainly true that the crisis as a whole, and not least Head's

[15]P.R.O., C.O. 42/615, Head to Lytton, September 27, 1858, minute by Lytton.
[16]O. D. Skelton, *Sir A. T. Galt*, pp. 234–35.

part in it, exacerbated political hostilities. But on the other hand, feeling was already very bitter and deadlock was already recognized on all sides to be approaching. The recurring crises of the late 1850's and the 1860's seem in themselves evidence that Head was right, and that only a middle-of-the-road administration, guided by a master of political subtlety—which Brown was not—could possibly keep the machinery of Canadian union from breaking down completely for long enough to enable the final solution of confederation to be worked out.

It may be that it was to direct attention to this solution of confederation that Head made his other personal contribution to the outcome of the crisis of 1858. On August 4, after accepting Brown's resignation, Head asked A. T. Galt to form a government. Galt was sitting as an independent and was recognized to be an able and influential individual. It was quite proper for Head to explore the possibility of forming a neutral government under Galt's leadership rather than turn back immediately to his old ministers. Such was the only motive Head ever admitted for calling upon Galt—and it may have been the only one he had. Nevertheless it would seem that he must have foreseen a further result from thus bringing Galt forward and preparing the way for his eventual entrance into the new Cartier–Macdonald ministry. Galt had been actively urging confederation since 1856. Only a few weeks before the seat-of-government crisis began, he had introduced in the assembly a resolution on this subject. No vote had been taken and the resolution was technically still before the House when the Government fell. Head can hardly have been surprised that Galt was unable to form a ministry, that he was asked instead to join the Cartier–Macdonald Government, and that he made their support for his confederation proposals the condition on which he agreed to do so. Moreover, the fact that Head was willing a week or so later to make his own well-known confederation announcement in the Speech from the Throne closing the session, suggests that he was now strongly in accord with Galt's opinions, and had deliberately decided to arrange for them to be brought into the field of practical politics at this time.

If this is so—and it seems the only reasonable explanation for Head's actions at this stage of the crisis—it means that Head's viewpoint had changed considerably since the year before when he had written his memorandum urging Maritime union but criticizing the idea of a wider confederation that would include Canada as well. The background for this change and for Head's new attitude is obscure. It was obscure at the time to the recently appointed colonial secretary, Sir E. B. Lytton, whose first reaction on reading Head's Speech was a violently scrawled minute, almost illegible in places, but not lacking even in its indignation the turgid fluency for which the popular novelist had become famous:

It is absolutely *necessary* to administer a reproof to Sir E. Head for his paragraph on 'Confederation'. It has caused the greatest displeasure, & I have been even urged to recall him on acct of it—unless there be producible evidence that he was in someway authorized by the Home Govt, for committing himself & us to the consideration of a measure which may be wise or not, against which I have no prejudice but which is not *departmental* alone, which would require the most anxious deliberation by the Cabinet, & which any sovereign of Gt. Britain would be likely to regard with apprehension. I think Sir E. Head has perpetrated a great indiscretion—I have great doubts of his conduct throughout the recent transactions.[17]

The explanation that Merivale was able to give Lytton, showing that Head's action was not as completely unauthorized as it appeared to be, offers the only glimpse we have of the development of Head's ideas on confederation in the earlier part of 1858—and even that explanation, which was partly oral, must now be pieced together from a number of related but in some cases improperly filed Colonial Office documents.[18] Merivale started from the fact that Head's conversations with Labouchere the summer before had resulted in Head's being asked to take the matter of some form of British North American union in hand "& rather encourage it than otherwise." He then made it clear

[17]P.R.O., C.O. 42/614, Head to Lytton, August 16, 1858, minute by Lytton.
[18]P.R.O., C.O. 42/614, Head to Lytton, July 31, August 9, and August 16, 1858; C.O. 42/615, Head to Lytton, September 9, September 27, and confidential, October 22, 1858. The following account is pieced together from Colonial Office minutes on all of these documents except where otherwise indicated. Lytton's minutes are not dated as a rule and the one which (from internal evidence and from the fact that it was used in drafting the reply to Head) clearly contains his final opinion was unfortunately written on a separate sheet of paper. Still more unfortunately this was bound after the despatch of July 31 instead of after the first set of minutes on the despatch of August 16 where a careful check shows beyond doubt that it really belongs. This confusion in the Colonial Office accounts for the different interpretation of this incident in W. M. Whitelaw, *The Maritimes and Canada*, p. 131.

that because of the delicacy of Canadian problems, "Communications between the Secretary of State and the Governor of Canada have been of late years carried on almost exclusively through private correspondence";[19] and he produced private letters, now missing, which Head and Lord Stanley had exchanged, when the latter was colonial secretary from February to May, 1858. These showed conclusively that Head had reason to suppose that his action in supporting confederation would be understood and approved by the Derby Government of which Stanley was still a member although he had transferred to another department and been replaced by Lytton as colonial secretary.

In the absence of all but a mere reference to the nature of the crucial private correspondence between Head and Stanley, some conjecture is necessary, but it seems highly probable that the modification of Head's views on confederation, since his conversations with Labouchere, had proceeded somewhat as follows. He had returned to Canada with a reasonably free hand to encourage any tendency that might show itself in the direction of at least Maritime union. He had been still convinced in his own mind that all was well with Canada, and that there was no need for a confederation that would include "Canada as now constituted." The virulence of the election campaign and of the debates in the new assembly, however, and the evident growth of sectionalism which resulted, had caused him to begin to doubt the stability of Canada, and sometime in the spring of 1858 he had entered into a correspondence with Stanley in which he suggested that more than just Maritime union might have to be seriously considered. He had been confirmed in this fear when the seat-of-government issue, which he had long regarded as most dangerous to Canadian unity, had been so unexpectedly revived, and particularly when it had resulted in an immediate and very bitter ministerial crisis. Aware of Stanley's support, and that although no longer colonial secretary he was still a member of the Government, Head had decided to go ahead without formal authorization and make an attempt at once, through the agency of A. T. Galt, to bring the idea of confederation into the forefront of Canadian politics.

It is not certain how far Head intended at first to become

openly involved himself in the confederation proposal. As a result of Galt's influence, the Cartier–Macdonald Government announced when it resumed office on Saturday, August 7, that as part of its programme "the expediency of a Federal Union of the British North American Provinces will be anxiously considered, and communications with the Home government and the Lower Provinces entered into forthwith on the subject."[20] Head may have hoped that this statement alone would be sufficient to launch the proposal, but by the Monday it was already clear that the Opposition was not convinced that the ministers' intentions were serious. The *Globe* commented: "The Federal Union correspondence, we presume, is to be the outward and visible sop to Mr. Galt; but that it will be carried on earnestly, or that it will practically advance the question, few can believe." The next day it hammered away at this point again:

... the action of the Government on the Federal Union ... is just as complete a piece of deception as the rest. Even the most ardent friends of the Federation of these Provinces admit that it is a thing too far distant to be at present considered as a practical question. Mr. John A. Macdonald and Mr. Sicotte, both expressed this view in the debate led by Mr. Galt the new Inspector General. There can be no Federation of these Provinces until there is a road to unite them, and that is not likely to be built for many years to come. ... The design, no doubt, is to hasten the construction of the railway in which many of the new Ministry are deeply interested, but as a proposition to get rid of the question of Representation by Population, and all the others which cluster around it, it is useless.

Under the circumstances, Head may have felt it desirable to help the ministers refute such charges of insincerity. Or, equally well, he may himself have doubted their sincerity and wanted to see them committed, by something more definite than their mere announcement, to a policy of confederation. Apparently, his first thought in this connection was that the Government might introduce a series of resolutions in the legislature favouring the union of British North America (including all or part of the Hudson's Bay Territories as well), and proposing an intercolonial conference at Toronto in October to draw up "a definite scheme or plan." A draft of such resolutions, in Head's handwriting, is among his papers in the Canadian Archives.[21]

[20]Skelton, *Galt*, p. 239.

[21]For a copy of these resolutions see Chester Martin, "Sir Edmund Head and Canadian Confederation, 1851–1858," Canadian Historical Association, *Report*, 1929, p. 14.

No doubt it was eventually judged politically inexpedient to give the Opposition the opportunity such resolutions would provide to prolong a session which had already lasted far beyond its normal term and which the ministers were desperately anxious to see done with. Instead therefore Head agreed to include in his Speech from the Throne the statement:

I propose in the course of the recess to communicate with Her Majesty's Government, and with the Governments of the sister Colonies, on another matter of very great importance. I am desirous of inviting them to discuss with us the principle on which a bond of a federal character, uniting the Provinces of British North America, may perhaps hereafter be practicable.

This statement committed not only the ministry which was responsible for writing it but also, and no less, the governor who read it and in whose name it was written, because it dealt with a matter of Imperial concern with regard to which the governor in that period was still answerable to the Imperial government. It is not surprising that Lytton, before he was aware of Head's private understanding with the Colonial Office, believed it "absolutely *necessary* to administer a reproof to Sir E. Head for his paragraph on 'Confederation.'" When the background of the situation, and its difficulty and delicacy had been explained to him, Lytton's views changed considerably. He then minuted for Merivale's consideration:

The Perusal of your Minute & Sir E. Head's private letters do modify my views as to the drfᵍ of a Despatch to the Govʳ.
The Public Despatch should be very brief & cautious . . . it must intimate some surprise or regret, but mildly, at the passage about Confederation, in such a way as you will know how to word it. . . . I should also wish a confˡ letter from myself to the Govʳ—requesting to have fully his views as to the policy of Confederation & its bearings on the connection with the Mother Country pro & con. Also what scheme of congress seems likely to be proposed & what is the state of popular opinion in the various colonies on this head. N.B. I should have to lay his answer before the Queen.

The concluding part of Lytton's minute contains detailed "Hints for Despatch to Sir E. Head," and it ends with the comment: "We must disapprove tho' courteously this passage in the Speech,—but I don't wish at this crisis to discredit Sir E. Head." The despatch itself, dated September 10, adhered to Lytton's minute very closely.[22]

²²P.R.O., C.O. 42/614, Head to Lytton, July 31, 1858, minute by Lytton bound after this despatch but obviously belonging elsewhere. (See note 18 above.)

Head did not know of course until he received this despatch that Lytton was inclined to look upon the prospect of confederation with greater distrust than his predecessors had done. In the meantime, however, he was highly conscious of the fact that the matter was of Imperial concern and that the way had not been adequately prepared—in public despatches at least—for the action he had authorized Canada to initiate. On September 9, therefore, while Lytton's despatch was still being drafted, Head sent from Toronto an official minute of the Canadian executive council which he hoped would help smooth over this awkwardness.[23] Very carefully worded, it stressed in each paragraph Canada's understanding that the sanction of the Imperial government was needed at all stages of any proposals and negotiations regarding confederation. Head noted later in his confidential explanation to Lytton:

The Minute of Council forwarded with my despatch of the 9th September Number 118 will sufficiently shew that I was not blind to the fact that any practical measures with regard to such a proposal must originate, not with the Government of Canada, but with that of the Queen. The substance of this Minute of Council was suggested by myself with the view of marking this important point.[24]

Unfortunately, the Colonial Office, extremely sensitive in any case in dealing with the notoriously intractable Canada, and with feelings particularly ruffled by the manner in which the subject of confederation had been raised, read quite a different meaning into the Canadian minute from the one Head had intended. The chief of the North American department expressed the general opinion of the Office when he wrote:

It seems to me that Her Majesty's Govt are asked to agree to a line of action to which, if they desire not to offend the Canadian Government, they have only the shadow of an option, and that this instance is strikingly illustrative of the very little weight which is attached in the present day to the opinions, whichever way they may incline, of the Home Govt on Canadian—and B.N.A. domestic policy.[25]

The parliamentary under-secretary added: " . . . they cannot guard as effectually against the jealousies of the several colonies

23P.R.O., C.O. 42/615, Head to Lytton, September 9, 1858, and enclosure.
24P.R.O., C.O. 42/615, Head to Lytton, confidential, October 22, 1858.
25P.R.O., C.O. 42/615, Head to Lytton, September 9, 1858, minute by A. Blackwood.

to be confederated and the differences of the delegates as they
can against the interposition of the Sec. of State."[26]

In fact, it did turn out that the hostility of the Colonial Office
to the Canadian proposals was shared generally by the other
colonial governments. The result was that, in spite of the efforts
of a strong delegation of Canadian ministers who went to London
in October, no steps were taken to authorize the intercolonial
conference Canada had asked for, and the whole matter of confederation was encouraged to die a natural death.[27]

Head's interest too appears gradually to have declined. In fact
from the beginning, apart from the reference in the Speech from
the Throne, he seems to have tried to stay in the background as
much as possible. In explaining confidentially to Lytton his
reasons for agreeing to make the confederation statement, he
was, for example, more concerned with excusing himself for thus
acting without full authority than with arguing in favour of confederation.[28] He may of course have included such arguments in
the private letter which he probably wrote in answer to Lytton's
request, and which is not now in the Colonial Office files.
Officially, however, he left the task of persuasion almost entirely
to Galt and the other Canadian ministers. That he was nevertheless keenly interested in the subject is indicated by great masses
of notes in his own handwriting among his papers in the Canadian Archives. These deal with the details of a plan for confederation including exact proposals for the division of powers
between the federal and provincial governments, the form of
these governments and of their courts of law, etc. They are just
the sort of notes he would have been likely to make in drafting
out a scheme to be considered by an intercolonial conference,
and they very likely date from the fall of 1858. As prospects for
the conference faded, Head seems to have set them aside un-
finished.

There remained one other outcome of the crisis of 1858 which
Head could not regard with the same philosophic detachment.
He was determined for personal as well as public reasons that
the seat-of-government question on which the Macdonald
Government had been defeated in the first place should now be

[26]*Ibid.*, minute by Lord Carnarvon.
[27]P.R.O., C.O. 42/616, Cartier, Ross, and Galt to Lytton, October 25, 1858;
same to same, private and confidential, October 25, 1858; C.O. 42/615, Lytton
to Head, November 26, 1858.
[28]P.R.O., C.O. 42/615, Head to Lytton, confidential, October 22, 1858.

permanently and satisfactorily settled. He felt most acutely the responsibility for having advised Queen Victoria to accede to the request of the legislature and choose a capital for Canada, only to have her choice summarily rejected. It became a "point of honour" with him to see that instead her decision was approved and carried into effect as soon as possible. "If this is done I care for nothing else," he wrote to Lewis. Accordingly, when the session of 1859 opened he got his ministers to face the question "boldly & openly" in the Speech from the Throne.[29] The result was that with surprisingly little difficulty suitable addresses in reply were passed and the problem finally solved. "The breach of faith therefore & insult implied by the vote of last session, on which no address or measure was founded, has been got rid of. This is a great relief to me. . . . If I have to leave Canada soon I shall do so with much more satisfaction after maintaining the Queen's decision."[30]

[29]Lewis Papers, Head to Lewis, February 12, 1859.
[30]Lewis Papers, Head to Lewis, February 16, 1859.

TEN

Concluding Years in Canada

T HE last three of Head's seven years in Canada are marked in some degree, though not entirely, by a sense of anticlimax. Earlier he had given much constructive thought to the basic problems of Imperial defence, the future of the Hudson's Bay Territories, and the relations between Upper and Lower Canada and between these and the rest of British North America. He had come to certain conclusions himself about these problems and had helped the Colonial Office to formulate general lines of policy. In 1858, when the political pot in Canada had boiled over, he had become personally involved in bitter public controversy. This crisis had underlined the weaknesses and dangers of Canadian government, and through Head's contrivance it had been made to point the way toward the ultimate solution of confederation. But it had produced no immediate positive result. When it ended, and when the seat-of-government issue which had caused it was finally settled in 1859, Canadian politics returned to a state of uneasy equilibrium maintained through the ministry's skill in avoiding rather than making major decisions.

Under these circumstances, Head's role became largely to watch and to wait—to re-state his opinions, or perhaps even revise them a little from time to time as the long-drawn-out discussions of such subjects as confederation or the Hudson's Bay Territories continued. This coincided very suitably with Head's personal inclinations during this period, and also with the fact that the stage was being reached when the Canadian ministers were tending more and more, in any case, to take charge not only of their own domestic policy but also of their relations with the mother country. Two exceptional events were the visit of the Prince of Wales to Canada and the crisis that arose in Grand Trunk Railway affairs. Both required the active participation of Head, and brought him into close contact with individuals who were to direct his subsequent career toward the governorship of the Hudson's Bay Company. Finally, the outbreak of Civil War in the United States raised again, at the very end of Head's term in Canada, defence problems not unlike those which had faced him at its beginning.

A matter of some urgency that required Head's attention in the early fall of 1858, immediately after the legislative session finally ended, was the Hudson's Bay question. Little progress had been made regarding this since Labouchere's proposals early in the year for the renewal of the licence under certain conditions. Resolutions in reply, introduced in the Canadian legislature in May had been vague and indecisive, and in any case their passage had been delayed until the last days of the session by the seat-of-government crisis.[1] An executive council minute outlining the policy the Cartier–Macdonald Government was prepared to support in furtherance of these resolutions was on Head's desk when he received, shortly after the prorogation, a confidential despatch from Lytton opening the subject again in a somewhat different form. Lytton had become increasingly conscious of the approaching deadline of May 31, 1859, when the company's licence had either to be renewed or allowed to expire. Aware of the inconclusive nature of the Canadian resolutions, he had decided not to wait to receive them formally before writing to Head to outline tentatively his own opinions and to ask for those of Head in return.[2]

The new emphasis in Lytton's viewpoint, which made it different from that of his predecessor, was that he wanted to "be enabled at once to commence that great work of civilization which must add so largely to the strength and prosperity of the Canadian population," namely, the creation into settled provinces of the Red River and Saskatchewan districts. Thinking in terms of relatively speedy action, Lytton tended to stress more than Labouchere had done the importance of reaching a decision as soon as possible with respect to the validity of the charter and the related question of compensation to the company for lands removed from its jurisdiction. He proposed, therefore, reference of these subjects to a judicial tribunal, preferably with the consent of the company. In the remainder of the company's ter-

[1] P.R.O., C.O. 42/614, Head to Lytton, August 16, 1858.
[2] P.R.O., C.O. 42/615, Lytton to Head, confidential, August 20, 1858.

ritories not required for settlement, he would be prepared to see its rights continue on a terminable basis.

When he answered this important despatch on September 8, 1858,[3] Head took into account not only the points raised by Lytton but also those dealt with in the Canadian minute of council which he had before him and which he forwarded in the same mail. The minute endorsed the resolutions recently passed by the legislature and added that these and the opening of a transcontinental line of communication through the Hudson's Bay Territories from Canada to the Pacific "by Railway, or otherwise" would be further urged upon the Imperial Government by Canadian ministers about to proceed to London.[4]

Head began by stating that on the main points that Lytton had dealt with "[my] own opinion fully coincides with the views expressed by yourself." He added, however, a warning which Lytton in subsequent negotiations failed to keep sufficiently in mind:

Canada will not readily undertake the Government of the Red River Settlement as a charge on her own revenues. She will assert her claims and rights in the abstract, but will object either to compensate the Company, or pay continuously for the maintenance of military protection or civil government.

Head did not believe therefore that much in the way of positive action should be expected of Canada for the time being. Instead, he re-stated the view he had put forward in the memorandum of 1857:

I am clearly of opinion that the reversion of the fee of the colony, if I may so call it, ought to be at once vested in Canada, and I would so frame the Council that two or three of its members should be Canadians changed from time to time. In this way the interest of Canada in the Red River would be kept up, and men would hereafter be found in the former who knew the wants and the character of the new colony.

With regard to the executive council's suggestion of a transcontinental line of communication—a subject also being widely discussed in the United States at that time—Head wrote:

It may be feared that the projects of railways and canals across this wild tract of many hundreds of miles are somewhat remote and misty, but I

[3]P.R.O., C.O. 42/615, Head to Lytton, confidential, September 8, 1858. This letter has been printed by G. deT. Glazebrook in the *Canadian Historical Review*, XXI (1940), 56–59. The file copy which he used is dated September 9.
[4]P.R.O., C.O. 42/615, Head to Lytton, September 9, 1858, enclosure.

think it might be feasible to establish within a given time telegraphic communication between Fraser's River and Halifax; or now, in fact, directly with Great Britain. For this purpose posts of some sort for the protection of the wires would be necessary at intervals, and each of these posts would of itself form the nucleus of a settlement of some kind.

These last sentences helped, no doubt, to confirm what Ellice called unsympathetically, Lytton's "dream of establishing British Settlement, from sea to sea,"[5] and they are of particular interest in view of Head's connection a few years later, as governor of the company, with an actual project for such telegraphic communication across the prairies.

Apart from this comment on the executive council suggestion, the one new, and very important, addition in this despatch to the ideas Head had expressed in the memorandum of 1857 was that he now linked the Hudson's Bay question and confederation. Writing only a few weeks after his confederation announcement in the Speech from the Throne, the interrelationship of these two great problems was clearly established in his mind:

If any approximation is made to an Union of a federal character among the several North American colonies, the new settlement might easily be aggregated to this Union, and it is, perhaps, one great recommendation of this scheme at the present moment that it will thus admit of extending westward the body of our North American colonies. It is evident that from the distance and natural impediments the real and active management of local affairs at the Red River or on the Saskatchewan must be exercised on the spot, but the notion of union, and of interests common with Canada and the other North American colonies would have a strong tendency to prevent any leaning towards the United States, and would ensure to Her Majesty's Government the support of those colonies against any effort in this direction.

After this preliminary exchange of views between Head and Lytton, Hudson's Bay affairs moved slowly toward the deadline of May 31, 1859, without much progress being made in the direction of a solution. Lytton remained obsessed with the need to obtain a legal decision on the charter. When the company refused to be a consenting party to any such action, he was antagonized to the extent that company officials believed him "to have declared 'War to the Knife.'"[6] He turned instead immediately to a scheme for getting Canada to follow up her hitherto vague protestations by actually challenging the validity

[5]H.B. Co., D 4/84a, Ellice to Berens, September 14, 1858.
[6]H.B. Co., D 4/84a, Simpson to Berens, private, November 29, 1858.

of the charter in the courts on a writ of *sciere facias*. He tried hard, and he thought successfully, to persuade the Canadian ministers when they came to London to adopt this course.[7]

The truth was, however, as Head had warned, that whatever she might say Canada was not yet prepared to do anything at all. Indeed, especially in responsible circles, agitation regarding the Hudson's Bay Territories was steadily dying down as the duties and expenses that would be involved in their annexation came to be set more realistically over against the immediate advantages to be gained. Lytton learned with dismay, therefore, in April, 1859, that "[the] Canadian members have broken faith on this subject,"[8] that the Canadian executive council would not recommend to the legislature application for a writ. And when an address to the Queen was passed by the legislature in May, it was so worded, a Colonial Office official noted, "that it is not easy to say whether the Canadian Parl[t] do or do not repudiate the claims urged on their behalf for geographical extension Westward."[9] Left to make the decision alone at the last minute, Lytton offered to renew the licence for one or two years only. When this offer was rejected by the company, and when the situation was further complicated by Lytton's ill health and a general election in Britain which was to bring in a new government, the licence finally expired on May 31 with no permanent solution for the Hudson's Bay problem as a whole having been found.

Apart from Hudson's Bay affairs and the solution of the seat-of-government question, there was little that concerned Head in the business of the session of 1859. Galt's famous tariff with its higher duties which aroused the protests of the Sheffield manufacturers and other British interests might have been expected to involve Head in the argument that followed, his office still being the regular channel of communication between the mother country and the colony. In fact, however, Galt's tariff was merely a further advance on that of Cayley who in 1858 had similarly raised rates, mainly and ostensibly for purposes of revenue, but with an eye to some protection as well. At that time Head had emphasized to the Colonial Office in language not unlike that he

[7]P.R.O., C.O. 42/617, Lytton to Head, February 11, 1859.
[8]P.R.O., C.O. 42/618, Head to Lytton, April 4, 1859, and minute by Lytton.
[9]P.R.O., C.O. 42/618, Head to Lytton, May 7, 1859, minute by Merivale.

had used years before with reference to bounties in New Bruns-wick:

. . . that however unsound the views of a community may be in matters of political economy, if that community substantially governs itself, we must expect to find such unsoundness reflected in its legislation. Self Government, which is only to operate when its acts agree with the opinions of others, is a contradiction in terms.[10]

In 1859, when Head forwarded Galt's tariff to the Colonial Office, he merely added, after noting that objections would likely be made to it:

I must necessarily leave the representatives of the people in Parliament to adopt that mode of raising supplies which they believe to be most bene-ficial to their constituents. There is nothing in the system adopted which professes to impose differential duties, or to fetter the freedom of trade.[11]

When the expected objections were made, Head left Galt to argue his own case, which the latter did very capably indeed.

The continuing repercussions of the excitement of the previous year, and the abuse which Head received from time to time in 1859, were not such as to cause any concern to a man of his ex-perience in the ways of politicians. "The debate on the min-isterial changes of last summer," he wrote to Lewis in February, "which has been mixed up with everything else, has not dam-aged or annoyed me at all. I am satisfied that the opinion of the Colony is strongly in my favour."[12] The whole affair, however, had unavoidably had the effect of bringing Head into closer association with one party and one group of ministers than was desirable for a governor under a system of complete Responsible Government such as existed in Canada. Fortunately, the Cartier-Macdonald ministry was to establish a record tenure of office for ministries under the Union—three years and nine months—so that it outlasted Head's term by a few months and he was spared the embarrassment of having to call on their—and his—opponents to form a government. An occurrence of the mid-summer of 1859 that might have altered this strangely was the near loss of the steamer *Plowboy* in Georgian Bay. Five members of the council were among other excursionists on board when the engines broke down and high winds almost drove the vessel on to a rocky and dangerous shore. Head's account of that

10P.A.C., G 180B, Head to Stanley, confidential, June 11, 1858.
11P.R.O., C.O. 42/617, Head to Lytton, March 26, 1859.
12Lewis Papers, Head to Lewis, February 12, 1859.

incident in a private letter to Merivale illustrates how close his personal association with his ministers had become:

> The enclosed extract from a paper will show you how near I have been to losing half my ministers. The event which it describes must have been a most fearful one. All the ladies behaved admirably. In fact the whole party went through the horrors of shipwreck of a most fearful kind. The holding of the anchor at the last moment was most singular. . . . Independently of the personal risk I really do not know what would have happened politically if the vessel had been lost. Probably not a soul would have been saved. McDonald, the Attorney General, the Ch. Comm^r of Public Works with his wife & daughter, the Ch. Comm^r of Crown Lands & the Post Master General were on board. Had I been in Toronto I should in all likelihood have joined the party.
> Brown's new card of dissolving the union is not succeeding at all.[13]

In September, 1859, after a pleasant summer which included holidays at Niagara Falls and a lengthy visit from the Ticknors,[14] Head started on a tour of Lower Canada prior to the transfer of the government to Quebec which was to take place in the fall and which would be the last before its final establishment in Ottawa. In the course of this trip he anticipated with some pleasure that it might be desirable to go to Portland to take part in the celebrations marking the arrival of the S.S. *Great Eastern*.[15] Just at this point, a sudden blow shattered many of his hopes and a dark shadow that would never be completely dissipated was cast over his life and that of Lady Head. On September 25, their only son, John, was drowned while swimming in the St. Maurice River. John's career and education had been a matter of major interest and some anxiety to Head ever since he had himself tried, unsuccessfully, to arouse the enthusiasm of the ten-year-old in the Greek and Latin classics. At Harrow and Upper Canada College, and more recently at Heidelberg from which he had returned only a month before, John had shown instead an unusual aptitude for science, and especially geology, stimulated originally in all probability as a result of the family's friendship with Sir Charles Lyell. Still in his teens, he had amassed a large collection of fossils, including two of a type not previously listed by geologists, and was planning to continue his

[13]P.R.O., C.O. 42/619, Head to Merivale, private, July 10, 1859.
[14]G. S. Hillard (ed.), *George Ticknor*, II, 424, Ticknor to E. Everett, August 22, 1859.
[15]P.A.C., G 463, Head to Newcastle, separate, September 14, 1859.

studies in this field at Oxford.[16] After John's death, Head "went through his work like a man,"[17] but there seems no doubt that his pleasure in it and his enthusiasm waned. The tendency toward irritability associated with his epilepsy seems also to have been more marked during the remaining time he spent in Canada, and large social functions became a burden that he felt less willing to undertake.

In 1859, one of the most important associations of Head's career was renewed when the Duke of Newcastle became colonial secretary for the second time. At the end of his first term, in 1854, Newcastle had been responsible for Head's appointment as governor general; during this second, he was to be in close touch with Head while the latter remained governor general and also when Head became governor of the Hudson's Bay Company; indeed, it was largely due to Newcastle's influence that Head was named to that post as well.[18] What degree of personal friendship developed between the two men is now impossible to say. In their general approach to colonial problems, however, they had much in common, and this no doubt was the primary factor in drawing them together. Like Head, Newcastle was inclined to take a long-range and comprehensive view of a subject, but to modify his theories when necessary by a soundly realistic judgment of what was immediately practicable. In particular, Newcastle shared Head's keen interest in the basic North American problems of confederation and the future government of the Hudson's Bay Territories.

The latter topic was of special importance when Newcastle took office. The licence having expired, the North West Territory was without a government and in Rupert's Land as well there was a growing conviction that company rule would soon have to end. After making interim arrangements and carefully studying the whole situation, Newcastle had a draft bill prepared for the removal of the Red River and Saskatchewan districts from the company's jurisdiction in return for certain compensation, and their creation into separate colonies. He submitted this bill to the

[16]Quebec *Chronicle*, September 30, 1859.
[17]Sir Joseph Pope, *Memoirs of Sir John Alexander Macdonald*, I, 217, Spence to Macdonald, October 14, 1859.
[18]E. W. Watkin, *Canada and the United States*, p. 147: "Sir Edmund Head was appointed Governor at the suggestion—almost the personal request—of the Duke of Newcastle."

company for consideration in May, 1860, and thus initiated lengthy negotiations which however led to no immediate result.[19]

While he was thus engaged Newcastle had also had his attention attracted to the subject of confederation. Following the failure of the Canadian efforts in this direction in 1858, discussion had been kept alive by two individuals in particular. These were Galt and Manners Sutton, the latter continuing to press instead for the alternative of Maritime union. In the autumn of 1859, Newcastle received a despatch from Manners Sutton informing him that union was being widely talked of in the Maritime provinces, and that the time would soon be ripe for some action. His interest aroused, Newcastle wrote confidentially to Head for the latter's views on the matter.[20] By way of reply, Head was at first content to refer back to his memorandum of 1857 which he had left with Labouchere at the Colonial Office, adding simply: "Although my views on one or two collateral points may have been slightly altered by my subsequent experience, they are not changed in any such a manner as to affect the opinion which I then expressed as to the expediency of such a project."[21] When a search at the Colonial Office failed to discover Head's original memorandum he was asked for a copy. He forwarded this in January, 1860, and along with it, a "Supplementary Memorandum" bringing his views up to date.[22]

Meanwhile, Maritime union had become linked again with attempts still being made by the Canadian executive council—and particularly by Galt who was in London in January—to keep alive interest in confederation and in the building of an inter-

[19]H.B. Co., A 8/10, Berens to Newcastle, May 30, 1860.

[20]P.R.O., C.O. 188/132, Manners Sutton to Newcastle, private and confidential, September 29, 1859; Newcastle to Head, confidential, November 5, 1859.

[21]P.R.O., C.O. 42/619, Head to Newcastle, confidential, December 1, 1859.

[22]See above, chapter VIII, note 23. The "Supplementary Memorandum," dated Quebec, January 21, 1860, is bound in C.O. 537/137 immediately following the memorandum of 1857. It is clear that the two memoranda were sent to Merivale at this time in answer to a private letter from him. Some confusion resulted from Merivale's transfer to the India Office but the memoranda reached Newcastle without undue delay. However, a covering despatch which Head wrote subsequently, after receiving an official request for his memorandum, never caught up with the documents it was supposed to enclose and was eventually filed separately. (P.R.O., C.O. 42/622, Head to Newcastle, confidential, February 9, 1860.) This contretemps was of no real importance at the time but tangles the skein of the historian. A copy of the "Supplementary Memorandum" with very slight verbal differences, although it is dated Quebec, May 28, 1860, is also to be found among the Head Papers in the Canadian Archives and it is from this that the quotations here are taken.

colonial railway. These circumstances, and Newcastle's current efforts to find a solution for the Hudson's Bay problem, must have made additionally welcome the arrival of a comprehensive expression of Head's opinions.

To one already familiar with the memorandum of 1857, however, and with the events that had taken place since, there is nothing unexpected in what Head now added in his "Supplementary Memorandum." Indeed it gives the impression of being a brief, almost cursory, summing-up of opinions so long and so firmly held that their author has ceased to feel any fresh enthusiasm for them. Head still believed, as he had ever since 1857, that a union of the Maritime provinces was highly to be desired. The experience of 1858, however, had shown the need for taking more into account one additional factor. If the severance of Upper and Lower Canada were to become inevitable "consequent on the cry of Repres^n by Population," then it would be "our duty to face the inconveniences & the objections which I believe to exist against an Union of these Provinces with Canada . . . for I think that the result of such a severance without an Union of the Colonies would be the absorption of Upper Canada into the United States." Nevertheless, Head now hoped again, as he had in 1857, that no such situation would develop. "The establishment of the seat of Govt at Ottawa & the growing importance of the central section of Canada as a unit of middle opinion between the extreme West & East," together with the strengthening of economic bonds through the opening of railways and the increase of trade, all of these tended in the direction of keeping the two sections together. Only if, in spite of these, dissolution of the Canadian union should become imminent would Head advise attempting the alternative of confederation, and then "only as the least of two evils & as a last recourse."

Head must have had many opportunities a few months after writing this supplementary memorandum to discuss confederation and other matters of common interest personally with the Duke of Newcastle when the latter, in the late summer of 1860, accompanied the Prince of Wales on his tour of the British provinces and parts of the United States. The Prince's tour was the outcome of an invitation by the Canadian legislature to the Queen and other members of the royal family to visit Canada in 1860 in connection with the opening of the Victoria Bridge, a great iron tube two miles long which was being built across the

St. Lawrence at Montreal—one of the engineering wonders of the time and the culminating effort of the Grand Trunk Railway. The Queen, being unable to come herself, had agreed that the Prince should come instead.

The Prince's visit, which Head would otherwise have greatly enjoyed, must have been in some ways a most trying experience, occurring as it did a little less than a year after his own son's death. John, just a year older than the Prince, would have been contemporary with him at Oxford. Unequal to the strain, Lady Head spent the time of the Prince's visit with friends in the United States. Sir Edmund, however, met the Prince on his arrival at Gaspé on August 12 and accompanied him throughout most of the next six weeks, until the Prince crossed into the United States at Detroit on September 20, participating in fishing and boating expeditions, dinners and balls, and in many special ceremonies including the laying of the corner-stone of the parliament building in Ottawa and the opening of the Victoria Bridge.[23] For Canada, the visit was a really great occasion, and all went well, amid enthusiastic expressions of popular loyalty to the Crown, except at Kingston and Belleville where Orange demonstrations gave such a partisan character to the welcome that the Prince's party refused to land. At Toronto where similar tendencies were barely restrained by firm action on the part of Head and Newcastle, both were burned in effigy in Colborne Street.[24]

[23]Dr. Acland, one of the Prince's party, has left behind one of the most intimate of all contemporary accounts of Sir Edmund Head. Writing in the course of this visit to Canada, he said: "I am quite in love with Sir Edmund Head . . . full of knowledge, classical, artistic, scientific. He lost his only son suddenly last year, and has since not rallied, and indeed takes very little interest in things compared to what formerly he did, or rather, is less willing to exert himself, and is in bad health. . . . I wish I could stereotype his conversations . . . such a varied store of knowledge—such memory—such quotations—such mildness—such taste and tenderness." J. B. Attlay, *Sir Henry Wentworth Acland, Bart.,* pp. 270 ff.

[24]J. C. Dent, *The Last Forty Years,* II, 403. Alluding to the performances of Blondin, the tightrope walker, at Niagara Falls (which the Prince's party visited on September 17) the Toronto *Globe,* still embittered by the events of 1858, said: " . . . it was out of the question allowing our beloved Prince to incur the dangers of such a journey [Blondin's offer to transport the Prince across the Falls in a wheelbarrow] but if it was the Governor-General, the thanks of the country should be given to Blondin if he wheeled Sir Edmund to American soil, never to return . . . the satisfaction would be increased if the wheeler was Old Nick himself wheeling the Governor-General to Hades amid the usual sulphurous smoke and flames." See T. B. Gough, *Boyish Reminiscences of His Majesty the King's Visit to Canada in 1860,* pp. 165–66.

Some two weeks before the Prince of Wales, on August 25, drove home the last rivet in the Victoria Bridge, and at a sumptuous luncheon gave "the health of the Governor-General, success to Canada, and prosperity to the Grand Trunk Railway,"[25] Head had received from the railway a memorial warning that it was in extreme financial difficulty and that unless speedy aid were given it would be unable to meet its obligations and a stoppage of the line would result. As soon, therefore, as the Prince went on to the American part of his tour Head and his ministers hastened back to Quebec to deal with this emergency.

Under ordinary circumstances the dealings of the Canadian Government with a Canadian railway should have been no concern of the governor general, but the affairs of the Grand Trunk never fell into any ordinary category. Since its incorporation in 1853, there had developed a most complicated pattern of relationships between the railway in Canada, its various English bond- and shareholders, and the Canadian Government, leading to corruption and inefficiency and much mutual recrimination. The English investors, represented in particular by the great banking empires of the Barings and the Glyns, suffered severely as a result of the company's misfortunes, and they felt at a special disadvantage vis-à-vis the Canadian Government because the latter not only shared their financial interest in the company but had a political interest too—and political authority. Accordingly, as early as 1856, Thomas Baring had initiated a private and confidential correspondence with Head in order to ensure that he was as familiar with the views of the shareholders as with those of his ministers on controversial issues.[26] Head's position above party politics, and his Imperial as well as Canadian responsibilities, would, Baring hoped, make him an impartial observer, and to some extent a referee in Grand Trunk affairs. As time went on, this hope seems to have been fulfilled, and Head seems to have been accepted into the counsels of all parties and to have been increasingly relied upon as adviser and arbiter.

Head's own explanation of why he was willing to undertake such responsibilities, and how he regarded them, is to be found

[25]G. D. Engleheart, *Journal of the Progress of H.R.H. the Prince of Wales*, p. 41.
[26]P.A.C., Baring Papers, Baring to Head, private and confidential, February 15, 1856.

in one of his early letters to Thomas Baring and G. C. Glyn. In it, Head emphasized that he could only look upon Grand Trunk questions from the point of view of the welfare of Canada. However:

I must admit that one great source of such welfare must be the credit and character of the Province as evinced by its readiness to meet all its legal liabilities and to fulfil—not the letter—but the spirit of its moral obligations. On these terms alone can Canada hope to assume the position which will entitle her to profit hereafter by the confidence of British Capital and enterprize. . . . For myself personally I can assure you Gentlemen, that I am deeply sensible of the importance of the whole question. I believe that the future prosperity of Canada is intimately connected with the speedy and successful conclusion of this great work.[27]

By 1860, Head's personal importance in Grand Trunk affairs had become such that when the financial emergency occurred at about the time of the Prince of Wales' visit, his participation in the attempt to find a solution was taken for granted by all concerned. In fact, it was generally felt that unless the difficulty could be tided over somehow, he would be unable to leave for England in October as he had planned to do. For a while the situation seemed to demand a special fall session of the legislature and it was even feared it might cause the Government to break up. "In either case," Baring was informed by his American representative, S. G. Ward, who had gone to Canada to keep in close touch with what was taking place, "it would seem that the Gov. General must remain in Canada. But possibly the whole matter may be postponed till the regular session and in that case it was thought that Sir Edmund Head would go home and not return to Canada."[28] A week later another letter from Ward contained the last-minute information that a way had been found (which need not concern us here) to avoid immediate disaster, and "that there will probably be no extra session no change in the Govt & that the Govr General goes home for a short time only and returns to attend to this business."[29]

When Head asked for leave of absence to go to England in the autumn of 1860, following the Prince of Wales' visit, his tenure of the highest office in the British colonial service had already exceeded its normal term, and he was aware that his successor would be named soon. In 1857, and again in 1859,

[27]P.A.C., Baring Papers, Head to Baring and Glyn, July 19, 1856.
[28]P.A.C., Baring Papers, Ward to Baring, October 2, 1860.
[29]P.A.C., Baring Papers, Ward to Baring, October 9, 1860.

there had been hints that he might be offered the difficult governorship of the Ionian Islands—"the renewal of my lease of office in an agreeable form," Head had commented at the time[30] —but nothing had come of these, and by 1860 there was no other suitable colonial post immediately in prospect. In his middle fifties, an exile from England for over twelve years except for brief holidays, and without any great private means, Head's purpose in visiting England from October, 1860, to February, 1861, was undoubtedly to renew old contacts and prepare the way for his permanent return.

There are chance references to his conferences with Colonial Office and other government officials while in England and to his meetings with his friends. A letter of Lyell's is of special interest in this connection: "It was like old times again to meet the Heads at the Milmans, but the loss of their son makes a great blank. There was no young man of all my acquaintance as able and enthusiastic as a geologist. The Heads will return in February to Canada, but I hope for no long time."[31] A letter Head himself wrote to Ticknor gives an interesting account of a week-end spent as guests of the Queen at Windsor:

I am able to say that everyone in this country sets the highest value on the courtesy and friendly bearing towards the Prince, shown in the United States. I may begin from the top, for I had the opportunity of talking both to the Queen and Prince Albert on the subject last week. . . . The Prince [of Wales] appeared in good spirits, and perfectly recovered from his long voyage. . . . Prince Albert expressed himself to me personally in terms much stronger than were necessary with reference to the Prince's visit. I attributed a large portion of its success to the Prince of Wales own courtesy and good-nature, which is strictly true. Palmerston and Lord John Russell were at the Castle—the former vigorous enough to walk upwards of three miles with me and Lord St. Germans in the afternoon of Sunday.[32]

When Head returned to Canada in February to wind up his administration, Grand Trunk business, as had been anticipated, claimed much of his attention. In fact, in London and in Boston on his way back, he had already talked over thoroughly with

[30]Lewis Papers, Head to Lewis, February 12, 1859.
[31]Mrs. Lyell (ed.), *Sir Charles Lyell*, II, 340.
[32]Hillard, *George Ticknor*, II, 429. The Prince of Wales was then still in residence at Frewen Hall, Oxford, where, earlier in the same week, Sir Edmund and Lady Head had dined with him. "Sir Edmund [the Prince wrote to the Queen] had been at Oxford with most of the present professors, so that it was very interesting to him to meet them again." Sir Sidney Lee, *King Edward VII*, p. 113.

Baring and Ward the various plans, including receivership, that
were being put forward to deal with the company's difficulties.[33]
At Quebec, he found his ministers in as complex and precarious
a situation as they had been in in the fall—made worse now perhaps by the fact that they had decided that a general election
would have to be called during the summer. They were most
anxious to postpone, until after that at least, any major action
regarding a railway whose continued operation was essential but
whose financial problems unfortunately were so extremely controversial.

In the weeks that followed Head remained close to the centre
of complicated negotiations aimed at working out some sort of
solution that would enable both the company and the Government to survive. Strangely enough the English interests had as
their agent at this stage no less typical an American than a certain
George Ashmun, recently chairman of the Republican National
Convention that had nominated Abraham Lincoln. Ashmun, a
skilled politician and lobbyist, had been introduced to Head in
Boston, and while in Quebec he kept Head carefully informed
of the English view by means of frequent interviews. Head
stressed always "that he could not form any definite opinion upon
the course to be pursued until some recommendation should be
made by his Council."[34] But he was willing to listen to all sides
of the case, and even to bring the disputants together, as for
example at a dinner party to which he invited Ashmun and a
number of others including Galt and Macdonald, and where,
according to Ashmun, "We had considerable conversation about
Grand Trunk, & I was gratified to see quite an improved state of
opinion."[35] Ward joined Ashmun in the latter part of the
negotiations, and another temporary solution was eventually
worked out. In his final report to Baring, Ward made clear how
he regarded Head's role: "Before leaving I addressed a note to
Sir Edmund stating in a few words what Mr. Galt had promised,
in order not to leave His Excellency under a false impression, &
also thinking it important that he should be apprised of the
understanding as he would not willingly look on at any thing
contravening it."[36] The role thus assigned to him of informed

[33]P.A.C., Baring Papers, Baring to Ward, February 1, 1861; Ward to Baring,
February 22, 1861.
[34]P.A.C., Baring Papers, Ashmun to Ward, March 5, 1861.
[35]P.A.C., Baring Papers, Ashmun to Ward, March 9, 1861.
[36]P.A.C., Baring Papers, Ward to Baring, April 4, 1861.

observer, influential from the very fact that he was known to be impartial and scrupulously fair-minded, was one that Head was well qualified to play. In his opinion it approximated to that of the sovereign in England and was one of the most important remaining to a governor under Responsible Government.

In the spring of 1861, defence problems more critical than any since the winter of 1855–56 were revived by the outbreak of the American Civil War. A letter to Lewis, written less than a fortnight after the attack on Fort Sumter, shows Head's clear appreciation of the ultimate danger: "The aspect of affairs is most serious & whenever their own fighting is over I do not think it will be a pleasant thing to have 100,000 or 200,000 men kicking their heels with arms in their hands on our frontier & all the habits acquired in a Southern Civil War."[37]

When he wrote this Head was already taking steps to make certain that his personal position would not be compromised through the activities of the energetic George Ashmun whom he had received and entertained a few weeks before on Grand Trunk business. Ashmun, Head learned, was about to return to Canada in the guise of a special agent of the new secretary of state, W. H. Seward, "to explain to the Canadian Government the true position of the United States in this crisis."[38] Forewarned by the newspapers, and no doubt recalling the dangers Crampton and Howe had become involved in during the potentially less serious recruiting crisis, Head was most scrupulous in his care to have Ashmun's status clarified by personal correspondence, and then, when he arrived, to explain that "all Official intercourse between the Govt of the United States and that of a British Colony must pass through Her Majesty's accredited representative at Washington."[39] Ashmun returned shortly afterwards to the United States, and Seward later admitted that his real mission had been "to ascertain the feeling in Canada with regard to fitting out Privateers on the St. Lawrence."[40]

The idea of privateers had apparently occurred to Confederate sympathizers as well, because on April 27, a few days before Ashmun's arrival, Head received a telegram from Governor

[37]Lewis Papers, Head to Lewis, April 24, 1861.
[38]P.A.C., Baring Papers, Ward to Head, May 1, 1861.
[39]P.A.C., G 463, Head to Newcastle, May 4, 1861.
[40]See L. B. Shippee, *Canadian-American Relations, 1849–1874*, p. 121.

Andrew of Massachusetts asserting that the steamer *Peerless* had been bought for the "rebels" in Lake Ontario, and demanding that "this piratical cruiser" be stopped at the canals or elsewhere. Head's answer, made typically through the more confidential medium of the mails, was that there would have to be some evidence of the vessel's piratical character before she could be stopped. At the same time, however, he ordered Canadian authorities to keep a careful but unobtrusive watch over the *Peerless* as she passed through Canadian waters to ensure that no breach of neutrality did take place. Explaining the whole affair in a despatch which he wrote immediately to Lord Lyons, Head made it clear that he had not neglected one final aspect of the matter:

I have not stated to the Governor of Massachusetts that the proper medium of communication with the Government of Canada was through Your Lordship, as Her Majesty's Minister at Washington, only because I feared such an intimation would seem a mockery at a time when the communications between the Northern States and the Capitol are at least interrupted, if not entirely cut off.[41]

Head showed equal tact and caution in avoiding controversy over selling or refusing to sell Canadian arms to one side or the other. The only stocks in Canada that might possibly have been disposed of belonged to the regular forces or the militia. To requests that some of the arms of the militia be made available against the "rebels," he was able to give the polite but conclusive answer that there was a clause in the Militia Act absolutely prohibiting them being taken out of Canada under any circumstances. The fact that this clause so fortunately existed was itself due to the great attention Head had always paid to every detail that might affect Canadian-American relations. It had been inserted in the first place, he noted on one occasion, "by my express desire with the view of preventing the Volunteer Corps from carrying their Arms into the United States on holiday visits."[42]

In military matters as in diplomacy, Head remained alert and careful throughout this period. Prompted no doubt by the *Peerless* incident, he wrote confidentially on April 29 to the commanding general, Sir Fenwick Williams, suggesting the need for

[41]P.A.C., Governor General's Letterbook, Head to Lyons, April 29, 1861.
[42]P.A.C., G 463, Head to Newcastle, April 25, 1861.

establishing guards on the canals *"as soon as possible."*[43] The next month, he took advantage of a short tour conducting the Queen's second son, Prince Alfred, through Upper Canada, to collect information personally and make a number of sketches showing American and Canadian defences on the Lakes. This material he forwarded to the Duke of Newcastle from Toronto.[44]

On the main defence question, the sending of reinforcements to Canada from Britain, there was much controversy in the summer of 1861, as there had been during the earlier crisis of 1856. The Imperial Government, acting on a request from Fenwick Williams, sent three regiments and a field battery to North America with great promptitude almost as soon as the fighting began. This caused immediate and severe criticism in the House of Commons where the trend of opinion was in the direction of leaving local colonial defence more and more to the colonial peoples themselves.[45] Toward the end of the summer, Head was asked for his advice regarding a second recommendation by Fenwick Williams to the effect that an additional force of artillery should be sent to Canada. He was also asked whether Canada might be willing to share the expense if this were done. Head's answer was firm and unhesitating: he insisted as he had done in 1856 that the responsibility for any decision on reinforcements must remain with the Imperial government.

If there is any great risk of a war with the United States I have no [doubt] of the expediency of sending an additional force of Artillery as suggested by the Lieutenant General Commanding. What the actual risk of such a war is Her Majesty's Government must judge.

Whether such a war occur will depend probably not on Canada, but on Great Britain. The colony would have no voice in determining this question and there exist no causes of difference with the Government of the United States arising out of the affairs or interests of Canada. The Colony would be involved in such a war only as part and an exposed part of the Empire. . . . There is nothing at present in the internal affairs of Canada which would make the presence of an increased force of artillery necessary or expedient.

The feeling of the Colony and its representatives in the Provincial Parliament would I believe be adverse to any contribution in money out of Colonial Funds towards the cost of such increased armament.

That our long exposed frontier is inaccessible by sea and not easily reinforced in winter, is a line of weakness through which an enemy might

43P.A.C., Governor General's Letterbook, Head to Fenwick Williams, April 29 and June 13, 1861.
44P.A.C., G 180B, Head to Newcastle, confidential, June 25, 1861.
45C. P. Stacey, *Canada and the British Army*, pp. 118 ff.

wound England is the misfortune of Canada as well as the Mother Country, but I doubt whether the people of Canada would see in this fact a sufficient reason for charging them with a large portion of the burthen of defence in a war caused by interests in no degree of a local or colonial character.[46]

The Trent Affair which occurred shortly after Head left Canada showed the justice of his opinion that war, if it came, would be the result of Imperial rather than Canadian causes and that reinforcement policy therefore was a continuing Imperial responsibility.

In the late summer and fall of 1861, just before Head's departure, a fresh series of Grand Trunk discussions began which were to result the next year, and after a change of government, in a comprehensive solution of the company's problems being finally reached. Head's part in these discussions was limited, but they were nevertheless important to him because they brought him into contact for the first time with the redoubtable Edward W. Watkin who two years later would be largely responsible for making him the governor of the Hudson's Bay Company. Moreover, Watkin's wider view of Grand Trunk policy, which included linking it with an intercolonial railway to Halifax on the one hand and with a line to the Pacific on the other, raised once again at the very end of Head's administration issues that had long been of special interest to him.

Watkin's trip to Canada at this time was made at the urgent request of the English bond- and shareholders and the London directors of the Grand Trunk Railway with the purpose of finding out what was wrong with the company and setting it right. He came too with a full-blown scheme of his own for a transcontinental line of communication across British territory to the Pacific. He had outlined this some months before his appointment in an article in the *Illustrated London News*, and had since discussed it in detail with the Duke of Newcastle.[47] It was not difficult, particularly when he found in Canada how unpopular further assistance to the Grand Trunk alone would be, for Watkin to combine his Grand Trunk salvage operation with his vision of Empire. In six weeks—during which he travelled as far west as the plains beyond Chicago and as far east as Halifax, by rail, boat, canoe, and spring-waggon, night and day—Watkin

[46]P.A.C., G 463, Head to Newcastle, September 9, 1861.
[47]Watkin, *Canada and the United States*, chap. v.

not only became familiar with Grand Trunk problems and advanced their solution as much as was possible at that time in negotiations with the Canadian Government, but he also got together at the end of September large and enthusiastic delegations from Nova Scotia and New Brunswick to meet with the Canadian executive council at Quebec and plan renewed efforts to build an intercolonial railway. Watkin's optimism and the perennial willingness of colonial leaders to try again to get this vital line built resulted, after a more than usually convivial conference, in a decision to send representatives to London with renewed offers from each of the colonial governments. Watkin himself was to precede them and prepare their way with the Imperial authorities.

Head had been in frequent contact with Watkin during his weeks in Canada. Watkin had been presented to him by Cartier on first arriving at Quebec in August, and had delivered a letter from Thomas Baring explaining his Grand Trunk mission. Head had called Macdonald in to join them in beginning preliminary discussions at once. Head's role in what followed had necessarily been a passive one, but as usual he had kept in close touch with all that took place, and on the eve of the intercolonial conference had entertained Watkin and a number of the delegates at a dinner.[48] His known interest in the success of the intercolonial scheme is shown by the fact that after his return to England the Canadian Government, with Monck's consent, took the unusual step of asking him to submit his views on the subject to the colonial secretary to reinforce those of the North American delegates. This Head did in due course.[49]

Apart from urgent military and Grand Trunk business, Head spent much of his last months in Canada in a round of farewell excursions and entertainments. There is an account for instance of a visit to Lake Memphremagog made by the Heads and their family and suite in late September. "He was looking exceedingly well, and . . . the simplicity of his manner set everyone at ease." Wearing a "Jim Crow hat" and a "farmer-cut coat." Head led the party on a sketching ramble and then back to the village for a large luncheon in which everyone took part.[50]

[48]*Ibid.*, pp. 501–3.
[49]P.A.C., G 464, Monck to Newcastle, November 15, 1861; G 166, Newcastle to Monck, December 9, 1861.
[50]Toronto *Leader*, September 28, 1861.

A more formal occasion was a farewell dinner offered by Cartier, the prime minister. Watkin was present and noted afterwards regarding Head: "In response to the toast to his health, he alluded to his infirmity of temper, admitted his suffering—before concealed from outside people—and expressed his apologies in a manner so feeling and so gentle that the tears came into everybody's eyes. I heard more than one sob from men whose rough exterior disguised the real tenderness of their hearts."[51]

Head's departure from Quebec took place on October 24, the day on which his successor, Lord Monck, assumed office. Through streets lined with troops, he drove in his carriage to the station, and after farewell ceremonies there, left by train for Montreal, and thence travelled to Boston for a final visit with the Ticknors before sailing for England on October 30. He was accompanied as far as Boston by G. E. Cartier, the prime minister, and John Ross, the president of the executive council.[52]

[51]Watkin, *Canada and the United States*, p. 503.
[52]Toronto *Leader*, October 28, 1861.

IV

LONDON, 1861–1868

ELEVEN

The Hudson's Bay Company and the Literary World of London

W HEN Sir Edmund Head returned to England late in 1861 at the age of fifty-seven, he had no certain plans for the future. Indeed almost two years were to pass before he would be elected governor of the Hudson's Bay Company, a post which he would then hold for the remainder of his life. Meanwhile, he was welcomed back into London society by his friends, and was accorded the honours due a man of his eminence and scholarship returning from more than twelve years of distinguished service in the colonies. Oxford granted him the honorary degree of D.C.L., and Cambridge, an LL.D. He was elected to the fellowship of the Royal Society, and of The Club, the famous literary and dining society founded in the eighteenth century by Johnson and Reynolds, and numbering among its members the leading figures in London's world of art and learning and politics. A little later, on the occasion of Merton College's 600th anniversary and the opening of its new buildings, Head was a principal guest at a dinner and replied to the toast: "The former fellows of the College." To mark this commemoration, a committee representing old members of the college offered to present four portraits, those of Lord Elgin, Dr. Robert Marsham (the then warden), Sir Edmund Head, and the Bishop of Salisbury. In 1867, Head's portrait was accordingly placed in the Hall, where it has since remained.

Not long after his return from Canada, Head made a brief and unsuccessful foray into party politics, standing for election in the Yorkshire riding of Pontefract. His defeat seems to have permanently discouraged what hopes he may have had along these lines, and in April, 1862, he accepted office as one of three unpaid Civil Service commissioners.[1] The work of the com-

[1]By a coincidence Head replaced Sir J. G. Shaw-Lefevre, whom he had succeeded as Poor Law commissioner in 1841.

mission in the course of its seven years' existence had become largely of a routine nature, though its functions were still being extended to cover important public departments. Head appears to have taken an ordinary share in its proceedings: it is interesting, however, and faintly ironic, to find a man of his "unusual" handwriting associating himself on one occasion with the statement that the quality most lacking in candidates for the public service was the ability to write a good hand with "the clear formation of all the letters of the alphabet and the essential quality of distinctness without the sacrifice of other desirable elements of a good official hand." Head remained a member of the commission for the rest of his life. When he died, his fellow-commissioners in their *Report* for 1868 paid tribute to: "our late colleague . . . whose long official experience, sound judgment, and extensive acquaintance with various branches of knowledge have frequently been of essential value to us on complicated and difficult questions which have arisen for our consideration and decision."

On July 2, 1863, Head was elected governor of the newly reorganized Hudson's Bay Company which had "largely changed its proprietary, and virtually amalgamated with some gentlemen, who, chiefly under the management of Mr. Watkin, projected a communication across the continent by road and telegraph from Canada to British Columbia."[2] To a considerable extent this event had its origin in Watkin's visit to Canada two years before at the very end of Head's administration.

The idea of communication across the continent goes back much further, of course, right to the time of Alexander Mackenzie himself. As early as 1848, the possibility of such communication taking the form of a railway had been seriously proposed. In 1858, when the subject was raised by the Canadian executive council, Head had expressed the opinion that the scheme of a railway was "somewhat remote and misty," but that a telegraph line might be a more immediately feasible alternative.[3] Watkin's arrival on the Canadian scene in 1861 tended, as his presence always did, to create the impression that even misty dreams were matters of practical, indeed urgent, reality—and

[2]H.B. Co., Stowe MSS, Confidential *précis* on the Hudson's Bay Company, by T. F. Elliot, January 21, 1858.
[3]See above, chap. x.

sometimes, by a still more remarkable alchemy, he was able to convert this impression into the truth. Watkin's interest at the time centred on the Grand Trunk and the extension of its activities both eastward to Halifax and westward to the Pacific. It may be that Head was partially responsible for the fact that at about this stage Watkin came to believe that the western part of the plan might be accomplished, in a preliminary way at least, by building a line of telegraph.

In 1861, however, discussions were concerned mainly with the intercolonial railway to Halifax. It was not until 1862, in the course of complicated negotiations in which Watkin and the Duke of Newcastle seem to have played the leading part, and in which Canadian ministers, London financiers, and the Hudson's Bay Company became involved, that the emphasis began to shift more and more to the western project. In that year, Watkin organized the Atlantic and Pacific Transit and Telegraph Company, and reached a large measure of understanding with the British and Canadian governments to the effect that the company's efforts to establish a line of road and telegraph communication through British territories to the Pacific would be subsidized by interest guarantees and land grants. And when he found the Hudson's Bay Company not sufficiently willing to add its support in connection with the part passing through its territories, he began as well, in December, negotiations that were to lead to its purchase and reorganization the following July.[4]

At what point Head resumed his participation in these events, with which he had been concerned in another role while in Canada, is not certain. It is known that at some stage his name was brought forward by the Duke of Newcastle as the potential governor of the new Hudson's Bay Company. When the offer was made, Head was no doubt glad to accept it for its financial advantages, and also because he knew that the company with its new objectives was likely to have an important influence on the welfare of British North America, a matter of long and sincere interest to him. Accordingly, on June 26, 1863, Head and others who were to be associated with him on the new committee of directors, met with the members of the International

---

[4]These events of the 1861–63 period are fully described in E. W. Watkin, *Canada and the United States*; R. G. Trotter, *Canadian Federation*; and E. A. Mitchell, "Edward Watkin and the Buying-out of the Hudson's Bay Company," *Canadian Historical Review*, XXXIV (1953), 219–44.

Financial Society, the body through which Watkin had arranged that the whole financial transaction for the transfer of the company's ownership would take place. The entire scheme was gone over in detail, the prospectus of the new company was studied and revised, and a final agreement reached. On July 2, when the transfer of shares took place, Head and the new directors were elected at a meeting of the General Court of the company, and Head took the oath of fidelity prescribed for the governor under the terms of the charter.

For the next six months or so, Head was fully occupied with two aspects of his new duties: the administration of the company's business including the communications project, and negotiations with the Colonial Office regarding the future of the charter rights. In both of these he was personally active, attending the weekly committee and sub-committee meetings regularly, keeping up an extensive private correspondence with Watkin and others on company matters, and normally drafting in his own handwriting important official letters. He was assisted particularly by Curtis Miranda Lampson, the deputy governor, formerly "a rival fur trader of eminence and knowledge, and an American,"[5] and by Eden Colville, one of the two members of the old committee who remained on in the new.

The conduct of the company's business brought Head into contact, and before long into conflict, with Watkin. The latter, rarely willing to wait on the completion of formalities, was already in Canada by the time the new governor and committee took office. His mission, informally agreed upon earlier, was regularized in the first business session of the new committee in the following terms:

Ordered that Mr. Edward Watkin be authorized to proceed to the Red River Settlement without delay for the purpose of reporting on the condition of the settlement, the condition of the neighbouring territory, the prospects of settlement therein, and the possibility of commencing operations for a Telegraph line across the southern district of Rupert's Land—that looking to the lateness of the season it will be impossible for Mr. Watkin to do more at present than make preliminary enquiries on these subjects with a view to a more exact and complete examination of them next spring.[6]

By the time these formal instructions reached him on July 20, Watkin had already accomplished much in Montreal. He had had

[5]Watkin, *Canada and the United States*, p. 147.
[6]H.B. Co., A 1/75, Minute of Committee, July 6, 1863.

long discussions with A. G. Dallas, Simpson's successor as governor of Rupert's Land, and with other company servants, finding out all he thought he would need to know for the time being without going to the Red River himself. He had made the important suggestion to Dallas that a circular be issued to all the company's employees explaining the recent change of proprietorship and assuring them that the trade would continue as before and their rights be safeguarded. Moreover, he had been in touch with members of the Canadian Government, and of the Opposition as well, sampling Canadian views on the annexation of the Territories, and making sure that the offer to subsidize the communication scheme would be continued. Finally, Watkin had already approached the manager of the Montreal Telegraph Company, Mr. O. S. Wood, with regard to the building of the telegraph line.[7]

Receipt of his instructions and knowledge that the governor and committee intended him only to make "preliminary enquiries" with a view to a fuller examination in the spring, did not slow Watkin down at all. A week or so later he completed two detailed agreements with Wood providing for the establishment of a telegraphic system all the way from Halifax to the Pacific.[8] There was, of course, a qualifying clause in each of these agreements—"subject to the approval of the Governor and Committee of the Hudson's Bay Company in England"—but Watkin did not take it too seriously. He instructed Wood to order immediately a small quantity of the material he would need first so that there would be no delay in actually starting the work in the spring.[9]

An energetic, aggressive, cutter-of-red-tape like Watkin was bound to alarm a man of Head's temperament, accustomed to scholarly analysis and to the world of officialdom. It was not by any means that Head was indecisive or procrastinating; he had shown more than once in New Brunswick and Canada his willingness to act firmly and even, if need be, in advance of formal authority. But he liked to see his way clearly, and there seemed many uncertainties ahead in the first months of his responsibility for the property and interests of the traders and

[7]Watkin, *Canada and the United States*, pp. 179–88, Watkin to Head, July 24, 1863.
[8]*Ibid.*, pp. 174–78, memoranda dated August 10, 1863.
[9]*Ibid.*, p. 178, Wood to Watkin, August 10, 1863.

shareholders of the Hudson's Bay Company. Head, and the committee as a whole, not unnaturally thought Watkin's actions "a little premature," as Head put it very mildly in a private note to Watkin on receiving the latter's first report from Montreal.[10] "I fear that we cannot move quite so fast as you would wish," he added a fortnight later on finding that Watkin, far from being in Montreal or at the Red River, was, with his usual disregard for the Atlantic Ocean, already back in London.[11] Watkin, on the other hand, with equal justice from his own standpoint, was disappointed that "the Governor and his Committee were not prepared to act with the energy and preciseness I had desired."[12] By the end of August, a mere two months after the new company had been formed, relations between it and its originator were already badly strained.

The issue went much deeper of course than a simple difference of personal temperament between Head and Watkin. Watkin's interest in the company from the beginning had been almost entirely confined to its usefulness or otherwise in furthering his telegraph and transit scheme. He thought essentially in terms of communications. Head's position as governor made it necessary for him to take a broader view. He was anxious to carry out the communications scheme, which after all was why the proprietorship had changed hands, but it nevertheless was only one of several branches of the activity even of the new company. And the success of it and of all the rest depended on what answer could be found to more fundamental problems relating to the future ownership and government of the charter territory and to its military protection against wandering Indian tribes or possibly the Americans. Head's view was that since the company's affairs were undergoing a very important transition in these respects, the thing to do was to bring this to a conclusion and get back on a sound and permanent basis of some sort as rapidly as possible: in the meantime, to carry on the ordinary business and plan thoroughly such future projects as the telegraph line, but to be slow and cautious in undertaking large and irretrievable commitments. It may be that Head was too inclined to concentrate on fundamentals to the neglect of immediate opportunities, but the contrast between his over-all responsibilities on the

[10]H.B. Co., A 7/4, Head to Watkin, private, August 13, 1863.
[11]H.B. Co., A 7/4, Head to Watkin, private, August 25, 1863.
[12]Watkin, *Canada and the United States,* p. 188.

one hand, and Watkin's special interest on the other, at least helps to explain their differences of opinion.

Reports from Watkin himself, and from Dallas and others, of conditions in Rupert's Land served to confirm Head's view that his most important task was to negotiate a satisfactory readjustment of the company's rights and responsibilities under the terms of its charter. There were rumours of gold discoveries east of the Rockies near the head waters of the Saskatchewan which, if they proved true, might result in problems similar to those that had arisen in connection with the gold rush to the Fraser a few years before. The Sioux war in Minnesota and the arrival of starving Indian refugees in the vicinity of the Red River were already a danger. And in the settlement itself agitation that had been growing for years was threatening the complete breakdown of company rule, as was shown by an incident that had occurred only a few months before Head took office. A clergyman, tried and jailed for an attempted abortion on his maidservant, but who also happened to have been a leading agitator against the company for years, was forcibly released in April, 1863, by his friends who believed him the victim of company persecution. The ringleader among his rescuers, a schoolmaster, on being in turn arrested, was publicly removed from the jail by a still larger mob, the authorities standing aside as the only way of avoiding bloodshed.[18] Head and Watkin alike, and all others concerned with the affairs of the company, were fully convinced that some alternative means of government had to be found. Head made this the main objective of his administration, and was most hesitant to proceed with major developments along other lines until it had been accomplished.

As a first step, he called a special meeting of the committee of directors on August 28, 1863, to consider a letter from Dallas and other papers describing conditions in the Red River Settlement and in the plains generally. At this meeting it was

Resolved that the time has come when, in the opinion of this Committee it is expedient that the authority, executive and judicial, over the Red River Settlement and the South Western portion of Rupert's Land should be vested in officers deriving such authority directly from the Crown and exercising it in the name of Her Majesty.

[18]H.B. Co., A 7/4, Head to Dallas, private, October 7, 1863: "The case of the fellow rescued from gaol is a scandalous one and would create a strong feeling here if discussed in Parliament. I have no doubt you did well to avoid bloodshed."

That the Governor be empowered to communicate this resolution to His Grace the Duke of Newcastle and to discuss the subject with him or with the under secretary of state for the Colonies—reporting from time to time to this Committee thereon.[14]

Acting under the terms of this resolution, Head presented the Hudson's Bay Company viewpoint to Colonial Office officials in discussions lasting through September and October, and in a final formal letter, seen and revised slightly by his committee before being sent on November 11.[15]

Head began by trying to correct certain public misconceptions regarding the company's role in the government of its territories. In particular, he emphasized the success it had had, up to very recent years at least:

The Company are fully competent to manage their own people, and they believe that they have proved themselves more competent to manage the Indians than any Government or Association which has yet tried its hand at this task in North America. They have preserved peace and good will on one side of a frontier when war and savage hatred have raged on the other. They have done so no doubt from interested motives, but the motives of those who have failed in accomplishing the same task have perhaps not been more pure.

The present difficulty was not in governing the company's servants or even, primarily, the Indians: it was caused by the settlement in the Hudson's Bay and adjacent territories of other subjects of Her Majesty. This was the reason that the company felt obliged to ask that the direct authority of the Crown be extended into these regions.

After some preliminary arguments designed to strengthen the company's claim to compensation for the abandonment of its exclusive ownership of the soil, Head went on to make a series of definite proposals for the creation of a crown colony to extend across the whole prairie region from the American border to the north branch of the Saskatchewan River. The company would be prepared to give up its exclusive rights in this territory in return for a money payment. Or, if this proved impracticable, it would agree to transfer half the land of the colony to the Crown on being allowed to keep the other half and on certain other conditions being met concerning, in particular, gold and silver revenues and the building by the company of the road and telegraph line from Canada to British Columbia.

[14]H.B. Co., A 1/76, Minute of Committee, August 28, 1863.
[15]H.B. Co., A 8/11, Head to Rogers, November 11, 1863.

Careful study of this scheme in the Colonial Office, delayed somewhat by the illness of the Duke of Newcastle (which was to lead to his retirement immediately afterwards), resulted finally in a reply being made on March 11, 1864. In it, Newcastle acknowledged in principle the necessity for creating a crown colony and compensating the company, but rejected both of Head's proposals as to how this latter might be done. The suggestion of an equal division of the land seemed as unacceptable to him as did the alternative of a very large money payment. It would reproduce on a greater scale the difficulties regarding "reserves" that had proved intolerable in Canada: and especially the fact that half the land of the colony would be held for the purpose of increasing the dividends of a private corporation, would be bound to mean growing discontent. Instead, Newcastle suggested that in return for all of the land being surrendered, the company should be given monetary compensation, within specified limits, in proportion as revenue was derived from the sale of the land and from the export of gold and silver. In addition, it should receive a land subsidy in connection with the building of the road and telegraph line to British Columbia.[16] There were obvious advantages in Newcastle's plan and it was accepted as the basis for further negotiation, although quite naturally the company protested that the amounts offered were too small and proposed some revision of them. Writing privately and confidentially to Dallas at this time, Head commented:

I daresay you are surprised at not having heard from me personally more often but the fact is that for the last two or three months I have been completely taken up with the negociations with the Colonial Office which of course fall on me. . . . We have now made a second proposal to the Government in reply to a counter-proposal which we received in answer to our first letter. The Duke of Newcastle's retirement may delay the decision but I doubt whether it will do so. You can easily imagine that it has not been easy to steer cautiously between frightening our shareholders by asking too little, and deterring the Government from treating with us at all, by asking too much.[17]

At this point, when it seemed that agreement was near on the creation of a crown colony, and when the company was also preparing to go ahead with the telegraph scheme,[18] the whole affair bogged down. This seems to have been partly because the

[16]H.B. Co., A 8/11, Fortescue to Head, March 11 and April 5, 1864.
[17]H.B. Co., A 7/4, Head to Dallas, private and confidential, April 19, 1864.
[18]H.B. Co., A 1/76, Minute of Committee, May 3, 1864.

new colonial secretary, Edward Cardwell, lacked Newcastle's keen interest in the plan;[19] even more because the Charlottetown Conference and the prospect of British North American union changed the picture completely, raising Colonial Office hopes that a separate crown colony might not be necessary and that immediate annexation of the Territories to the new federation might take place instead. Although Head continued intermittently to press for a decision, and although various further negotiations were attempted, there was no real possibility of their success until after Confederation.[20] Then, only three days before his sudden death in January, 1868, Head wrote his last letter on the subject, outlining the company's position at the beginning of the final series of discussions that were to lead to the settlement that had so long been the major objective of his administration of the company's affairs.[21] That he did not quite live to see this does not minimize the importance of the part he played in bringing it about.

From the personal point of view, Head seems to have been well content during these last years with his position as governor of the Hudson's Bay Company. That he had no wish to return to the colonial service was made evident when, late in 1864, after he had been associated with the company for more than a year, he was asked by Cardwell to become governor of Ceylon, an important and very well-paid appointment. Cardwell thought "a practical hand" was needed just then to deal with Ceylon's problems and, as he explained to a correspondent: "The first person in the Colonial service to whom I thought it right to address myself was Head. He was gratified by the offer, but after taking time to consider, ultimately declined it, on the ground chiefly of Lady Head's health."[22] Lady Head's health (she was to survive her husband for over twenty years) can have been only one reason for Head's decision. For some time he had been "very much dissatisfied" with the colonial service as such, especially because of its failure to provide for retired governors— a weakness in the system which he and others by vigorous cam-

[19]H.B. Co., A 8/11, Rogers to Head, June 6, 1864.
[20]H.B. Co., Stowe MSS, Confidential *précis* on the Hudson's Bay Company, by T. F. Elliot, January 21, 1868.
[21]H.B. Co., Stowe MSS, Head to the Duke of Buckingham and Chandos, January 25, 1868.
[22]P.R.O., P.R.O. 30/48/39, Cardwell to Gordon, private, October 14, 1864.

paigning were eventually to remedy.[23] The Hudson's Bay Company employment was not only remunerative but it allowed him, moreover, to continue his association with British North America while still living in London.

Life in London had always had its attractions for Head. In particular, it provided the opportunity so long denied him of enjoying the society of a large circle of friends and acquaintants sharing his interest in literature and the arts. With Lewis, his closest friend, the time was limited, because Lewis died in the spring of 1863 while still in his fifty-eighth year. Most of the others, however, whom Head had known well since his earlier days in Oxford and London survived him, and there are numerous indications of the high esteem with which Head was regarded in the literary world of London generally in these years. This seems to have been particularly on account of the extraordinary breadth of his learning and the richness of his conversation. "It is not many weeks ago," one friend wrote of Head, at the time of his death, "since the Bishop of M—— expressed to me his sense of the deep and vast stores of information which came out from him in the most agreeable way, and specially at any private sitting."[24] A new, but close friend of these later years, Sir Charles Bunbury, wrote of Head:

I have scarcely known a man of more extensive and varied knowledge, or of a more powerful grasp of mind, and with this he had a remarkably refined taste and feeling for poetry. On a slight acquaintance his manner struck one as dry. I was quite surprised when I came to know him better, to find him full of humour and fun—often as merry and light-hearted as a boy. He was a thoroughly genial man, and a most kind-hearted one.[25]

For a man whose career had been administrative rather than academic to win tributes of this sort is most unusual; but Head's interest and his phenomenal memory had enabled him continually to broaden and deepen his scholarship and his artistic perceptions in spite of other heavy responsibilities. He was not able to the same extent, of course, to maintain a large output of

[23]P.R.O., C.O. 449/1, memorandum by Cardwell, April 30, 1864.
[24]*Notes and Queries*, 4th series, I, 180.
[25]Mrs. Henry Lyell (ed.), *The Life of Sir Charles J. F. Bunbury, Bart.*, II, 228. The London *Times* (January 30, 1868) in its obituary notice confirmed this impression of Head's role in London society: "He was a most accomplished scholar both in classical and modern languages, and no one perhaps of our time had greater mastery over English. His loss will be severely felt by a wide circle of political and literary friends."

written work. He published a number of articles and poems from time to time, but apart from these and his famous *"Shall"* and *"Will"* he devoted what leisure he had for this type of activity mainly to translating or editing the work of others, although usually with copious notes and observations of his own.

The subject-matter of Head's writings normally lay in the field of the remote and the abstruse: he enjoyed investigating and trying to solve the more difficult problems of philology and art criticism. But through it all there runs a broad humane philosophy which finds expression, frequently, in memorable sentences. In his editorial introduction to Kugler's *Handbook*, for example, he wrote:

In art, as in many other branches of human knowledge and industry, exclusiveness or the tendency to depreciate that which does not at once conform to our own tastes and feelings, is a fertile source of error and of mischief. Such a disposition deprives mankind of the free and unrestrained enjoyment of much which is calculated to cheer and improve them.[26]

Again in *"Shall"* and *"Will"*, philosophy and philology both emerge in the following comment:

Whether it be that our thoughts are not easily directed to the future because the present is too absorbing, or that there is "an awful, irrepressible, and almost instinctive consciousness of the uncertainty of the future which makes men avoid the appearance of speaking presumptuously of it"—the fact is certain—the want of a future tense as an organic part of the conjugation of verbs is a common defect in many modern languages.

At another place in this same work, Head's common-sense judgment of men and things, and his rejection of woolly sentimentality are shown in his comment on the attempts of some philologists to found their theories on a relationship between words and human character:

I do not attach much value to the consideration that a certain idiom in language is based on "the brighter side of human nature". Conventional forms of speech are current enough in all tongues, and courteous phrases are consistent with uncourteous acts. The red Indian wore the scalping-knife, and called every man "brother"; and where human nature fails is not in words.[27]

During these last years in London, Head's major works included, in 1864, his editing of Lewis's *Essays on the Administrations of Great Britain from 1783 to 1830*. These essays had

[26]F. T. Kugler, *A Handbook of Painting*, ed. E. W. Head (1854), I, vii.
[27]*"Shall"* and *"Will"* (1858), pp. 54, 35.

originally appeared in the *Edinburgh Review*, and Head collected and annotated them and wrote a moving preface as a memorial to his friend. He undertook a similar work of friendship in the last year of his life on behalf of Mrs. Sarah Austin who at the time of her death had been long engaged in making a translation of *Essays on Political History of the 15th, 16th, and 17th Centuries*, by Jules Van Praet. Head's own death supervened at the moment when he had completed the revision and correction of all except the last eight pages.

In 1866, Head published his translation from the Icelandic of *Viga Glum's Saga*. His interest was not alone in the robust descriptions of this tale, but in the fact that the sagas were the literature of men "who have left their mark in every corner of Europe, and whose language and laws are at this moment important elements in the speech and institutions of England, America, and Australia." They were in addition, "the first prose literature which exists in any modern language spoken by the people." It is indicative of the pioneer nature of Head's work in this field that he should have felt it necessary to explain these things, and to add that the remoteness of insignificant Iceland afforded no adequate measure of the interest which belonged to its language, its literature, and its history.

Shortly before his death Head collected a number of his original and translated poems, which had appeared from time to time in *Fraser's Magazine*, with a view to having them printed for private distribution among his friends. Included among them were translations from Propertius, from a number of Spanish ballads, and from Icelandic and German folk-tales. When he died, Henry Taylor prepared them for a wider public[28]—for "all to whom any record of his mind, even in its lighter and more excursive operations, or any traces of his steps on earth, will have a value." In his preface, Taylor pointed out that these poems represented not more than "one or two of the bye-paths," apart from the main business and purposes of Head's life, "for—though loving literature with an exceeding love, and knowing the literature of divers times and countries with the knowledge to which only love can lead, and with an extent of knowledge to which few, even through love, have found their way—he gave his life, after his first youth, to the public service at home and abroad,

[28]No editor's name is given in the volume itself, but that it was Henry Taylor is made clear in his *Autobiography*, I, 257–58.

and such productions as these were merely the fruits of occasional
retirement into literature when resting from public labours."

During his last years, Head's interest in Canadian affairs continued, and the whole family had many pleasant memories,
together with some sad ones, of their life in North America. In
October, 1866, for example, following a disastrous fire at Quebec
City, Head wrote a strong letter to *The Times* urging help for
the sufferers.

At a moment when the loyalty of Canada has been proved by their
efforts against the Fenians, and when England is looking to the con-
solidation of her North American possessions, it seems to me on every
account desirable to show our sympathy with the victims of such a calamity.

My special interest in Canada induces me to trouble you with this letter,
in the hope that those whose high position enables them to take the lead
and those who are actually connected with the Colony by relations of office
or business will unite in setting on foot a movement by which contributions
in aid of the sufferers at Quebec may at once be made available.[29]

On January 9, 1867, Head was one of the guests at a dinner
given by the Canada Club for the Canadian delegates then in
London to discuss confederation. Sir Francis Bond Head was
also present, Edward Watkin presided, and the colonial secretary,
Lord Carnarvon, was the principal speaker.

In the last year of his life, Head was appointed to serve on a
royal commission to inquire into the organization and rules of
trade unions and other similar associations. With him on this
commission were two men with whom he had long been on terms
of close friendship, Herman Merivale and J. A. Roebuck. Head
was present at many of the sessions when evidence was heard,
but did not live to see the report published.

For some considerable time, Head's health had been a growing
anxiety to himself and his friends. His greatest fear was that as
he grew older his epileptic tendencies would increase and that
there would result "a slow decay of his faculties, with, perhaps,
a long life."[30] Verses of Robert Bland the Younger which he had
read twenty-five years earlier, came back into his mind in this
connection as an example of another's different foreboding, and
on one occasion he repeated them almost word for word to a
close friend:

[29]London *Times*, October 31, 1866.
[30]G. S. Hillard (ed.), *George Ticknor*, II, 482–83, Ticknor to Twisleton, March
22, 1868.

While others set, thy sun shall fall,
Night without eve shall close on thee;
And he who made, with sudden call
Shall bid, and thou shalt cease to be.

So whispers Nature, whispers sorrow,
And I would greet the things they say
But for the thought of those whose morrow
Hangs trembling on my little day.[31]

In a sense, therefore, death came as a friend, because it came suddenly in his sixty-third year when his powers were still undiminished. On the morning of January 28, 1868, after breakfast at his home in Eaton Square, Head went into another room, and shortly afterwards was found dead of a sudden heart attack. He was buried in Kensal Green cemetery, in London. In Rochester Cathedral, beneath the memorials of his ancestors, there is a brass tablet with these words:

In memory of the Right Hon[ble] Sir Edmund Walker Head K.C.B.: the last Baronet of an ancient Kentish family. Fellow of Merton College Oxford 1830. Commissioner of Poor Laws 1841.

Lieut[t] Governor of New Brunswick 1848–1854. Governor General of British North America 1854–1861.

As Colonial Governor sagacious, firm, just, conciliatory; earnest in the advancement of the Provinces under his charge; in industry, wealth, arts and sciences;

Gifted with rare accomplishments, a scholar deeply versed in the literature of all ages and many languages. With an exquisite judgment in the fine arts:

In manners genial, in conversation easy, rich, and various; beloved by many, most loved by those who knew him best.

Born 1805. Died Jan[y] 28, 1868.

These lines, according to family tradition, were the tribute of Amabel Head, "the young American," to the father whose memory she particularly cherished right up to the time of her own death in 1914.[32] Although drafted by so loving a hand, they constitute a remarkably concise and penetrating analysis of the career and character of Sir Edmund Head.

[31]*Ibid.*
[32]Lady Head lived on until the age of eighty-two, dying on August 25, 1890. The elder daughter, Caroline, married and her descendants are still living. Amabel, the younger daughter, remained unmarried. It was on her death in 1914 that Head's remaining personal papers were destroyed. Some, along with books, paintings, furniture, etc., had been lost in the burning of the Pantechnicon in London in 1874 (Mrs. Henry Lyell (ed.), *Bunbury*, II, 304).

BIBLIOGRAPHY

BIBLIOGRAPHY

NOTE: Apart from sources specifically referred to in footnotes, only a few that were of the greatest general importance in connection with Head or the background of his work have been included in this bibliography.

MANUSCRIPT SOURCES

ENGLAND

Public Record Office

Home Office files of the H.O. 39 and 73 series, and the M.H. 1–4 series were of the greatest value in connection with Head's poor-law administration. The main Colonial Office series used were C.O. 188–191 (New Brunswick), C.O. 217–221 (Nova Scotia), and C.O. 42–45 (Canada). Other material for the study of Head's administrations in North America was found in the Foreign Office and War Office series, F.O. 5, 97, and W.O. 1, and in special Colonial Office volumes, C.O. 449/1 and C.O. 537/137. The Cardwell Papers, Carnarvon Papers, Eyre Papers, and Russell Papers also contained important information.

British Museum

Babbage Correspondence; Bliss Correspondence; Layard Correspondence.

Hudson's Bay Company Archives

Important material dealing with Head's administration in Canada and his government of the Hudson's Bay Company is to be found in the Governor's Letterbooks, the Simpson Papers, and the Stowe Manuscripts.

Oxford University

Merton College, Register; Oriel College, Buttery Books.

Harpton Court, Kington, Herefordshire

Lewis Papers.

CANADA

Public Archives of Canada

The principal series of official documents used were: C.O. 188–189 (New Brunswick), G (Canada), S (Canada), the Governor General's Letterbooks, the Governor General's Secretary's Correspondence, and the New Brunswick and Canadian Executive Council Minutes. In addition material of value was found in the Baring Papers, the Ellice Papers, the Head Papers, the Howe Papers, and the Macdonald Papers.

GOVERNMENT DOCUMENTARY SERIES

GREAT BRITAIN
Hansard; Poor Law Commmission Reports.

NEW BRUNSWICK
House of Assembly Journals; Statutes.

CANADA (Province)
House of Assembly Journals; Statutes.

NEWSPAPERS AND PERIODICALS

Edinburgh: *Edinburgh Review*, CXVIII (1863).
Fredericton: *New Brunswick Reporter.*
Halifax: *British North American; Nova Scotian; Sun.*
London: *Foreign Quarterly Review*, XXVI (1834); *Illustrated London News*, 1868; *Notes and Queries*, 4th series, I (1868); *Quarterly Review*, CLXV (1848); *The Times.*
Miramichi: *Gleaner.*
Quebec: *Chronicle.*
Saint John, New Brunswick: *Chronicle; Loyalist and Protestant Vindicator; New Brunswick Courier.*
Toronto: *Globe; Leader.*

PUBLISHED WORKS

ALBION, R. G. *Forests and Sea Power: The Timber Problem of the Royal Navy, 1652–1862.* Cambridge, Mass.: 1926.
ANDREWS, ISRAEL D. *Report . . . in relation to the Trade and Commerce of the British American Colonies . . . since 1829.* Washington: 1851.
—— *Report on the Trade and Commerce of the British North American Colonies. . . .* Washington: 1854.
Annual Register, 1838, 1840, 1859.
ATTLAY, J. B. *Sir Henry Wentworth Acland, Bart., a Memoir.* London: 1903.
BELL, K. N. and W. P. MORRELL, eds. *Select Documents on British Colonial Policy, 1830–60.* Oxford: 1928.
BENTON, PHILIP. *History of the Rochford Hundred.* London: 1882.
BUTLER, J. R. M. "Note on the Origin of Lord John Russell's Despatch of October 16, 1839, on the Tenure of Crown Offices in the Colonies," *Cambridge Historical Journal*, II (1926–28).
Cambridge History of the British Empire, J. H. ROSE, A. P. NEWTON, and E. A. BENIANS, general eds. VI, *Canada and Newfoundland.* Cambridge: 1930.
CHISHOLM, J. A., ed. *The Speeches and Public Letters of Joseph Howe.* 2 vols. Halifax: 1909.
CIVIL SERVICE COMMISSIONERS. *Eighth Report.* London: 1863.
CREIGHTON, DONALD. *John A. Macdonald: The Young Politician.* Toronto: 1952.

DAWSON, R., ed. *Fifty Years of Work in Canada, Scientific and Educational, being Autobiographical Notes by Sir William Dawson.* London: 1901.

DENT, J. C. *Canadian Portrait Gallery.* 4 vols. Toronto: 1880.

—— *The Last Forty Years: Canada since the Union of 1841.* 2 vols. Toronto: 1881.

Dictionary of National Biography, edited by L. STEPHEN and SIR S. LEE. London: 1921.

DOUGHTY, A. G., ed. *The Elgin-Grey Papers, 1846–1852.* 4 vols. Ottawa: 1937.

DOWDEN, E., ed. *Correspondence of Henry Taylor.* London: 1880.

ENGLEHEART, G. D. *Journal of the Progress of H.R.H. the Prince of Wales.* Privately printed: n.d.

FENETY, G. E. *Political Notes and Observations.* Fredericton: 1867.

FINER, S. E. *The Life and Times of Sir Edwin Chadwick.* London: 1952.

FOSTER, JOSEPH. *Alumni Oxonienses.* London: 1888.

GANONG, W. F. "Monograph of the Origins of Settlements in the Province of New Brunswick," *Transactions of the Royal Society of Canada,* 2nd series, VI (1904).

GIBSON, JAMES A. "Sir Edmund Head's Memorandum on the Choice of Ottawa as the Seat of Government of Canada," *Canadian Historical Review,* XVI (1935).

GLAZEBROOK, G. DET., ed. "A Letter on the West by Sir Edmund Head," *Canadian Historical Review,* XXI (1940).

GOUGH, T. B. *Boyish Reminiscences of His Majesty the King's Visit to Canada in 1860.* London: 1910.

GREVILLE, C. C. F. *A Journal of the Reign of Queen Victoria from 1837–1852,* edited by HENRY REEVE. 3 vols. London: 1885.

GREY, EARL. *The Colonial Policy of Lord John Russell's Administration.* 2 vols. London: 1853.

HANNAY, J. *History of New Brunswick.* 2 vols. Saint John: 1909.

—— *Lemuel Allan Wilmot.* Makers of Canada Series. Toronto: 1926.

HEAD, F. B. *A Narrative.* London: 1839.

HILLARD, G. S., ed. *Life, Letters, and Journals of George Ticknor.* 2 vols. Boston: 1876.

HINCKS, FRANCIS. *Reminiscences of his Public Life.* Montreal: 1884.

HOGAN, J. S. *Canada.* Montreal: 1855.

IRELAND, W. H. *History of Kent.* London: 1829–30.

JOHNSTON, J. F. W. *Notes on North America.* 2 vols. Boston and Edinburgh: 1851.

—— *Report on the Agricultural Capabilities of the Province of New Brunswick.* Fredericton: 1850.

KENNEDY, W. P. M. *Documents of the Canadian Constitution.* 2nd ed., Oxford: 1930.

KERR, D. G. G. "Edmund Head, Robert Lowe, and Confederation," *Canadian Historical Review,* XX (1939).

—— "Head and Responsible Government in New Brunswick," *Canadian Historical Association Report,* 1938.

—— "The New Brunswick Background of Sir Edmund Head's Views on Confederation," *ibid.,* 1949.

LAUGHTON, J. K. *Memoirs of the Life and Correspondence of Henry Reeve.* 2 vols. London: 1898.

LAWRENCE, J. W. *The Judges of New Brunswick and their Times.* Saint John: 1907.

LEE, SIR SIDNEY. *King Edward VII.* London: 1925.

LEWIS, G. F., ed. *Letters of Sir George Cornewall Lewis.* London: 1870.

LONGLEY, J. W. *Joseph Howe.* Makers of Canada Series. Toronto: 1926.

LOWER, A. R. M. *The North American Assault on the Canadian Forest.* Toronto: 1938.

LYELL, MRS. HENRY, ed. *Life, Letters, and Journals of Sir Charles Lyell.* 2 vols. London: 1881.

—— *The Life of Sir Charles J. F. Bunbury, Bart.* 2 vols. London: 1906.

MACKENZIE, A. *Life and Speeches of George Brown.* Toronto: 1882.

MARSTON, MAURICE. *Sir Edwin Chadwick.* London: 1925.

MARTIN, A. PATCHETT. *Life and Letters of the Right Hon. Robert Lowe, Viscount Sherbrooke.* 2 vols. London: 1893.

MARTIN, CHESTER. "Sir Edmund Head and Canadian Confederation, 1851–1858," *Canadian Historical Association Report,* 1929.

—— "Sir Edmund Head's First Project of Federation, 1851," *ibid.,* 1928.

MARTINEAU, J. *The Life of Henry Pelham, Fifth Duke of Newcastle, 1811–1864.* London: 1908.

MASTERS, D. C. *The Reciprocity Treaty of 1854.* London: 1936.

MITCHELL, E. A. "Edward Watkin and the Buying-out of the Hudson's Bay Company," *Canadian Historical Review,* XXXIV (1953).

MORGAN, H. J. *Sketches of Celebrated Canadians and Persons Connected with Canada.* Quebec: 1862.

MORISON, J. L. *British Supremacy and Canadian Self-Government, 1839–1854.* Glasgow: 1919.

MORRELL, W. P. *British Colonial Policy in the Age of Peel and Russell.* Oxford: 1930.

MORTON, A. S. *A History of the Canadian West to 1870–71.* London: n.d.

NICHOLLS, SIR G. *A History of the English Poor Laws.* 2 vols. London: 1854.

Oxford University Commission Report. See *Report of H.M. Commissioners. . . .*

PARKER, C. S. *Life and Letters of Sir James Graham.* 2 vols. London: 1907.

PERLEY, M. H. *Reports on the Sea and River Fisheries of New Brunswick.* Fredericton: 1852.

PLAYFAIR, W. *British Family Antiquity.* London: 1811.

POPE, SIR JOSEPH. *Correspondence of Sir John Macdonald.* Toronto: 1921.

—— *Memoirs of Sir John Alexander Macdonald.* 2 vols. Ottawa: 1894.

PORRITT, E. *Sixty Years of Protection in Canada, 1846–1907.* 2nd ed., Winnipeg: 1913.

PROTHERO, R. E., ed. *The Letters of Richard Ford, 1797–1858.* London: 1905.

Report of H.M. Commissioners Appointed to Enquire into the State of Discipline, Studies and Revenue of the University of Oxford, together with an Appendix. London: 1852.

SCOTT, R. W. *The Choice of the Capital.* Ottawa: 1907.
SHIPPEE, L. B. *Canadian-American Relations, 1849–1874.* New Haven and Toronto: 1939.
SHORTT, A. and A. G. DOUGHTY, eds. *Canada and its Provinces.* 23 vols. Toronto: 1914.
SKELTON, O. D. *Life and Times of Sir A. T. Galt.* Toronto: 1920.
STACEY, C. P. *Canada and the British Army, 1846–1871.* London: 1936.
STANLEY, G. F. G. *The Birth of Western Canada.* London: 1936.
STEWART, ALICE B. "Sir Edmund Head's Memorandum of 1857 on Maritime Union: A Lost Confederation Document," *Canadian Historical Review,* XXVI (1945).
TAYLOR, HENRY. *Autobiography, 1801–1875.* 2 vols. New York: 1885.
TORRENS, W. T. M. *Life and Times of Sir James Graham.* 2 vols. London: 1863.
TROTTER, R. G. *Canadian Federation: Its Origins and Achievement.* London: 1924.
TUCKER, G. N. *The Canadian Commercial Revolution, 1845–51.* Yale Historical Publications. New Haven: 1936.
WATKIN, E. W. *Canada and the United States: Recollections 1851 to 1886.* London: 1887.
WEBB, SIDNEY and BEATRICE. *English Poor Law History.* Part II. London: 1929.
WHITELAW, W. M. *The Maritimes and Canada before Confederation.* Toronto: 1934.

WORKS OF SIR EDMUND HEAD

A Few Words on the Bodleian Library. Oxford: 1833.
Report on the Law of Bastardy: A Supplementary Report on a Cheap Civil Remedy for Seduction. London: 1840.
A Handbook of the History of Painting. Part II, *The German, Flemish, and Dutch Schools of Painting,* by F. T. KUGLER. Edited by Sir E. HEAD. London: 1846.
A Handbook of the History of the Spanish and French Schools of Painting. London: 1848.
A Handbook of Painting: The German, Flemish, Dutch, Spanish, and French Schools, by F. T. KUGLER. Edited by Sir E. HEAD. 2 vols. London: 1854.
"Shall" and "Will"; or, Two Chapters on Future Auxiliary Verbs. London: 1856.
"Shall" and "Will". . . . *To which are added,* 1. *An essay on certain affirmative and negative particles in the English language.* 2. *An essay on the provincial word "songle."* 2nd ed. London: 1858.
Essays on the Administrations of Great Britain from 1783 to 1830, by G. C. LEWIS. Edited by Sir E. HEAD. London: 1864.
Essays on the Political History of the 15th, 16th, and 17th Centuries, by J. VAN PRAET. Edited by Sir E. HEAD. London: 1868.

INDEX

Lightning Source UK Ltd.
Milton Keynes UK
UKHW010004210722
406167UK00001B/152